# Chambers
# pardon
# my english!

## an exploration of slang
## and informal language

Michael Munro

Chambers

CHAMBERS
An imprint of Chambers Harrap Publishers Ltd
7 Hopetoun Crescent
Edinburgh, EH7 4AY

First published by Chambers Harrap Publishers Ltd 2007

A CIP catalogue record for this book is available from the British
Library.

ISBN 978 0550 10286 7


*Editors*: Ian Brookes, Lorna Gilmour
*Prepress Controllers*: Nicolas Echallier, Becky Pickard

Thanks are due to the following people for their help in the
preparation of this book: Vicky Aldus, Paul Cook, Patrick
Gaherty, Orin Hargraves, Mairéad Hegarty, Heather Macpherson,
Elaine O'Donoghue, Ruth O'Donovan, Georges Pilard, Kate
Seymour, Lianne Vella, Patrick White.


Designed and typeset by Chambers Harrap Publishers Ltd,
Edinburgh
Printed by Clays Ltd, St Ives plc

# CONTENTS

An Introduction to Slang                                vii
How to Use This Book                                    xii


## *Part One: The Language of Particular Groups*
### Professions
Military slang                                            2
Nautical slang                                            6
Legal slang                                               9
Medical slang                                            11
Police slang                                             13
Journalists' and printers' slang                        17
Musicians' slang                                        20
Show business slang                                     22
Pornography slang                                       27
Stock-exchange slang                                    29
Commercial and business jargon                          32
Bookmakers' slang                                       35

### Sections of society
Criminal slang                                          39
Gangland slang                                          46
Prison slang                                            49
Drug world slang                                        52
Yoof slang                                              57
School slang                                            59
Campus slang                                            61
Computer and Internet users' slang                      63
Hip-hop slang                                           68
Gay slang                                               70

## Activities

General sporting slang                                                74
Football slang                                                       75
Rugby slang                                                          79
Cricket slang                                                        80
Boxing slang                                                         84
Golf slang                                                           86
Horse-racing slang                                                  88
Motor-sport slang                                                   90
American football slang                                             92
Baseball slang                                                      94
Basketball slang                                                    96
Climbers' slang                                                     98
Surfers' slang                                                      100
Skateboarding slang                                                102
Hunting slang                                                       103
Poker slang                                                         105
Bingo slang                                                         107

## *Part Two: Slang in Areas of Everyday Life*

Booze                                                               110
Food                                                                116
Money                                                               119
Violence                                                            122
Oaths                                                               127
Euphemisms                                                          130
Insults                                                             135
Rhyming slang                                                       141
The weather                                                         144
Work                                                                146
Unemployment                                                        150
Class and social concerns                                           152
Politics                                                            155

Clothing and fashion                              158
Transport                                         163
Nationality                                       167
Race                                              170
Religion                                          172
Places                                            175
Animals                                           179
The human body                                    181
Bodily functions                                  186
Sex                                               189
Relationships                                     198
Illness                                           202
Death                                             205
Insanity                                          207
Television                                         210

## Part Three: Slang of Particular Places and Times
### Slang in English-speaking countries around the world

United States slang                               214
Canadian slang                                    221
Australian slang                                  224
New Zealand slang                                 232
South African slang                              234
Caribbean slang                                   236
Irish slang                                       238
South Asian slang                                 242

### Regional slang within the United Kingdom

Scottish slang                                    245
Ulster slang                                      248
Scouse slang                                      250
Geordie slang                                     252

Northern English slang                                          253
Midlands slang                                                 255
West Country slang                                             257
Southern English slang                                         258
London slang                                                  259

## Slang through the ages
The 16th century                                              263
The 17th century                                              265
The 18th century                                              268
The 19th century                                              271
World War I                                                   276
The 1920s                                                     278
The 1930s                                                     280
World War II and the 1940s                                    283
The 1950s                                                     286
The 1960s                                                     288
The 1970s                                                     291
The 1980s                                                     293
The 1990s                                                     296
The 21st century                                              297

Index                                                         301

# AN INTRODUCTION TO SLANG

What exactly is slang? Most people will have their own ideas about what it constitutes, but perhaps we should begin from an authoritative definition. *The Chambers Dictionary* puts it this way:

> words and usages not forming part of standard language, only used very informally, *esp* in speech; *orig* a jargon of thieves and disreputable people; the jargon of any class, profession, or set.

The word itself is of doubtful origin. Some make a connection between *slang* and *sling*, the idea being that people sling words at one another in a devil-may-care manner. However, this etymology is largely conjectural and the truth of it is unlikely to be established one way or the other. To return to the definition, it is clear that the essence of slang is its informality: it is language that is never appropriate in a formal context. Why is this? The key is in the 'speech' element of the definition. Slang is about direct verbal communication between speakers, both of whom are familiar with the vocabulary used. They each know what the other means. The problem is that other people may not understand, because the style of language is not their own. Clearly, any risk of ambiguity cannot be allowed in a formal situation where it is imperative (or it ought to be) that what is said or written is clear to all and not open to misinterpretation.

How did slang come to evolve? Again, the dictionary definition points in the right direction. The first serious attempts to record English slang took place in the Elizabethan era when glossaries of what was known as 'thieves' cant' were published. This is not to say that no-one used slang before this period, only that it was never recorded in any systematic way. What these glossaries were concerned with was the language of the robber and the 'fence', the whore and the pimp, the pickpocket and the confidence trickster, and it was noted down, not from purely philological interest, but as a kind of protection for the innocent against the wickedness of the urban criminal element. While being thus forearmed may have truly been of use to those literate enough to benefit, no doubt the gentle reader also enjoyed the *frisson* of being able to 'slum it', at least in linguistic terms. While the rough-and-ready vocabulary of slang would have been glaringly out of place in the Latinate prose and poetry of the time, contemporary playwrights, working in the immediate and intimate world of the spoken word, were able to use slang expressions to give a racy feel to their dialogue, or as convincing 'colour' in their portrayals of the underworld that was fermenting anarchically beneath the ordered ranks of society. In fact, to the 'groundlings', members of the lower classes standing in the pit at the theatre, much of this slang would have been familiar; they would get the jokes, and join in the laughter of those 'in the know'.

The whole point of 'thieves' cant' was, of course, to disguise what was being said, to screen illegal activities from unwelcome listeners, not only from among the potential victims but those seeking to enforce the law. This trait of including some people and excluding others has continued to be typical of slang and characterizes the jargon of many different types of human associations. As the dictionary again says, many classes, sets and professions evolved their own slang, almost as a shibboleth, a sign of being among the freemasonry of the initiated.

The common use of slang inevitably generates a sense of belonging to a group, of identity, of having shared interests and concerns that are important in life. If you know the slang you are obviously an insider; if you don't, you belong among the excluded 'others'. Such jargoneering continues to this day, with, to name only a few examples, the slang of the Internet that drives the World Wide Web, the 'business-speak' of the world of trade and commerce, the 'gangsta' speech of hip-hop performers, and the abbreviated code beloved of text messagers and e-mailers that streams continuously through the atmosphere.

Slang has always been produced in towns and cities rather than in rural contexts. Presumably in order to flourish it needs the contiguity of large numbers of people and at the same time the existence of distinct groupings within the community as a whole. It is no different in the 21st century, with people who generate slang tending to be both young and urban. Slang is as much a part of the process of defining who they are as the music they listen to and the styles of clothes they wear. However, apart from issues of identity and belonging, we should not leave out the element of fun and creativity involved in the coining of new slang terms. Slang has been called the poetry of the illiterate; indeed the English writer G K Chesterton went so far as to say that slang is 'the one stream of poetry which is continually flowing'.

Perhaps this is overdoing it. Certainly, much of the slang to be heard on the streets is far from being pleasing to the ear, let alone the stuff of poetry. Yet an undeniable creativity remains. Many people seem to have a natural desire to make their speech more lively and memorable, to be seen as different from the ordinary and clichéd. The young tend to become bored with what is old and seek to replace dated language with expressions that speak directly to their own generation. They rename the familiar in more exciting (or 'sexy') terms and create vibrant expressions for what is new. Individuals who have no other claim to fame may make themselves noticed by using striking turns of phrase. At worst it is a form of showing off; at best such linguistic inventiveness represents a vital strand in the future development of the language.

What is invented by one lively mind can be adopted by others who are less creative but equally keen to be seen as being at the forefront of fashion. Not every new expression catches on; some remain too specific to particular people or situations; others are too awkwardly made or unmemorable to lodge themselves in the popular imagination. However, many slang terms genuinely fulfil a function (in the words of the US poet Carl Sandburg, slang 'takes off its coat, spits on its hands – and goes to work') and it is these that find a niche in the language and are soon adopted and spread, particularly in the current age of instant mass communication.

Again the question of 'in-groups' is important. If you are not au fait with the latest slang you are an outsider – what the beatniks of the 1950s would have called a 'square' – as much to be pitied as despised, but definitely to be kept at arm's length. It is a truism that people of earlier generations are ill-advised to adopt the latest slang coinages. Indeed, few things are more laughable than an older person trying to use the latest slang, inevitably and ludicrously getting it wrong.

While slang is decried by many as substandard and to be deplored, there can be no doubt that the language is enriched by new slang, and it should be borne in mind that an expression that begins as slang may not always remain as such. The great lexicographer of slang Eric Partridge illustrated this phenomenon by the development of the word 'queer'. In his work of 1950 entitled *Here, There and Everywhere: Essays upon Language*, Partridge explains how 'queer' began as a term used in the 16th-century underworld to mean 'useless' or 'bad'. Through regular usage it evolved from slang to become colloquial (ie to be found in informal conversation) before being adopted into standard English with its modern senses including 'odd', 'vaguely unwell' and 'homosexual'. Partridge did not live to see the latest chapter added to the biography of this little word, in which, from the 1990s onwards, it was claimed by the gay community not as a pejorative term but as a badge of identity.

Slang is not a monolithic entity. There are, of course, many slangs, whether they arise from distinct communities, professions or classes or from different parts of the world. Most of us will come into contact with, and use or at least understand, several varieties of slang every day. This will be through our work (from medical jargon to commercial jargon), our environment or milieu (from school slang to gay slang) or the activities we prefer to devote time to (from football to bingo). Our daily lives are filled with slang relating to every intimate detail: the food we eat, the way we express our emotions, and the way we deal with the various aspects of sexuality.

English is one of the great world languages and wherever it is spoken as a first language it has generated its particular slang, not just in different parts of the British Isles but from North America to Asia and Australasia. It should also be borne in mind that time is an important dimension in slang: what is up-to-the-minute and fashionable may soon become behind the times. Many slang terms that are coined during one period may often come to be identified with and trapped in that era, while, often surprisingly, others never wholly lose their currency. Any book that tries to capture the latest slang is unavoidably out of date by the time it is printed. Yet the attempt must be made, and if slang continues to proliferate in the 21st century at the rate at which it has begun, there will certainly be no shortage of new material for those who seek to record it.

# HOW TO USE THIS BOOK

This book is not exactly a dictionary of slang, although it does explain the meanings of thousands of slang terms. The material has been arranged so that readers can find the slang words associated with a particular group, subject, region or period in one place. It has to be admitted that some slang words do not fit neatly into any of the sections of the book, whereas other words may crop up in more than one section.

For most readers, the table of contents on pages iii–vi will offer the best route into the book, showing as it does where each of the different areas of slang is discussed. However, for readers who are in search of a particular word, there is an alphabetical index at the back of the book. This lists all of the terms discussed in this book and shows the page on which each is defined.

# Part One

# The Language of Particular Groups

# *PROFESSIONS*

## *Military slang*

Life in the armed forces can be tough and, especially in time of war, downright dangerous. It is the job of the regular officers and NCOs to take a bunch of disparate individuals and turn them into a cohesive formation able to fight as a team. One of the unofficial ways in which new recruits achieve a sense of belonging is through learning the distinctive lingo, knowledge of which separates the initiated from the greenhorns. In such an artificial and arduous environment, it can be no surprise that a strain of black humour and cynicism runs through the slang of the services, as well as a desire to put a more human face on any threatening situation. So it is that dead people are labelled as having 'gone for a Burton' or having 'bought the farm'; deadly weapons are seemingly scorned by being given belittling names, such as 'Archibald', 'eggs', 'pineapples' or 'moaning minnies'; those in authority, often with the power of life or death over their charges, are quietly brought down to size by being thought of as 'brass hats', 'chicken colonels' or 'top-kicks'. The traditional disdain felt by one branch of the services for another also finds expression in dismissive (although sometimes not unfriendly) nicknames, with the infantry being disparaged as 'beetle-crushers' or 'grunts' and the RAF being scorned by those on the ground as 'Brylcreem Boys'.

## *Glossary*

**ablutions** a room or building for washing yourself

**ace** an airman of the highest quality, especially one who has downed several enemy aircraft

**ack emma** before midday (from the old signallers' name for the letters AM)

**ammo** ammunition

**Archibald** an anti-aircraft gun or its fire (also called **Archie**)

**bandit** an enemy aircraft

**beetle-crusher** an infantryman

**beetle off** in the RAF, 'beetling off' means flying away

**biscuit** a square mattress

**black ops** covert operations

**blighty** home (often referring to Britain as the home country, especially in World War I, when a 'blighty' or 'blighty one' was a wound necessitating a return home)

**Blue Beret** a soldier in a United Nations peacekeeping force

**blue on blue** friendly fire, the accidental firing on one's own side rather than the enemy

**boffin** a research scientist employed by the armed forces

**boot** a new recruit to the US Marine Corps

**boot camp** a training centre for new recruits

**bootie** or **bootee** a Royal Marine (shortened from the earlier term 'boot-neck')

**bowler-hat** to discharge someone from the armed forces

**brass hat** a staff officer

**Brylcreem Boys** a disparaging term used by other forces for members of the RAF, whether or not they actually used the proprietary brand of hair cream in question

**bull** tediously excessive discipline, such as unnecessary drill or polishing of kit

**bundook** a rifle

**Burton** in the RAF, if a flier or aircraft has 'gone for a Burton', this means they are dead or destroyed

**bust** to demote

**buy it** or **buy the farm** to be killed

**carpet** in RAF slang, 'on the carpet' means at or near ground level

**Charlie** a name given by US forces in Vietnam for the Vietcong or a member of the Vietcong (from 'Victor Charlie', the communications code letters for VC)

**chaser** an aeroplane for pursuing hostile aircraft

**chicken colonel** a full colonel in the US Army (from the use of an eagle as a badge of rank)

**chocko** or **choco** an Australian term for a conscripted member of the Australian armed forces in World War II, especially one who never left the country (shortened from 'chocolate soldier')

**click** a kilometre

**coalbox** a shell that emits black smoke

**daisy-cutter** a powerful bomb designed to explode close to the ground

**demob happy** excited by the prospect of release from the armed forces

**ditch** to 'ditch' an aircraft is to bring it down in the sea

**dog-soldier** a soldier who acts as a last line of defence

**dog tag** a soldier's metal identity disc

**doughboy** an American infantryman

**egg** a bomb or mine

**erk** RAF slang for an aircraftman

**fizzer** if a serviceman is 'put on a fizzer', he is officially accused of some transgression

**flak** anti-aircraft fire

**frag** to kill or wound with a fragmentation grenade (especially as in the Vietnam War)

**funkhole** a dugout

**galoot** an inexperienced soldier or marine

**gippo** a cook

**glasshouse** barracks used for the detention of military prisoners

**golden bowler** dismissal from the army followed by a job in Whitehall

**gong** a medal

**Green Beret** a commando

**greenhouse** the cockpit of an aircraft

**grunt** an infantry soldier

**guardee** a guardsman

**gunfire** an early-morning cup of tea

**hedgehog** a small, strongly fortified, defensive position

**hill** if a soldier 'goes over the hill', he deserts from the army

**hitch** a term of service in the US and Canadian forces

**iddy-umpty** Morse code

**imshi!** go away!

**jankers** punishment for defaulting

**jock** a soldier in a Scottish regiment

**jolly** a Royal Marine

**Kate** or **Kate Carney** the British Army (a piece of near-rhyming slang)

**kitchen police** in the American military, the 'kitchen police' are soldiers detailed to help with kitchen duties, especially as punishment

**kite** RAF slang for an aircraft

**lancejack** a lance corporal in the British Army

**leatherneck** a Royal Marine

**lobster** a British soldier (from the red coats formerly worn by them)

**loot** an American abbreviation for 'lieutenant'

**milk run** a routine flight

**milk train** an early-morning flight or patrol

**moaning minnie** a World War II German mortar that produced a shrieking noise when fired

**nig-nog** a raw recruit

**noddy suit** a suit designed to protect the wearer against nuclear, biological and chemical weapons

**non-com** a non-commissioned officer

**number nine** a purgative pill

**old sweat** an experienced soldier

**penguin** RAF slang for a member of the Women's Royal Air Force (because they were 'flappers who did not fly')

**pineapple** a hand grenade or a bomb

**pip** a star as a mark of rank

**pip emma** in the afternoon (from the old signallers' name for the letters PM)

**plebe** a first-year cadet at a naval or military academy

**plunger** a cavalryman

**pom-pom** an automatic quick-firing gun

**pongo** a British Army soldier

**prang** in the RAF, to 'prang' means to crash or shoot down an aircraft, or to bomb a place

**prune** RAF slang for a dud pilot

**rag-fair** a kit inspection

**recce**, **reccy** or (in the US) **recon** reconnaissance

**redcap** a military policeman

**Red Devils** the Parachute Regiment

**red hat** a staff officer

**Roman candle** a landing by parachute when the parachute fails to open

**rooty** bread

**Sammy** an American expeditionary soldier

**sarge** a sergeant

**scrambled eggs** the gold braid on a military officer's cap

**sitrep** a situation report, a report on the current military position

**skrimshank** or **scrimshank** someone who 'skrimshanks' is evading work or duty

**sky pilot** a military chaplain

**slot** to 'slot' an enemy is to shoot them dead

**snafu** a chaotic situation (an American acronym for *situation normal all fouled (or fucked) up*)

**spike** a bayonet

**sprog** a raw recruit

**spud-bashing** the job of peeling potatoes

**squaddie** a private or ordinary soldier

**square-bashing** parade-ground drill

**stonk** an intense bombardment

**sweat** a soldier

**swing the lead** to invent specious reasons for evading duty

**tail-end Charlie** the aircraft bringing up the rear in an air-force formation

**take out** to 'take out' an enemy target is to destroy it

**tankbuster** an aircraft designed to attack and destroy tanks

**tapes** the stripes on a non-commissioned officer's sleeve

**Terries** the Territorial Army

**ticket** a certificate of discharge from the army

**turkey-shoot** a battle involving large-scale killing or destruction of easy targets

**top-kick** a first sergeant in the US Army

**up the pole** in favour

**winger** a pal, colleague or favourite

**write yourself off** in RAF slang, to 'write yourself off' means to get yourself killed

**yomp** to carry heavy equipment on foot over difficult terrain

## *Nautical slang*

Britain has a long history of seagoing and this has generated substantial amounts of slang, much of which has made the transition into everyday use. For example, most of us will have no idea of what the crew of a sailing vessel understood literally when ordered to 'splice the mainbrace', but the slang meaning of the phrase is widely known, as would be its frequent consequence of being 'three sheets in the wind'. A common proverb is 'worse things happen at sea' (and they do), but that fearsome and untamed element, on which all sailors must spend most of their time, is made to seem less daunting by being called by more homely names, such as 'the briny', 'the drink' or 'the oggin'; even that dreaded end for mariners, a watery grave, is drained of some of its terror by being referred to as 'Davy Jones's locker'. Those in command are to be respected, of course, but orders are perhaps easier to accept if you think of your superiors in terms of humanizing nicknames, such as 'the bloke' or 'Jimmy-the-one'. A ship has always been something of a world unto itself, particularly before the age of telecommunications, and it is noticeable that nautical terms often came to be used for things equally known to land-lubbers, as in 'bilge' meaning nonsense, or 'adrift' meaning not in the right place at the right time. In the following list naval slang is included amongst more common nautical slang, as there are many usages common to both military and civilian mariners.

## Glossary

**adrift** absent or late

**andrew** 'the andrew' is a name for the Royal Navy (the name is sometimes said to derive from Andrew Miller, a well-known officer in the 19th century)

**baby spanner** a Royal Navy term for a penis

**bilge** rubbish, drivel (originally the foul water collecting at the bottom of a ship)

**bloke** the commander

**briny** the sea

**bucko** a swaggerer or domineering bully

**can** a depth charge

**caulk** to snooze

**Davy Jones** a sailors' name for the malignant spirit of the sea

**Davy Jones's locker** the sea, especially when thought of as the grave of drowned sailors

**deck ape** a US term for an enlisted sailor in the US Navy

**doctor** a ship's cook

**dog's-body** pease pudding

**drink** 'the drink' is the sea

**fantod** a fidgety, fussy person, especially a ship's officer

**full blues** full formal naval uniform

**gash** something that is 'gash'

is spare or extra

**gob** a sailor in the US Navy

**greaser** a ship's engineer

**grey funnel line** the Royal Navy

**head** or **heads** a ship's toilet

**Irish lager** stout, especially Guinness

**Jack Dusty** a Royal Navy storeman

**Jack tar** a sailor

**Jimmy-the-one** a first lieutenant in the Royal Navy

**jonty** a naval master-at-arms

**jump ship** to leave one's ship while still officially employed or in service

**middy** a midshipman in the Royal Navy

**mudhook** an anchor

**muslin** a collective term for a ship's sails, or the canvas from which they are made

**number one** a lieutenant, or ship's first officer under its commander

**oggin** the sea

**on the beach** if a sailor is 'on the beach', he is unemployed or has been dismissed from the Navy

**owner** the captain of a warship

**part brass rags** to quarrel

**pigboat** a US term for a submarine

**pusser** a 'pusser' is a naval supply officer (or purser); something described as being 'pusser' is considered to be smart, genuine, official, or formal

**quarterdecker** a stickler for naval etiquette (the quarterdeck being the part of the deck used by superior officers)

**reefer** a midshipman in the Royal Navy

**salt** a sailor, especially an experienced one (an 'old salt')

**scattermouch** an old term for a person from the Mediterranean

**sea lawyer** a (low-ranking) sailor who is versed in the intricacies of maritime law and who disputatiously stands on his rights or finds fault with the decisions of his superiors

**snotty** a midshipman in the Royal Navy

**sparks** a ship's radio operator

**spitcher** if something or someone is described as 'spitcher', it is done for

**splice the mainbrace** to serve out (or partake of) an allowance of alcoholic spirits

**stew-can** a destroyer

**stinker** a fulmar or petrel (which ejects a foul-smelling oil from its stomach)

**striper** a naval officer (from the bands or stripes on the sleeve of an officer's uniform)

**sun dodger** a submariner

**swab** a clumsy person; in old naval slang, a 'swab' also meant an officer's epaulette

**swabby** a US term for a seaman, especially a new recruit

**tar** a sailor

**tarpaulin** a sailor

**three sheets in the wind** somewhat drunk (the expression comes from the nautical use of 'sheet' to mean a rope securing a sail; if sheets are flapping in the wind, the sail is not properly secured)

**tiddley** a person or thing described as 'tiddley' is smart or trim

**tin fish** a torpedo

**water dog** an experienced sailor

## Legal slang

The legal profession tends to be a closed book to most laymen, and it is often said that members of the profession prefer to keep things that way. Legal language is required to be particularly precise so as not to be open to misinterpretation, but its Norman French, its Latin and its hedges of conditions and provisos do not concern us here. Like other professions, the law has its own slang and the list below is intended to be a representative selection of this. While laymen would hope to avoid first-hand acquaintance with the workings of the courts, they are nevertheless likely to encounter much of its less formal terminology through the medium of fiction, especially in film and television drama, from *Rumpole of the Bailey* to *Ally McBeal*. In this way, many of us who really have no business knowing such things can say what it is to 'cop a plea'. The Atlantic is no barrier, and we have long known what it is to 'take the Fifth' or when we are face with a 'Philadelphia lawyer'. Some of the following items are used equally by criminals ('brief' for example) and it may be that readers searching for a specific word may find it under the section of the book that deals with **Criminal slang**.

# Glossary

**ABH** the offence of actual bodily harm

**ambulance-chaser** a lawyer on the lookout for accidents in order to instigate actions for damages

**beak** a magistrate

**brief** a lawyer, especially a barrister

**cab-rank principle** or **rule** a rule requiring barristers to take the first case offered to them, regardless of their opinion of it

**cop a plea** to plead guilty to a lesser charge in order to speed up the judicial process or avoid a heavier sentence

**GBH** the offence of grievous bodily harm

**John** or **Jane Doe** a name used for an unidentified suspect or victim

**jump bail** to abscond while on bail

**kangaroo court** a court operated by a mob, by prisoners in jail, or by any improperly constituted body

**legal eagle** a bright, discerning lawyer

**McKenzie Friend** a person who attends court with an unrepresented litigant in person to render assistance in presenting the case, but is not qualified to address the court

**mopery** a US term for a minor or imagined violation of the law

**NAI** non-accidental injury

**notchel** notice that one will not be responsible for another's debts

**palimony** alimony or its equivalent demanded by one partner when the couple have been cohabiting without being married

**Philadelphia lawyer** a very able, shrewd or sharp lawyer

**scofflaw** a US term for a person who is contemptuous of, or flouts, the law

**shoulder knot** a bailiff

**shyster** an unscrupulous or disreputable lawyer

**silk** a Queen's Counsel or King's Counsel

**sus laws** laws allowing a person to be arrested on suspicion of having committed a crime

**take the Fifth** to refuse to testify (in accordance with the Fifth Amendment to the

Constitution of the USA, which allows persons on trial not to testify against themselves)

**third degree** to give someone 'the third degree' is to subject them to intense cross-examination

**walk** to go free after being tried in a court of law

**wig** a judge

**wingman** a person who hears a case alongside a judge, under the judge's chairmanship

## *Medical slang*

The medical profession has been described as having a great need for insiders' language. For one thing, it is often thought better not to further upset those who are already unwell (or their concerned relatives or friends) by emphasizing gory details. Thus, deliberately obscure language and euphemism are often part of any medical practitioner's kit. From another point of view, a certain amount of black humour is usually brought into play as a means of dealing with distressing experiences on a daily basis. While it seems that increasing numbers of us are willing to contemplate a bit of 'nip and tuck', even 'the snip', who would want to fall into the category of 'LOBNH'? Readers may find some of this language offensive or worryingly flippant, but medical professionals would no doubt argue that it has always been like this and that standards of care are in no way diminished by less-than-respectful language.

### *Glossary*

**angel** a nurse

**baby catcher** an obstetrician

**basket case** a person with all four limbs amputated

**bleeder** a haemophiliac

**blood work** the results of a patient's blood tests

**bones** a nickname for a doctor

**bug** a viral disease

**caesar** a Caesarean section

**chemo** chemotherapy, the treatment of disease (especially cancer) by means of chemical compounds selectively directed

**clotbuster** any drug used to dissolve blood clots

**CPR** cardiopulmonary resuscitation

**crocus** a quack doctor

**elderly prim** a woman of 25 or over who is pregnant for the first time

**ENT** ear, nose and throat

**Freud Squad** psychiatrists collectively

**gasser** an anaesthetist

**gum digger** an old Australian term for a dentist

**heartsink** a person who causes medical practitioners to become exasperated because he or she makes repeated requests for medical attention, but is not able to be treated effectively

**hype** a hypodermic needle

**IC** intensive care

**jab** an injection

**larry** to 'do a larry' is to work as a locum

**nip and tuck** cosmetic surgery

**ob-gyn** the branch of medicine dealing with obstetrics and gynaecology, or a medical practitioner specializing in this

**orthopod** an orthopaedic surgeon

**pill-pusher** a doctor

**preemie** a premature baby

**prim** a primigravida, ie a woman who is due to give birth for the first time

**pumpkin positive** a description of a patient as unintelligent (from the idea that a light shone into the patient's mouth lights up their supposedly empty head like a Hallowe'en pumpkin)

**sawbones** a surgeon or doctor

**shot** an injection

**slasher** a surgeon

**snip** 'the snip' is a vasectomy

**stat** immediately (short for the Latin word *statim*)

**strep** any of the Streptococcus bacteria

**strep throat** an acute streptococcal infection of the throat

**tubes** if a woman 'has her tubes tied', she undergoes a sterilizing procedure on her Fallopian tubes

**tummy tuck** a plastic surgery procedure for the stomach

**whopper with cheese** an overweight woman suffering from thrush

One distinctive area of medical slang comprises the cryptic abbreviations made on patients' notes by doctors in hospitals or surgeries. These are often far from complimentary, although sometimes they are simply in-jokes scribbled down to relieve tedium. A few of these are shown below:

**BUNDY** but unfortunately not dead yet: suggesting that the demise of a troublesome patient would not be unwelcome

**CNS-QNS** central nervous system – quantity not sufficient: suggesting that a patient is unintelligent

**DBI** dirt bag index: used with a number from a scale to suggest how long it has been since a patient washed

**DIFFC** dropped in for friendly chat: not actually suffering from anything

**FLK** funny-looking kid: relating to a child with a strange appearance

**GLM** good-looking mum: suggesting a child's mother is worth attention

**GOK** God only knows: relating to a puzzling case

**GOMER** get out of my emergency room: used by US doctors to stigmatize patients who are uncooperative or unable to explain what is wrong with them

**LOBNH** lights on but nobody home: a low assessment of a patient's intelligence

**LOL** little old lady

**PFO** pissed, fell over: referring to a patient injured while drunk

**PGT** pissed, got thumped: the patient was injured in a drunken fight

**TATT** tired all the time

**TTFO** told to fuck off: relating to a patient dismissed without treatment

# Police slang

The fact that many of us who have never served in the police force are familiar with at least some of its slang again has to be attributed to fiction. The Victorian era saw a rapid growth in crime fiction, with the immortal Sherlock Holmes representing only the pinnacle of the genre. In the 20th century the 'police procedural' (a style of crime novel that deals with the details of police investigation) came to rival the exploits of the great maverick private detectives. Crime stories also proliferated in the movies and on television screens, encouraging generations of kids to play at 'cops and robbers'. In the UK, TV programmes from *Z-Cars* to *The Sweeney* to *The Bill* introduced a largely unsuspecting public to the slang used by both police and their criminal adversaries, and we became quite accustomed to the perpetrator of 'an inside job' being caught 'bang to rights' and ending up in 'the nick'. The British public, through a long exposure to imported cop shows, has become acquainted with American slang that would otherwise remain completely opaque, and many know immediately what is meant by an 'APB', 'ten-four' and 'officer down'. Much of the slang used by the police is, inevitably, equally familiar to the criminal element (and vice versa) and it may be that terms not found here will be included under the section on **Criminal slang**.

## *Glossary*

**APB** an all-points bulletin, a report giving details of a wanted person, crime, etc issued by one police station and transmitted to all others in the region or state of the USA

**back-up** assistance from other police officers

**bang to rights** someone who is caught 'bang to rights' is caught red-handed in the act of committing a crime

**bone** to seize or arrest someone

**bust** a police raid

**canary** an informer (so called because they 'sing' to the police)

**chummy** a criminal, especially a thief

**collar** to arrest someone

**cop** a capture or arrest

**cuffs** handcuffs

**dabs** fingerprints

**darbies** handcuffs

**dee-wee** a US term for 'driving while intoxicated'

**domestic** a row between

people living in the same house, usually a couple

**drop a dime** in the USA, to 'drop a dime' means to make a phone call to the police, especially to inform on someone

**drunk tank** a US term for a police cell where drunks are held

**face** a well-known criminal

**firm** a criminal gang

**floater** a corpse found floating in a river or other body of water

**form** a person who 'has form' has a criminal record

**gangbanger** a member of a US street gang

**gangbuster** a special police agent working to combat criminal gangs in the USA

**go down** to be sent to prison

**goon** a US term for a hired thug

**gov** or **guv** a detective's term of address for his boss (shortened from 'governor')

**hard man** a criminal specializing in acts of violence

**helmet** a uniformed officer

**hot** recently stolen or obtained dishonestly

**inside** someone who is 'inside' is serving a prison sentence

**inside job** a crime carried out by or with the help of someone trusted or employed by the victim

**job** US police officers often describe working for the police force as being 'on the job'

**lids** a collection of uniformed officers

**lift** someone who gets 'lifted' is arrested

**manor** a police district

**Met** 'The Met' is the London Metropolitan Police force

**Mister Big** the head of a criminal organization

**MO** a criminal's 'MO' is his typical method of working (an abbreviation of the Latin phrase *modus operandi*)

**Mob** in the USA, 'the Mob' means the Mafia, or organized crime in general

**mobster** a US gangster

**mug shot** a photograph of a person's face taken for police records

**mule** a person who smuggles drugs into a country for a dealer

**narc** a US term for a narcotics agent

**nark** an informant

**nick** 'the nick' is a prison or police station; to 'nick' someone is to arrest them

**nose** a police nformer

**nostrils** a sawn-off shotgun

**obbo** observation carried out on suspected criminals

**officer down** a term used on police radio in the USA to notify that an officer has been wounded

**one-eight-seven** the code for a homicide used by the Los Angeles Police Department

**paddy wagon** a van for transporting prisoners

**perp** a US term for the perpetrator of a crime

**pinch** to arrest someone

**previous** someone who has 'got previous' has had previous convictions

**prior** a US term for a previous conviction

**pull** or **pull up** to arrest someone

**puppy-walker** an experienced police officer who introduces a new recruit to his or her beat

**rabbit** a suspect who runs away

**rap sheet** a record of a person's arrests and convictions or a charge sheet

**rogues' gallery** a police collection of photographs of criminals

**Saturday night special** a US term for a small, inexpensive handgun

**shooter** a firearm

**sing** to confess or inform on someone to the police

**skell** a homeless person who lives on the streets and begs for money

**snout** a police informer

**stake out** to put a person or place under surveillance

**sting** a trap for criminals set up by the police

**Sweeney** 'the Sweeney' is a name for the flying squad (shortened from the rhyming slang 'Sweeney Todd')

**ten-four** a code word used to acknowledge receipt of a radio message

**tom** a prostitute

**twoccing** the practice of stealing cars (from the initials of the technical term *taking without owner's consent*)

**verbal** an arrested suspect's oral confession of guilt

**vic** a US term for the victim of a crime

**villain** a criminal

**walk** to go free from a court of law

**wire** a portable recording device, as worn by someone

taking part in a police surveillance or evidence-gathering operation

**wolly** a uniformed policeman, especially a raw young constable

**woodentop** a uniformed officer

## Journalists' and printers' slang

While reporting the news, as a branch of writing (a news report is still 'a story'), is considered a profession, the business of producing newspapers is undoubtedly a trade. For this reason, slang connected with the field contains elements of both the literary (albeit rather disrespectful, as in 'hack' or 'ink-slinger') and the commercial (as in 'glossies' or 'scandal sheet'). Over the last couple of centuries newspapers have evolved a language of their own, largely arising out of the constraints of headline-writing. When you want to make important words as large as possible in print, you have to keep them short. Thus, on the front pages of newspapers, people are not criticized or censured but 'rapped'; things are not scrutinized or investigated but 'probed'. Certain tabloids take this to extremes, such as in one-word headlines like *The Sun*'s infamous 'Gotcha'. While, in the past, more challenging vocabulary would be used in the full articles within the august publication, increasingly the lazy hacks concerned simply repeat the monosyllabic terms as if no alternative were available.

News reporting became multi-media in the 20th century, especially on radio and television, and this also generated specific slang, such as 'bong' and 'noddy'.

The glossary below also contains slang traditionally used by printers in the newspaper industry. Although much of this became obsolete with the introduction of computer typesetting, some of the terms remain in use.

# Glossary

**advance** an 'advance' is a news story about an event that has yet to happen

**agony aunt** a person, usually a woman, who gives advice in a newspaper column or in a radio or television programme

**agony column** the part of a newspaper or magazine in which readers submit, and receive advice about, personal problems

**antimony** a printers' term for metal type

**back bench** a collective term for a newspaper's senior journalists

**Balaam** unimportant paragraphs kept in readiness to fill up blank space in a newspaper

**bang** an exclamation mark

**bed** when a newspaper or magazine 'goes to bed' or is 'put to bed', this means that it is sent to be printed

**blatt** a newspaper

**blind interview** an interview with someone whose name, for reasons such as privacy or security, is not disclosed

**bong** a headline on a television news programme

(from the original use by ITN of an individual 'chime' of Big Ben to signal a new headline being read out)

**bulks** copies of a newspaper that are distributed free for promotional purposes

**bump** if a news story is 'bumped', it is moved from its original position in print or in a broadcast running order to accommodate a more recent or important development

**cub** a young trainee reporter

**glossies** magazines printed on glossy paper

**goss** gossip, as reported in newspapers or magazines

**graf** a paragraph

**Grauniad** a nickname for the *Guardian* newspaper, based on its allegedly large number of typographical errors

**griff** the true facts, accurate information

**hack** any journalist

**hackette** a female journalist

**hatches, matches and dispatches** newspaper announcements of births, marriages and deaths

**heavies** those newspapers regarded as serious or

highbrow may be referred to collectively as 'the heavies'

**Indie** a nickname for the *Independent* newspaper (its Sunday edition being known as the 'Sindie')

**ink-jerker** or **ink-slinger** a journalist

**kicker** the opening lines or paragraph of a story, often printed in a different font in order to grab the reader's attention

**kill fee** a fee paid to the writer of an article that was commissioned but not published (for whatever reason), usually being less than the sum paid for a published piece

**lead** the first sentence or two of a news report, whether in print or broadcast, which 'leads' the reader or audience into the story by providing many of the major points

**lockout** the final words of a broadcast report, usually identifying the reporter and the station or programme as well as the location

**mag** a magazine

**newshound** a reporter

**News of the Screws** a nickname for the *News of the World* newspaper, based on its alleged tendency to focus on salacious stories

**noddy** a sequence in a filmed interview in which the interviewer is photographed nodding in acknowledgement of what the interviewee is saying

**pap** a member of the paparazzi, photographers who specialize in spying on or harassing famous people in order to obtain photographs of them in unguarded moments

**penny-a-liner** a hack writer

**pull-out quote** a quotation from a story displayed beside or within it in prominent type to grab the attention of casual readers

**qualities** newspapers considered to contain a high standard of journalism may be referred to collectively as 'the qualities'

**rag** a newspaper

**rag-out** a newspaper article or headline reproduced in a later issue with a ragged edge as if torn out

**ratpack** a group of photographers aggressively pursuing famous people

**red-top** any tabloid newspaper whose masthead is printed in red, noted especially for sensationalism and prurience

**scandal sheet** a newspaper with a reputation for publishing scandal or gossip

**screamer** a sensational headline, or an exclamation mark

**shoutline** a short line of text, usually in bold type, drawing attention to an important point

**sling ink** to write for the press

**smoot** a compositor who does odd jobs in various printing houses

**snapper** a photographer

**sob sister** an agony aunt

**squeak** a feeble newspaper

**stalkerazzi** members of the paparazzi who pursue celebrities to an extreme degree in order to obtain photographs and information

**sub** a subeditor

**Thunderer** 'The Thunderer' is an old nickname for *The Times* newspaper

**tired and emotional** a phrase used as a euphemism to indicate that a person was drunk

**top of the hour** the first minutes after the hour, when many news reports are broadcast

**topspin** extra, not always reliable or well-attested, information

**Torygraph** a nickname for the *Daily Telegraph* newspaper, based on its alleged bias towards the Conservative Party

**tweak** to 'tweak' another journalist's copy is to edit or rewrite it

**typo** a typographical error

**visibly moved** a phrase used as a euphemism to indicate that a person was weeping or in tears

**zinger** a US term for a humorous barb at the end of a news report

# *Musicians' slang*

At its more exalted levels, music is indeed an art. However, to many musicians not talented or fortunate enough to operate in these higher regions it is first and foremost a means of earning a living, and it is among journeyman musicians that slang especially flourishes. A working musician has to master his or her 'chops' and 'licks' to have any hope of one day becoming a 'chart-buster'. The musicians' instruments are the tools of their trade and they are often given familiar, shorter and zippier names. Thus a guitar becomes an 'axe', a harmonica becomes a 'harp' and piano keys become 'ivories'.

Among younger people in particular, music can be so intimately integral to everyday life that many of the terms first used by musicians become part of both a wider cultural movement and general language use. Music remains, of course, a branch of the entertainment industry and it may be that many terms relating to this aspect of the art will be found under the section on **Show business slang**.

## *Glossary*

**axe** a guitar (in rock music) or a saxophone (in jazz)

**axeman** a guitarist (in rock music) or saxophonist (in jazz)

**blow off the stage** if a band or performer 'blows someone off the stage', they play better, louder or more impressively than another band or performer

**cat** a fan of jazz

**chart-buster** a recording artist or a recording that is very successful

**chops** skill or ability at playing

**cook** musicians who are playing skilfully and generating excitement are often said to be 'cooking'

**cut** a recording, or an individual track on a recording

**deejay** a disc jockey

**demo** a musical recording made to demonstrate the quality of a performer to a prospective recording company

**gig** an engagement, especially of a band or pop group for one performance only, or such a performance

**groove** to listen or dance to pop or jazz music

**groupie** a (usually female) fan who follows pop groups wherever they appear, often in the hope of having sexual relations with them

**harp** a harmonica or mouth-organ

**in the groove** music or playing that is 'in the groove' is excellent

**ivories** piano keys

**kitchen** the percussion section of an orchestra

**lick** a short instrumental passage or flourish

**muso** a musician or music enthusiast

**noodle** to improvise on a musical instrument in a casual or desultory way

**one-night stand** a performance given on one single evening in one place by one or more people who then travel on to another place

**on the road** travelling from place to place giving performances

**plank spanker** a player of an electric guitar

**roadie** a member of the crew who transport, set up and dismantle equipment for musicians on tour

**skins** drums

**skinsman** a drummer

**squiffer** a concertina

**Strat** a Fender Stratocaster, a proprietary model of electric guitar

**thrash** short for **thrash metal**, a type of very fast, loud rock music, often with violent themes

**tickle the ivories** to play the piano

**traps** drums or other percussion instruments

**vee-jay** or **veejay** a broadcaster who introduces and plays music videos (a phonetic spelling of the initials 'VJ' for 'video jockey')

**woodshedding** a period of intensive private practice or rehearsal

## Show business slang

The term 'show business' covers a fairly wide range of activities, from theatre to cinema, from variety shows to television and radio, and the following list contains industry-specific terms from many of these different genres. However, many of the slang terms included are used by entertainers across several different fields, as being part of the generalized experience of professional performers. Like many other types of slang, that of show business creates a sense of being an insider, of belonging to a community that is somehow special. This is important particularly to those struggling in low-paid, usually temporary, employment, or 'resting'. By far the greatest number of professionals never reach the glamorous heights of the major stars, but they are still in the same business, still members of the freemasonry of performers. Show business can be inward-looking, and it is to stage shows about putting on a show, or films about the movie industry, that the general public owes its familiarity with some of the terms included here.

## Glossary

**Abby Singer** the second-last shot of a day's filming (named after Abner E Singer, a Hollywood production manager and assistant director, who was notorious for pretending that the second-last shot of the day was actually the last shot)

**actioner** a film with plenty of action scenes

**am-dram** amateur dramatics

**angel** someone who gives financial backing to a theatrical venture

**baddy** a villain in a film, television show, etc

**bird** to 'give the bird' to an act is to hiss it off the stage (the bird in question being the goose, which makes a hissing noise)

**Bollywood** the Indian commercial film industry (a blend of 'Bombay', now Mumbai, a centre of the industry, and 'Hollywood')

**bomb** a film that is a commercial failure

**borsch belt** or **circuit** the group of summer resort hotels in the Catskill Mountains in the eastern USA, known as traditional venues for comedians (so called because they attract a predominantly Jewish clientele)

**bring the house down** to evoke very loud applause in a place of entertainment

**casting couch** a couch on which actresses are said to be seduced with the promise of a part in a film or play

**chew** or **chew up the scenery** to overact

**chick flick** a film likely to appeal only to women

**chopsocky** a genre of films featuring martial arts

**corpse** an actor 'corpses' when he or she forgets his or her lines or can't speak them because of uncontrollable laughter

**deepie** a film projected in three dimensions

**die** to flop, especially on stage

**dry** when an actor 'dries' he or she forgets his or her lines

**egg** a joke

**flick** a cinema film

**gagster** a comedian

**give it up for** to show one's appreciation of a performer by cheering or applause

**goody** a hero of a film, television show, etc

**Great White Way** Broadway, a street in New York City noted for its theatres

**ham** an actor who overacts

**helm** to direct a film

**helmer** a film director

**hoofer** a professional dancer

**horse opera** a Western film

**improv** improvised comedy

**in the can** if a film or scene is 'in the can', it has been successfully shot (a 'can' is a cylindrical container for storing film)

**lay an egg** if a comedian or performance 'lays an egg', they flop

**leg-business** ballet-dancing

**lensman** a cameraman

**luvvie** or **luvvy** an actor or other member of the entertainment industry, especially when regarded as overly pretentious or affected

**MacGuffin** or **McGuffin** a term coined by Alfred Hitchcock for the element of a film that drives, or provides an excuse for, the action, of supreme importance to the main characters but hardly noticed by the audience

**martini shot** the last shot of a day's filming (so called because the next item on the agenda would be a drink)

**nabes** a US term for local or neighbourhood cinemas

**nut** the amount of money a film must earn in order to break even

**oater** a Western film

**niterie** a nightclub

**open** if an actor can 'open a movie' this means his or her presence in it is enough to guarantee its success at the box office

**paper the house** to fill a theatre by issuing free passes

**peeler** a striptease artist

**plant** a performer pretending to be an ordinary member of an audience to assist a performer (such as a comedian or illusionist) on stage

**prequel** a film produced as a follow-up to one that has proved a success, based on the same leading characters but showing what happened before the start of the original story

**resting** an actor who is out of work is said to be 'resting'

**romcom** a romantic comedy

**showbiz** show business

**shtick** a comedian's familiar routine or line of chat

**silver screen** a cinema screen, or the film industry as a whole

**skin flick** a cinema film in which there is much nudity and sexual activity, especially a cheaply made pornographic film

**slasher film** or **movie** a horror film in which people are slashed with knives, razors, etc

**sleeper** a film which becomes popular after an initial period of not being so

**soap** a soap opera, a sentimental, melodramatic television or radio serial concerned with the day-to-day lives of a family or other small group

**space opera** a science-fiction film

**spear carrier** an actor in a minor, non-speaking role

**splatter film** or **movie** a film in which graphic scenes of gory mutilation are depicted, employing various special effects

**straight man** an actor who feeds lines to a comedian and is used as the butt of the jokes

**ten-percenter** an agent

**thesp** an actor (a shortened from of 'thespian')

**threequel** the third film in a series, a sequel to a sequel

**Tinseltown** Hollywood, the centre of the US film industry

**top banana** the star entertainer in a line-up, especially of comedians

**turkey** a film or play that is a complete failure

**weepie** a highly emotional film or play

**yok** or **yock** a laugh

One specialized field of show business slang is that known as 'Variety-speak'. This is the distinctive vocabulary used by the magazine *Variety*, the trade paper that is the 'house journal' of the US entertainment industry. It specializes in shortening words to make snappy headlines, nicknaming people and places, and using abbreviations. Here are a few of its typical expressions:

**Beantown** Boston, Massachusetts
**Beertown** Milwaukee, Wisconsin
**b.f.** boyfriend
**boffo** very good or successful
**cleffer** a songwriter
**coin** money
**competish** competition
**crix** critics
**g.f.** girlfriend
**horse opera** a Western film
**legs** a film or stage production having a good run at the box-office is said to 'have legs'
**lensman** cameraman
**moppet** a child actor
**nsg** not so good
**oater** a Western film
**p.a.** personal appearance
**pour** a cocktail party
**praiser** a publicist
**socko** very good or successful
**the o.o.** the once-over
**whammo** very good or successful

Polari or Parlyaree is a variety of slang that is most commonly used among members of the theatrical profession. It is believed to have evolved out of the lingua franca used around Mediterranean ports and brought to Britain by British sailors. Other influences include the Romany encountered by strolling players and back-slang. Some of its words and phrases have achieved a wider currency, most notably among the gay community. Here are just a few examples:

**Aunt Nells** the ears
**Aunt Nellie fakes** earrings
**bona** good
**buvare** a drink
**carsey** a toilet, or a house
**charper** to search
**charpering omi** a policeman

**charver** to have sexual intercourse
**dinarly** money
**dolly** nice, pleasant, attractive
**dona** a woman
**eek** the face
**feele** a child
**lallie** a leg
**letty** or **latty** a bed or lodgings
**mangarly** or **mangary** food
**naff** inferior, worthless
**nantee** or **nanti** nothing

**ogle-fakes** spectacles
**omi** a man
**park** to give
**polone** or **paloney** a young woman, or an effeminate man
**riah** hair
**sharpy** a police officer
**strill** a musical instrument, especially a piano
**tober** road
**varda** or **vada** to look or see
**zhoosh** to fix, titivate or tidy
**zhooshy** showy

## Pornography Slang

Readers should note that much of the language in the list below, not to mention the practices described, may be highly offensive to many. Pornographic images have been created for centuries – sexually explicit wall paintings were discovered when the ancient Roman town of Pompeii was being excavated, for example – but what we usually think of as pornography involves film, whether as still photographs or moving pictures.

The pornography industry has come a long way since the days when it was associated with filthy postcards and men in macs furtively slipping in and out of seedy cinemas and 'pornshops'. If the morality of the whole thing is left to one side, the production of pornography must be seen as a trade in which people work and earn a living. This explains the creation of terms like 'money shot'. It may be part of the erotic illusion that what is being shown is real passion, but professionals in the business know that 'fluffers' are often necessary, that certain elements must be included in any shoot, and there are specific slang terms for all of them, from 'reverse cowboy' to 'golden showers' to 'pearl necklace'.

The Internet has done much to make pornography more universally available, and many of the slang expressions have become more widely known as netsurfers either seek out or accidentally happen upon porn sites spelling out exactly what they have on offer.

## Glossary

**all-natural** used to describe a woman who has not had breast implants or other body augmentation procedures

**back scuttle** to 'back scuttle' a woman is to penetrate her from behind

**barely legal** a term applied to women (or material featuring them) supposed to be only just old enough legally to take part in sexual activity

**bukkake** a genre of film in which a group of men masturbate over and ejaculate onto a single woman (originally a Japanese term)

**bunghole** the anus

**bust a nut** to ejaculate

**come shot** or **cum shot** a photograph or shot in a film in which a man is seen to ejaculate

**cowboy** a sexual position in which the woman sits astride the man, facing him

**cream pie** a film ending in which the man ejaculates inside the woman, often featuring shots of semen oozing from the vagina

**cum shot** see **come shot**

**doggy fashion** when people are filmed having sex 'doggy fashion' the man penetrates the woman from behind

**domme** a dominatrix

**double penetration** penetration of a woman by the penises of two men simultaneously, one in her vagina and one in her anus

**DP** an abbreviation for **double penetration**

**facial** an act of ejaculating semen onto a woman's face, following fellatio

**fisting** the insertion of the whole hand into a vagina or anus

**fluffer** someone whose job it is to arouse a male actor on a film set before filming begins or keep his penis erect between takes

**frosting** ejaculated semen

(from the US term for cake icing)

**golden showers** scenes in which urination on a sexual partner is shown (also called **water sports**)

**hentai** a Japanese genre of pornographic animation

**jazz mag** a pornographic magazine

**money shot** another term for **come shot** (so called because it is regarded as the culminating shot without which consumers are not getting their money's worth)

**naturals** female breasts that have not been surgically augmented

**pearl necklace** drops of ejaculated semen around the neck and upper chest of a woman following fellatio

**pop shot** same as **come shot**

**porn** or **porno** pornography

**pornshop** a shop selling pornographic literature, films, etc

**reverse cowboy** a sexual position in which the woman sits astride the man, facing away from him

**S and M** sadomasochistic practices

**solo** involving masturbation only

**split beaver** a sexually aroused, and therefore open, vagina

**stag film** a pornographic film

**stroke mag** a pornographic magazine

**stunt cock** a penis filmed only in close-ups during sexual activity, standing in for that of the main actor

**upskirt** a voyeuristic shot from below a (usually unsuspecting) woman wearing a short skirt

**water sports** same as **golden showers**

## Stock-exchange slang

Most people, even those who own no stocks or shares, will have heard of the activities of stock-market 'bulls' and 'bears'. However, there is a lot more to this area of slang than these legendary creatures. The specialized language used by stock market traders is often colourful, and can convey a picture of a world in which exciting events take place daily. A whiff of aggression, even violence, is never far away, with powerful buyers being labelled as 'dawn raiders', and 'poison pills' being employed to deter undesirable takeover bids. The world of myth and romance can also be conjured up by the contest between 'black knights' and 'white knights' and the occurrence of 'witching hours', whether double or treble. However, there is still room for the prosaic and day-to-day activities of what, for many, is simply a means of earning a living, perhaps as a 'bottom fisher' or in a 'bucket shop', with a weather eye on the 'Footsie' and a dread of being 'naked'.

## *Glossary*

**bear** a person who sells stocks for delivery at a future date, anticipating a fall in price

**bear market** a market in which prices are falling

**bed-and-breakfast deal** the purchase of stock to be held overnight only

**Big Bang** the changes in the system and rules of the British Stock Exchange instituted on 27 October 1986, in effect deregulating many of its practices

**black knight** a person making an unwelcome bid to take over a company

**black Monday** the international stock-market crash in October 1987

**blue-chip shares** the most reliable class of industrial shares

**bottom fisher** an investor who seeks to buy shares in badly performing companies in the hope that they will increase in value

**bottomish** appearing to have reached its lowest value

**bucket shop** the office of an unregistered stockbroker, a mere agent for bets on the rise or fall of prices of stock

**bull** a person who seeks to raise the price of stocks and speculates on a rise

**bull market** a market in which prices are rising

**concert party** a group of people working together to buy shares separately, in order to use them later as one holding

**corporate raider** a company or individual that seeks to gain control of a business by acquiring a large proportion of its stock

**daisy chain** a group of dealers who buy and sell a commodity among themselves in order to inflate the price to outside buyers

**dawn raid** a stock market operation in which a large proportion of a company's shares are suddenly bought, often in anticipation of a takeover bid

**dead-cat bounce** a temporary recovery of share prices following a sharp fall, not indicative of a true upturn but merely caused by some reinvestment by speculators who had already sold shares

**double witching hour** the final hour of certain periods of trading, when two kinds of future and option contracts expire and the market is exposed to volatility

**Fannie Mae** a security issued by the US Federal National Mortgage Association

**Footsie** the Financial Times Stock Exchange 100-Share Index

**gnome** an obscure but powerful international financier or banker

**grey knight** a third party who makes a counteroffer to buy a company that is subject to an unwanted takeover bid, without making their own ultimate intentions clear

**grey market** a financial market trading in shares not yet officially listed

**hammer** if a person or company is 'hammered' they are declared a defaulter

**junk bond** a bond offering high yield but with high risk

**kaffirs** South African mining shares

**kangaroos** Australian mining shares

**Lady Macbeth strategy** a strategy in a takeover battle in which a third party appears to act as a white knight, but in the end allies with the party making an unwelcome takeover bid

**naked** lacking the financial backing necessary to complete a contract or make it valid

**paper** stocks and shares

**park** to register securities under some other name in order to hide their true ownership

**poison pill** a clause or clauses in a company's articles of association put into effect by an unwanted takeover bid, and making such a takeover less attractive

**quant** a person who uses complex statistical models to predict fluctuations in the stock market

**raid** concerted selling by a group of speculators in order to lower the price of a particular stock

**rocket scientist** a mathematical expert who devises schemes to take advantage of price differentials on money markets

**shark repellents** strategies adopted by a business organization to avoid an unwanted takeover

**stag** a person who applies for shares in order to sell them at once at a profit

**ticker** a telegraph instrument that prints signals, such as stock-market prices, on a tape

**tipsheet** a newsletter containing advice on the buying and selling of shares

**toppy** appearing to have reached its highest value

**triple witching hour** the final hour of certain periods of trading, when three kinds of future and option contracts expire and the market is exposed to extreme volatility

**valium picnic** a day on the New York Stock Exchange when business is slow

**waddle** to become a defaulter

**Wall-Streeter** a financier based on Wall Street in New York City

**white knight** a person who rescues a company from an unwanted takeover bid

**white squire** a friendly party to whom a company chooses to transfer the bulk of its shares as a defence against a takeover move

## Commercial and business jargon

The world of commerce and business touches most of us in one form or another, whether as a customer or client buying anything from a computer mouse to a new home, as an employee in a shop or office, or even as a captain of industry. And we all know that the business world is notorious for its use of jargon. As in other professions, such language facilitates communication between those in the know, but it also acts as a means of obscuring the truth to inquisitive members of the public.

There does seem to be another dimension to business jargon, however, which is that of topicality. Much is made of the notional 'level playing field', but those who are not completely up to date with the current slang and jargon expressions risk revealing themselves as already being at a disadvantage, of being 'out of the loop'. At times there seems to be an almost perverse mania for coining neologisms when perfectly serviceable and plain English expressions could be used without needlessly mystifying anyone. Why else would anyone feel the need to come up with the likes of 'mission-critical', 'facetime' or 'helicopter view'?

## *Glossary*

**appro** when a product is made available to a customer 'on appro', this means that they can try it out without obligation to buy (the phrase is a shortening of 'on approval')

**bang for your buck** value for money

**bean counter** an accountant

**blue-sky thinking** speculation with no immediate practical function

**bricks-and-mortar** used to describe an enterprise that does not use the Internet to conduct its business

**bring to the table** to contribute or offer, especially in business negotiations

**clicks and mortar** retailing that combines traditional outlets with use of the Internet

**come on stream** to go into operation or production

**company doctor** an adviser, consultant or businessman who turns unprofitable or inefficient companies into profitable or efficient businesses

**cook the books** to falsify accounts

**corridor work** discussion

behind the scenes at a meeting

**creative accountancy** accountancy characterized by an imaginative re-interpretation or dubious manipulation of established rules of procedure for personal benefit or ease of operation

**exes** expenses

**facetime** time spent dealing with another person face-to-face

**featherbed** to provide with financial inducements

**filer** a filing cabinet

**gazump** a prospective house buyer is 'gazumped' when the seller raises the price of the property after accepting the buyer's offer but before the contract has been signed

**gazunder** the seller of a house is 'gazundered' when the buyer lowers the sum offered just before the contract is due to be signed

**get into bed with** to adopt as a partner in business

**get your ducks in a row** to become properly organized

**go bust** to become bankrupt

**go under** when a business fails or folds it is said to 'go under'

**gravy train** a job or scheme which offers high rewards for little effort

**grey pound** the spending power attributed to retired people

**guinea pig** a token company director who does not actually do anything

**helicopter view** a general view of a subject, lacking in specific detail

**honcho** a boss or manager

**hot-desking** the practice of allocating a desk in an office only to a worker who needs it at the time, rather than to each worker as a matter of course

**knock out** to make or sell

**level playing field** a position of equality, from which rivals may compete without anyone having an unfair advantage

**loop** if you are 'in the loop' you are included in a group to whom information is made available; being 'out of the loop' is being excluded from such a group

**lowballing** the business practice of tendering an unrealistically low price in order to secure a contract

**magalogue** or **magalog** a

large mail-order catalogue in the form of a magazine

**mission-critical** vital to the interests of a business

**outfit** a business organization

**perk** the 'perks of a job' are the incidental benefits that having the job brings, such as being provided with a company car

**pink pound** the spending power attributed to the gay community

**plug** to 'plug' a product is to give it a favourable mention in public, especially to do so persistently to force the item into familiarity

**power breakfast** or **lunch** a high-level business discussion held over breakfast or lunch respectively

**power dressing** the wearing, by businesswomen, of smart suits tailored on austerely masculine lines, so as to give an impression of confident efficiency and have a daunting effect on colleagues and contacts

**push the envelope** to attempt more than seems possible

**put up the shutters** to stop trading, either for the day or permanently

**roll out** to launch a new product or service

**shaper** a decisive, somewhat bullying manager who carries others along with his or her dynamism

**swindle-sheet** an employee's claim for expenses

**touch base** someone who 'touches base' with another makes contact with them, often without any specific reason

**wash** if a business or undertaking is said to 'wash its face' this means it just pays its way

# Bookmakers' slang

Much of the slang connected with bookmaking and betting in general consists of shorthand and codewords, largely arising from the times when bookmaking activities were illegal and bookies had to be careful of who was listening. Much of bookies' slang therefore consists of various types of disguised language, including rhyming slang (like 'Burlington Bertie') and back-slang, as in 'enin', 'rouf' and 'net'. Many people are part-time 'punters', with the odd 'flutter' on the big horse races such as the Grand National, and regular televising of racing has made at least some of the bookies' terms more familiar.

When bookies at racecourses are seen making elaborate hand gestures to one another and the punters, often touching a specific part of their bodies, they are using 'tick-tack', their very own method of telegraphic signalling. Humour has its place in this world, as expressions such as a 'Bismarck' illustrate. Perhaps this is not surprising, given the number of 'mug punters' there are out there. After all, as the popular saying has it, 'When did you ever see a poor bookie?'

## Glossary

**bag swinger** an Australian term for a bookmaker or bookmaker's clerk

**banker** a certainty

**beard** someone who places a bet on behalf of someone else who prefers to remain anonymous

**Bismarck** a favourite that bookmakers do not expect to win (the term derives from the German battleship of the same name, which was sent to the bottom of the Atlantic by the Royal Navy in World War II despite being considered 'unsinkable')

**blue bet** a phoney bet made to encourage credulous punters to follow suit

**bookie** a bookmaker

**bottle** odds of two to one

**Burlington Bertie** odds of one hundred to thirty

**carpet** odds of three to one (borrowed from the criminal slang for a three-month prison sentence)

**chalk** the favourite in a race

**chalk player** someone who habitually bets on favourites

**cockle** odds of ten to one

**dead cert** a certain winner

**dog** the underdog in a race

**dog player** someone who habitually bets on underdogs

**double carpet** odds of thirty-three to one

**each way** to place a bet 'each way' means you are betting for a win and for a place

**earhole** odds of six to four

**egg** an Australian term for a bookmaker who refuses to take a particular bet

**enin** odds of nine to one

**face** odds of five to two

**flutter** a bet or wager

**hand** or **handful** odds of five to one

**jolly** 'the jolly' is the favourite in a race

**leg** a swindler, especially at a racecourse

**levels you devils** odds of even money

**motser** an Australian term for a large amount of money, especially the proceeds of a gambling win

**mug punter** someone who makes bets that have very little chance of winning

**nailed on** if a horse in a race is said to be 'nailed on', it is considered a near-certainty to win

**nap** a racing tip that professes to be a certainty

**net** odds of ten to one

**neves** or **nevis** odds of seven to one

**no offers** a term that is marked (often in the abbreviation **n/o**) on a board by a bookmaker who is not prepared to offer any odds on a particular horse

**on the nose** if a bet is placed 'on the nose', this means the contestant is being backed to win only (and not to come second or third)

**parcel** a sum of money lost or won

**place** a position among the leading finishers (usually the first three) in a race

**pot** a large stake or bet

**pound** to 'pound' a horse or other runner in a race is to bet on it as almost a certainty

**prophet** a tipster

**punter** someone who places a bet

**rampsman** a person who gains money from bookmakers by deception (from the word 'ramp' meaning 'to swindle')

**roof** or **rouf** odds of four to one

**rort** in Australia, someone who 'rorts' calls the odds at a race meeting

**runner** a 'bookie's runner' is someone who takes bets or collects winnings on behalf of a bookmaker

**settler** someone who calculates the winnings on

bets for a bookmaker

**shoulder** odds of seven to four

**SP** the 'SP' is the starting price of a competitor (ie the odds at the time the race begins)

**springer** same as **steamer**

**steamer** a horse that quickly attracts numerous bets, leading to fast shortening of the odds against it

**stiff** a racehorse that is a poor bet

**thick** a 'thick' bet is one involving a large amount of money

**tick-tack** or **tic-tac** bookmakers' telegraphy by arm signals

**tips** odds of eleven to ten

**tissue** a bookmaker's forecast

**top of the head** odds of nine to four

**turf accountant** a bookmaker

**velvet** gains or winnings

**vigorish** a percentage of a gambler's winnings taken by the bookmaker

**wrist** odds of five to four

**xis** odds of six to one

# SECTIONS OF SOCIETY

## Criminal slang

Criminals, probably more than any other section of society, have always had good reason to keep their activities as clandestine as possible, and referring to things in a language all of their own was an obvious way to do this. There are collections of 'thieves' cant' dating back to Elizabethan times, and criminal slang has continued to evolve in order to deal with new activities and opportunities. Some of this 'secret' vocabulary has always leaked out into the common domain, markedly through crime fiction and latterly through films and television series based on the old formula of 'cops and robbers'. A common thread in this particular slang is the hatred and contempt expressed for the traditional enemy, the police (referred to in such graphic terms as 'beasts' or 'filth'), who are always eager to 'fit' or 'stitch you up' on a 'bum rap'. Another focus of animosity are traitors such as the 'grass' or 'nark', or 'canaries' who are only too ready to 'sing'. The close association of police and criminals means that some of the slang concerning crime is common to both, and it may be that some of the items listed in this book under **Police slang** would be equally at home here, and vice versa. Slang that is more common to the world of organized crime may be found under **Gangland slang**, and that occupational hazard of the professional criminal, prison, is listed separately under **Prison slang**.

## Glossary

**banana** a corrupt police officer (a play on the idea of being 'bent')

**bang to rights** someone who is caught 'bang to rights' is caught red-handed in the act of committing a crime

**bang up** to imprison or shut someone in a cell

**beak** a magistrate

**beast** a police officer

**bent** crooked, criminal or stolen

**betty** an old word for a burglar's jemmy

**Bill** 'the Bill' or 'the Old Bill' are members of the police force (the jury is still out on the origin of this term, perhaps the most likely explanation being that police officers in the 1920s and 1930s were often World War I veterans who reminded people of the moustached old soldier called 'Old Bill' in cartoons by the artist Bruce Bairnsfather)

**bin** a jail

**bird** to 'do bird' is to serve time in prison

**bizzy** a police officer

**black** to 'black' someone, or 'put the black on' them, is to blackmail them

**blag** to steal

**blow** to act as an informer

**boost** a US term meaning to shoplift or steal

**boys in blue** the police

**bracelets** handcuffs

**brass** a prostitute

**brief** a lawyer, especially a barrister

**bull** a US term for a prison guard

**bum rap** a false criminal charge

**bung** an old word for a purse

**burn** in the USA, someone who 'gets burned' is swindled in a transaction

**cabbage** to steal

**canary** an informer (so called because they 'sing' to the police)

**caper** a crime or illegal activity

**carry** someone who is 'carrying' has drugs or an illegal weapon on their person

**case** someone who 'cases a joint' reconnoitres or examines it, usually with a view to burglary

**cheat** an old term for a thing in general, especially the gallows

**cheese it** to run away, or stop doing something

**chiv** or **shiv** a knife

**choky** or **chokey** prison

**clean** someone who is 'clean' has nothing of an incriminating nature, such as a weapon or illegal drugs, on their person

**clink** prison

**clip joint** a place of entertainment, such as a night-club, where customers are overcharged or cheated

**clone** to copy the number of a stolen mobile phone onto a microchip which is then used in a different phone, so that the owner of the original phone is billed for any calls

**cockatoo** an Australian and New Zealand term for a lookout

**con** a swindle (also called a **con game** or **con trick**)

**con artist**, **con man** or **con woman** someone who swindles people by first gaining their confidence

**copper** a police officer

**copshop** a police station

**crack a crib** to break into a building

**crim** a criminal

**dabs** fingerprints

**darbies** handcuffs

**darkmans** an old word for night

**dick** a detective

**dip** a pickpocket

**diver** a pickpocket

**do** to 'do' a place, such as a bank, is to rob it; to 'get done' is to be prosecuted

**dob** in Australia, to 'dob in' a person is to inform on them

**drink** a monetary inducement, bribe or reward

**face** a well-known criminal

**Fed** an agent of the US Federal Bureau of Investigation

**fence** a receiver of stolen goods, or a place where one of these operates

**filth** 'the filth' is a derogatory name for the police force

**firebug** an arsonist

**fit up** to frame someone for a crime they did not commit

**five-finger discount** shoplifting

**fizgig** or **fizzgig** an old Australian term for a police informer

**flash** of or relating to criminals

**flimp** to rob someone while a partner distracts their attention

**form** a person who 'has form' has a criminal record

**frame-up** a false criminal charge made against an innocent person

**frightener** to 'put the frighteners on' someone is to attempt to make them afraid

**fry** a US term meaning to execute or be executed by electrocution

**fuzz** 'the fuzz' are the police

**game** 'the game' refers to thieving

**gill** a policewoman

**G-man** an agent of the US Federal Bureau of Investigation

**go down** to be sent to prison

**graft** illicit profit by corrupt means, especially in public life

**grass** an informer, especially to the police on a fellow criminal

**grass up** to 'grass someone up' is to inform on them

**gravy** money or profit obtained by corrupt practices

**grift** a US term meaning to swindle

**grifter** a US term for a swindler or con man

**gumshoe** a US term for a detective or policeman

**gun** a US term for a professional gunman or killer

**gun moll** a woman who associates with criminals

**gunsel** a US term for a gunman

**gyp** to swindle

**hard man** a criminal specializing in acts of violence

**harman** an old term for a constable

**harmans** the stocks in which criminals were formerly placed

**hatchet man** a man paid to use violence on others

**have nothing on** if the police 'have nothing on' someone, they have no incriminating evidence against him or her

**have your collar felt** to be arrested or apprehended by the police

**heat** a term with various meanings in the USA: 'the heat' can mean the police force itself, or a period of intensive search for a criminal after a crime has been committed (as in the phrase 'the heat is on'); to be 'packing heat' is to be carrying a firearm

**heater** a pistol

**heavy** a large, strong man employed for purposes of a violent and often criminal nature, or to deter others

**heist** a robbery or theft, especially an armed hold-up, or a particularly clever or spectacular theft

**hit** a murder by a criminal or criminals

**hitman** a person employed to kill or attack others

**hoister** a shoplifter

**hood** a violent criminal

**hooker** a prostitute

**hooky** stolen or illegal

**hot** recently stolen or obtained dishonestly

**hot seat** the electric chair

**hotting** the practice of attempting high-speed stunts in a stolen powerful car, often as a display

**hot-wire** to start the engine of a motor vehicle without a key by manipulating the wiring

**hustle** to obtain money illicitly, for example by swindling or working as a prostitute

**hustler** a swindler or a prostitute

**ice** diamonds or other precious stones

**iceman** a jewel thief

**illywhacker** an Australian word for a conman

**inside** someone who is 'inside' is serving a prison sentence

**inside job** a crime carried out by or with the help of someone trusted or employed by the victim

**job** a criminal enterprise, especially theft

**john** a prostitute's client

**John Hop** an Australian and New Zealand term for a police officer (rhyming slang for 'cop')

**jump bail** to abscond while on bail

**kinchin** a child

**knocking shop** a brothel

**knock off** to steal or rob

**launder** to 'launder' money

is to handle it in such a way that the identity or illegality of its source, the illegality of the transfer or the identity or criminality of the people involved remains undetected

**law** 'the law' means the police force or a police officer

**lift** someone who gets 'lifted' is arrested

**loid** to 'loid' a lock is to spring it using a strip of Celluloid®

**lorry** someone who has possession of something that does not belong to him might say that it 'fell off the back of a lorry'

**mack** a pimp

**manor** a police district

**mark** a suitable victim for trickery or theft

**mill** to rob or steal

**Mister Big** the head of a criminal organization or operation

**mittens** handcuffs

**moody** fake or counterfeit

**nab** to arrest someone, especially in the act of committing a crime

**narc** a US term for a narcotics agent

**nark** an informant

**nick** 'the nick' is a prison or police station; to 'nick' someone is to arrest them

**nip** to arrest or steal

**nipper** a pickpocket

**nippers** handcuffs

**nobble** a word with quite a range of meanings: to 'nobble' a racehorse is to injure or drug it to prevent it from winning; to 'nobble' something is to obtain it dishonestly; to 'nobble' a person is to persuade or dissuade them by bribery or coercion, or it can mean to arrest them

**nose** a police informer

**Old Bill** see **Bill**

**on the game** earning money as a prostitute (also **on the streets** or **on the bash**)

**on the run** fleeing from the police

**on the take** someone who is 'on the take' is corrupt (ie taking bribes)

**pack** someone who is 'packing' is carrying a gun

**paperhanger** a US term for a person who makes or deals in forged cheques

**peach** to inform on someone

**peter** a safe

**peterman** a safe-blower

**piece** a gun

**pig** a derogatory term for a police officer

**pigeon** the victim of a swindle or con trick

**pinch** to arrest

**plod** a police officer, or the police force in general

**plug-ugly** a US term for a ruffian or thug

**ponce** a pimp

**previous** someone who has 'got previous' has had previous convictions

**prig** to steal

**pro** a prostitute

**pull** or **pull up** to arrest someone

**ramp** to rob or swindle

**rap** a criminal charge (someone who 'beats the rap' escapes conviction, whereas someone who 'takes the rap' takes the blame or punishment, especially in place of another)

**reader** a pocketbook

**receiver** a person who receives stolen goods

**ring** to disguise a stolen vehicle by exchanging its frame, engine number, etc with those of a legitimate vehicle

**ringer** a stolen vehicle whose identity has been disguised

**roll** to rob a person who is

helpless, especially drunk or asleep

**rozzer** a police officer

**scam** a swindle

**scream** an appeal against conviction

**screw** to burgle or rob a place

**shake down** to extort money from someone by threats or blackmail

**shamus** a US term for a detective

**shelf** in Australia, to 'shelf' a person is to inform on them

**shill** a US term for a con man's accomplice

**shooter** a firearm

**shop** to inform on someone to the police

**shoulder surfing** the practice of looking over the shoulder of someone who is using a cash machine, in an attempt to learn their PIN

**sing** to confess or inform on someone to the police

**skim** to copy information stored on a credit card in order to create a counterfeit card with the same account data

**skin game** a swindling trick

**snatch** a robbery or kidnapping

**snitch** an informer

**snitchers** handcuffs

**snout** a police informer

**snowdropper** or **snow-gatherer** a person who steals laundry from a clothes line

**soup** stolen plate that has been melted down

**souvenir** in Australia and New Zealand, to 'souvenir' something is to steal it

**squeal** to turn informer

**squeeze** to 'put the squeeze on' someone is to extort money from them

**steaming** a form of mugging used by gangs, eg on the London Underground, who rush through crowds, snatching whatever they can

**stick up** to rob a person or place at gunpoint

**stiff** to rob or cheat

**sting** a theft or piece of deception designed to make money

**stitch up** to incriminate someone by informing on them to the police

**stool pigeon** a police informer (often shortened to **stoolie**)

**straight** someone who is 'straight' is honest and respectable; to 'go straight' is to give up criminal activities

**straightener** a bribe

**swag** plunder or stolen goods

**swagsman** a burglar's accomplice who carries the plunder

**sweetener** a bribe

**swing** to be executed by hanging

**swipe** to steal

**time** to 'do time' is to serve a sentence of imprisonment

**tom** a prostitute

**tooled up** carrying a weapon, especially a gun

**torch** to set a place alight deliberately

**touch** a theft or a sum got by theft

**trap** a person who catches offenders

**trick** to 'turn tricks' is to earn money as a prostitute

**turn over** to 'turn over' a place is to rob it

**tweedle** to swindle or con someone

**tweedler** a con man, or a stolen vehicle sold as though legitimate

**vig** or **vigorish** excessive interest charged on a loan, especially an illegal one

**walloper** an Australian term for a policeman

**wash** same as **launder**

**weigh off** to 'weigh off' a criminal is to sentence him, especially to imprisonment

**whizzer** a pickpocket

**wire** a pickpocket

**working girl** a prostitute

**wristlets** handcuffs

**yegg** a US term for a burglar or safe-cracker

## Gangland slang

Much of what is considered gangland slang in the United Kingdom is common to other areas of crime. It is really to the USA that we have to look for slang that is truly and vividly specific to the world of organized crime. Since the rise to power of the likes of Al Capone in the 1920s, the activities of US gangsters have filled the media, with periodic waves of new interest being generated by films such as the *Godfather* trilogy, Martin Scorsese's *Goodfellas* and the more recent TV series *The Sopranos*. So prominent and colourful was the slang being used in these fictional depictions (and indeed in highly-publicized Mafia trials) that the term 'Mobspeak' was coined to categorize it. Much of it is, of course, given the Italian–American ethnicity of the Mafia families, derived from Italian or Sicilian dialect, lending it a further degree of opacity for 'civilians' who can never aspire to be 'wise guys'.

## Glossary

**bada-bing, bada-boom** a term, fairly meaningless in itself, used as a kind of verbal embellishment to emphasize how easy or automatic some process is supposed to be

**bagman** a man who collects or distributes money as part of racketeering

**bones** see **make your bones**

**borgata** a Mafia family

**button** or **button man** a member of the Mafia who kills on orders from above

**capo** the head of a branch of the Mafia (the overall boss is known as the 'capo di tutti capi')

**cement overshoes** what a victim of American gangster assassination is said to get when his feet are encased in cement and he is sunk in a river

**civilian** an ordinary member of the public

**clip** to murder

**Colombian necktie** a form of punishment killing in which the victim's tongue is pulled through the gap in his cut throat

**comare** the mistress of a Mafia member

**compare** a friend or fellow family member

**consigliere** an advisor, especially on legal matters

**contract** an undertaking or agreement to kill a particular person, especially for an agreed sum of money

**Cosa Nostra** another name for the Mafia (an Italian phrase literally meaning 'our thing')

**don** a Mafia boss

**enforcer** a member of a gang who uses strong-arm tactics to enforce the power of the gang or its leaders

**family** an individual Mafia organization or clan

**friend of mine** a phrase used by a family member to introduce a member of another family

**friend of ours** a phrase used by a family member to introduce one 'made man' to another

**gangbanger** a member of a US street gang

**gangsta** a US term for a member of a criminal gang

**gangster's moll** the girlfriend of a gangster

**godfather** the head of a criminal organization, especially a Mafia family

**goodfella** a gangster, especially a member of the Mafia

**goomare** same as **comare**

**goombah** someone who belongs to an American criminal gang, especially the Mafia

**hit** a murder by a criminal or criminals

**hitman** a person employed to kill or attack others

**homeboy** a (fellow) member of a US street gang (often shortened to **homie**)

**ice** to 'ice' a person is to kill them

**iceman** a professional killer

**made man** or **guy** a man who has been initiated into the higher ranks of the Mafia

**make your bones** to become a fully-fledged member of the Mafia, usually by killing someone on their behalf

**Mob** in the USA, 'the Mob' means the Mafia, or organized crime in general

**mobbed up** someone who is 'mobbed up' is a member of the Mafia

**mobster** a US gangster

**numbers game** or **racket** an illegal form of gambling in which players bet on the appearance of a chosen sequence of numbers in the financial pages of a newspaper, etc

**outfit** a gang

**pop** to kill

**protection** money extorted from shopkeepers, businessmen, etc as a bribe for leaving their property or business unharmed

**rub out** to murder

**soldier** an ordinary member of the Mafia

**taste** a percentage of the profits of an operation paid

to one's superior
**underboss** a high-ranking Mafia member, second only to a boss or 'don'
**wet your beak** to be given a share of the profits from an activity
**whack** to murder
**wise guy** a member of the US Mafia

## Prison slang

Imprisonment is one of the hazards of the criminal life and in some ways, prison slang is simply an extension 'inside' of the criminal slang current on the streets. However, rather like a branch of the armed forces, a prison is a community, no matter how transient and shifting its population sometimes is, and communities always tend to generate their own slang. A mastery of this language is, of course, one of the things that separate the old 'lags' from the 'stars', whether they are in for a 'haircut' or a 'nickel', and it is vital for inmates wishing to keep their concerns secret from the 'screws'. Below is a selection of prison-related slang from past and present, from Britain, America and elsewhere.

### Glossary

**all day and night** a US term for a life sentence
**badge** a US term for a prison guard
**bang up** to imprison or shut someone in a cell
**Barlinnie drumstick** a home-made weapon, usually a metal pipe with nails protruding from it (named after Barlinnie prison in Glasgow)
**beast** a sex offender, especially one convicted of assaulting children
**bed-leg** any improvised weapon
**big house** in the USA, 'the big house' is a term for a prison
**bird** to 'do bird' is to serve time in prison
**bit** a US term for a prison sentence

**boof** in US prisons, to 'boof' something is to smuggle it concealed in one's rectum

**brig** a US term for a prison

**bull** a US term for a prison guard

**bullet** a US term for a one-year prison sentence

**calaboose** a US term for a prison

**calendar** a prison sentence of one year

**can** a US term for a jail or prison

**canary** an old Australian term for a convict

**canary-bird** a jailbird or convict

**carpet** a prison sentence of three months (some say this is rhyming slang, with the full form 'carpet bag' meaning a drag; others believe it originates in the fact that three months was the time needed to weave a certain kind of carpet)

**cheese-eater** a US term for an informer

**choky** or **chokey** prison

**clink** prison

**college** prison

**cooler** a jail

**daddy** 'the daddy' is a title given to the dominant inmate in a particular part of a prison

**deuce** a US term for a two-year prison sentence

**digger** a solitary-confinement or segregation cell

**dime** a US term for a ten-year prison sentence

**double-bubble** 100% interest charged on a loan

**dub** to lock

**fish** a US term for someone who has only recently been imprisoned

**gate fever** a neurotic or restless condition affecting long-term prisoners nearing the end of their sentence

**go down** to be sent to prison

**guest of Her Majesty** someone who is serving a prison sentence

**haircut** a short prison sentence

**hit the bricks** a US phrase meaning to be released from prison

**hitch** a North American word for a term of imprisonment

**hole** 'the hole' is a solitary-confinement cell

**hoosegow** a US term for a prison or jail

**in hock** in prison

**joint** 'the joint' is a prison

**jug** a prison

**juvie** in the USA, a detention centre for juvenile offenders

**inside** someone who is 'inside' is serving a prison sentence

**knockback** a refusal of parole

**lag** a prisoner

**lifer** a prisoner serving a term of life imprisonment

**L-plate** a prisoner serving a term of life imprisonment

**lumber** someone in prison may be said to be 'in lumber'

**nick** a prison

**nickel** a US term for a five-year prison sentence

**nonce** a sex offender, especially one convicted of assaulting children

**on ice** in prison, especially in solitary confinement

**on the in** in prison

**on tour with the National** a British prisoner who is 'on tour with the National' has been an inmate in several of the country's prisons

**pad** a cell

**passman** a prisoner who is permitted to leave his cell in order to carry out certain duties

**pen** a US term for a prison (a shortened form of 'penitentiary')

**poky** or **pokey** jail

**pontoon** a sentence of twenty-one months

**porridge** to 'do porridge' is to serve a jail sentence

**quod** a prison

**ruck** a fight

**screw** a prison officer

**shank** a home-made weapon

**shit and a shave** a short prison sentence

**shop** prison

**slammer** a prison

**snout** tobacco

**spin** to 'spin' a prisoner's cell is to search it

**spring** to 'spring' someone is to procure their escape from prison or jail

**star** someone who is in prison for the first time

**stiff** an illegal letter sent or received by a prisoner

**stir** prison

**stretch** a term of imprisonment

**swy** an Australian term for a two-year prison sentence

**tank** a US term for a prison cell

**time** to 'do time' is to serve a sentence of imprisonment

**up the river** in the USA, to be sent or to go 'up the river' means to go to prison

## Drug world slang

The use of natural substances for their intoxicating or narcotic effects is probably as old as humankind itself. As medical science developed, so did the ability to manufacture artificial drugs and the resulting abuse of these. Especially from the 20th century onwards, with drug abuse being increasingly outlawed and penalized, the slang of the illicit drug world could be described as illustrating one of the archetypal functions of slang: to prevent undesirable listeners from knowing what is being spoken about.

New drugs arrive on the scene periodically and often come, in some ways, to define an era, as LSD did for the 1960s and ecstasy did for the 1990s. New slang terms are coined to refer not only to the substances themselves, but the people who use them habitually and the effects they produce. Many and varied are the ways in which to describe someone who is under the influence of drugs – as the glossary below demonstrates.

Because of the illegal nature of drug abuse and drug-trafficking, there are several areas of crossover between drug world slang and **Criminal slang**, and many of the terms listed in that section might also have found a home here.

### Glossary

**acid** LSD
**acid-head** or **acid freak**
  a person who takes LSD
  habitually
**angel dust** the drug
  phencyclidine, a hallucinogen
**bag** or **baggie** a quantity of
  drugs, especially heroin, in a
  paper bag or other container
**bang** an injection of a drug

**benny** an amphetamine tablet
  (from benzedrine)
**bindle** a packet containing
  drugs
**blow** cannabis or cocaine
**blow someone's mind** to
  cause someone to go into
  a state of ecstasy under the
  influence of a drug
**body packer** someone who

smuggles drugs by concealing them inside their body

**bombed** intoxicated by drugs

**bomber** a pill or capsule of an illicit drug such as amphetamine, or a cigarette containing marijuana

**brown sugar** heroin

**bummer** a bad trip on drugs

**candyman** a North American term for a drug pusher

**carry** someone who is 'carrying' has illegal drugs on their person

**Charlie** cocaine

**chase the dragon** to inhale the fumes of melting powdered heroin

**chronic** a potent form of marijuana

**clocker** a drug dealer who is available at any time (ie around the clock)

**coke** cocaine

**coked up** under the influence of cocaine

**cokehead** someone who takes cocaine habitually

**cold turkey** the sudden withdrawal of narcotics from a habitual user, accompanied by unpleasant symptoms

**come down** to emerge from the state induced by a hallucinogenic or addictive drug

**connection** a source of illicit drugs

**cook** a person who manufactures illegal drugs in a home-made laboratory

**cook up** to prepare a drug prior to injecting oneself with it

**crack** a form of cocaine mixed with other substances

**crackhead** a user or addict of crack

**crank** any amphetamine drug

**crash** to suffer the unpleasant after-effects of a drug high

**dealer** someone who sells drugs

**disco biscuit** a tablet of ecstasy

**doobie** a marijuana cigarette

**dope** a drug, especially marijuana

**dove** a tablet of ecstasy

**downer** a depressant drug

**E** the drug ecstasy or a tablet of this

**face** if you are 'off your face', you are under the influence of drugs

**fantasy** a mixture of hallucinogenic drugs,

or, in particular, gamma hydroxybutyrate

**fix** a shot of heroin or another drug

**flake** cocaine

**freak out** to have a hallucinatory experience on drugs

**freebase** cocaine refined for smoking by being heated with ether, which is often also inhaled during the process

**gage** marijuana

**gear** any illicit drugs

**goofball** a North American term for a barbiturate pill

**gouch out** to become unconscious through the effects of drugs

**grass** marijuana

**H** heroin

**hash** hashish

**head** someone who takes hallucinogenic drugs

**herb** a West Indian term for marijuana

**high** in a drug-induced state of euphoria

**hit** a dose of a hard drug

**hop** an old US term for opium or any narcotic

**hophead** someone who habitually takes narcotics

**horse** heroin

**hype** a hypodermic needle

**ice** a highly synthesized form of methamphetamine

**J** a joint or marijuana cigarette

**jack up** to inject oneself with a drug

**jelly** a capsule of the drug Temazepam®

**joint** a marijuana cigarette

**junkie** a drug addict

**leaf** marijuana

**line** a small amount of a powdered drug (usually cocaine) laid out in a narrow channel so that someone can sniff it

**magic mushrooms** mushrooms with naturally hallucinogenic qualities (sometimes shortened to **shrooms**)

**mainline** to take a narcotic drug intravenously

**makings** materials used to prepare drugs

**marching powder** cocaine, sometimes with the presumed country of origin specified, as in 'Colombian marching powder' or 'Peruvian marching powder'

**Mary Jane** marijuana

**meth** the drug methamphetamine

**microdot** a small pill of concentrated LSD

**monkey** to 'have a monkey on your back' is to be addicted to drugs

**moonrock** a combination of heroin and crack

**mule** a person who smuggles drugs into a country for a dealer

**munchies** 'the munchies' is a popular name for a drug-induced craving for food

**nose candy** cocaine

**number** a marijuana cigarette

**OD** a drug overdose

**pop** someone who 'pops a pill' swallows a drug in pill form

**poppers** amyl nitrate or butyl nitrate inhaled from a crushed capsule

**pot** marijuana

**pothead** someone who habitually smokes marijuana

**reefer** a marijuana cigarette

**roach** a marijuana cigarette, or its butt

**roach clip** a clip used to hold a marijuana cigarette when it has become too short to hold without burning the fingers

**rock** another name for crack cocaine or a piece of this

**rock house** the den of a dealer in crack cocaine

**roofie** a tablet of the sedative drug Rohypnol, known as the 'date-rape drug'

**rush** the euphoria experienced after taking a drug

**scag** or **skag** a North American term for heroin

**score** to successfully obtain illegal drugs

**shit** marijuana or heroin

**shooting gallery** a place where addicts gather to inject drugs

**shoot up** to inject a drug, especially heroin

**shrooms** see **magic mushrooms**

**skin-pop** to injects drugs into the skin, rather than into a vein

**skins** cigarette papers used to make marijuana cigarettes

**skin up** to make up a marijuana cigarette

**skunk** a type of cannabis smoked for its particularly strong narcotic effects

**slanger** a US term for a dealer in illegal drugs

**smack** heroin

**smackhead** a heroin addict

**snort** to inhale a powdered drug, especially cocaine, through the nose

**snow** a name used for various white powdered drugs, such as cocaine, morphine or heroin

**snowball** a mixture of cocaine and heroin

**snowbird** a cocaine addict or user

**sorted** well-provided with drugs

**space cadet** someone who regularly takes drugs, and is often 'spaced out'

**spaced out** or **spacey** in a dazed or stupefied state caused by taking drugs

**special K** ketamine

**speed** amphetamine

**speedball** a mixture of cocaine and opiates, especially heroin or morphine

**speedfreak** a habitual user of amphetamine

**spliff** a marijuana cigarette

**stash** a hidden supply of a drug

**stoned** high on drugs

**stoner** a habitual taker of drugs

**straight** not on drugs; also used to refer to a cigarette that contains no marijuana

**strung out** suffering from drug-withdrawal symptoms

**stuffer** a person who smuggles drugs in a bodily passage

**sugar** heroin or LSD

**tab** a tablet of ecstasy or a small square of paper containing LSD

**tea** an old US word for marijuana

**toke** a puff on a marijuana cigarette

**toot** a North American term for a quantity of a drug (especially cocaine) for inhaling, or the act of inhaling this

**tracks** or **tramlines** red marks on the skin caused by taking drugs intravenously

**trip** a drug-induced hallucinatory experience

**turn** someone who 'turns on' or is 'turned on' gains a sense of heightened awareness and vitality through hallucinogenic drugs

**upper** a drug or pill producing a stimulant or euphoric effect

**wasted** high on drugs

**weed** marijuana

**white stuff** heroin, morphine or cocaine

**whizz** amphetamine

**wired** high on drugs

**works** the syringe and other drug-injecting paraphernalia of an intravenous drug user

**XTC** the drug ecstasy

**zonked** under the influence of drugs

## Yoof slang

The use of 'yoof' rather than 'youth' in the heading for this section is a deliberate attempt to demonstrate the pervasiveness of this branch of slang (the term 'yoof' itself is discussed more fully in the glossary below). Many sections of the media go out of their way to attract and hold the attention of adolescents, acting in the knowledge that this demographic group is in possession of significant amounts of disposable income. Keen to appear 'happening' and up to date, they strive to express themselves in the latest slang of their target audience, sometimes with ludicrous results. To be fair, keeping abreast of the latest expressions is never easy for those who are not completely immersed in their use. The slang of the young people on the streets is perhaps the most universal of all types of slang, but it is undoubtedly also the most protean. No sooner has a term become fashionable and current than it is superseded by something newer and is soon forgotten. By the time a youth slang term reaches the point of being noticed by the media and recorded in print, it may well already have been consigned to oblivion by those who created and popularized it. For this reason, no dictionary of youth slang can ever be completely up to date, but can really only offer a snapshot of what was current at the time of compilation. As with many categories of slang, there will be overlaps with other areas. Youth slang will include terms from the drug users' world, campus slang and even criminal slang.

## Glossary

**all that** used to describe anything or anyone considered very good or attractive

**back in the day** at an earlier time, especially a period pleasurably remembered

**bag off** to have a romantic or sexual encounter

**bait** obvious

**bang** a party

**bangin'** excellent

**baphead** an idiot

**bare** very

**butters** ugly or unattractive

**beast** used to describe anything excellent; cool

**bling** jewellery, especially of a large and conspicuous style

**boyf** boyfriend

**buff** attractive or sexy

**cheese** to smile

**chill** to relax

**chill pill** a supposed pill that will make someone calm down, as in the phrase 'take a chill pill'

**chirps** to 'chirps' someone is to chat them up

**chung** sexually attractive

**cop off** to have a romantic or sexual encounter

**cotch** a bed, or the place where someone sleeps

**cotched** relaxed

**crib** someone's home

**crovey** excellent

**crump** excellent

**deebo** to steal, or to beat someone up

**deep** excellent

**disco biscuit** a tablet of the drug ecstasy

**down** to be 'down with' something is to be aware of or comfortable with it

**dry** dull, not amusing at all

**fave** favourite

**feel** in the US, if someone asks 'do you feel me?' this means 'do you understand what I am saying?'

**fit** sexually desirable

**fugly** extremely ugly

**gay** unfashionable, worthless or inferior (this is just the latest meaning adopted by this extraordinarily mutable little word)

**geezergirl** or **geezerbird** a young woman who enjoys aggressive social behaviour of a kind more usually associated with young men

**gonk** a foolish or stupid person

**go off on one** to become angry and make a fuss

**happy slapping** the practice of physically attacking an unsuspecting victim while an accomplice records the incident on a camera-equipped mobile phone

**hottie** a sexually attractive person

**kicking** extremely lively and enjoyable

**large it** or **have it large** to enjoy yourself unrestrainedly or boisterously

**lush** this can mean sexually attractive, or can be used more generally to describe anything considered good

**mentalist** to call someone a 'mentalist' is to say they are crazy

**minger** an unattractive or undesirable person or thing

**minging** dirty or unpleasant

**mong** an idiot

**monged** highly intoxicated by drink or drugs

**munter** an unattractive person, especially a woman

**muppet** a foolish or stupid person

**nang** excellent or cool

**off your face** or **tits** highly intoxicated by drink or drugs

**on the razz** having a spree or bout of heavy drinking

**safe** very good

**skank** a dirty or promiscuous woman

**skanky** dirty and unattractive

**spaz** or **spazz out** to lapse into a delirious state or lose control

**spazzy** clumsy or stupid

**talk to the hand** a dismissive remark made by an uninterested listener (the implication is along the lines of '...because the face isn't listening')

**taxing** the practice of mugging a person for his or her fashionable footwear

**Trev** a generic name for someone considered stupid or unfashionable

**tunes** music

**whip** a car

**wigger** or **wigga** a white person who adopts elements of urban black culture (ie a 'white nigger')

**wix** excellent or admirable

**yard** someone's home

**yoof** a phonetic pronunciation of 'youth', as in certain forms of London speech (as an adjective, 'yoof' is applied to magazines and programmes aimed at, pandering to, or dealing with topics that are presumed to be of interest to modern youth)

**your mother** or **mum** a retort to an insult, implying that anything derogatory that has been said also applies to the mother of the person who uttered the insult

## School slang

The slang we learn at school is probably the first slang that most of us are exposed to. The period of our schooldays is an intense time, full of friendships, alliances and animosities that at the time seem the most important things in the world. Again, it can often be very much about fitting in, belonging to a peer group. It undoubtedly helps mitigate the fear of authority figures such as the head teacher if they can be referred to behind their backs by names that are less than respectful, such as 'beak'. Much schoolyard slang is transient and most is left behind when we grow out of it, but some terms may remain part of our vocabularies for most of our lives. While some expressions seem to be universal, others vary from school to school. Public schools in particular are well known for their distinctive and often unique slang, and it is interesting to note that some extremely familiar terms (for example, 'soccer') were originally public-school coinages.

This list attempts to capture playground slang of the past and present, but it should be remembered that those who toil at the 'chalkface' are part of the school community too. For this reason, a few expressions are included that pupils might not recognize, being essentially teachers' slang.

## Glossary

**ace** to 'ace' a test or exam is to perform very well in it

**apple polisher** same as **teacher's pet**

**bags I** I lay claim to

**beak** a school teacher, especially a head teacher

**brainiac** a highly intelligent person

**bunk off** to play truant

**cave** beware

**chalkface** the classroom, regarded as the scene of a teacher's exertions

**Chinese burn** the burning pain caused by gripping another person's lower arm with two hands and deliberately twisting the flesh in opposite directions

**chizz** or **chiz** a cheat, swindle or nuisance

**chronic** a student who repeatedly fails in examinations

**co-ed** a US term for a girl at a mixed-sex school

**cut** in the USA, to 'cut class'

means to deliberately fail to attend a class

**egghead** a studious or brainy pupil

**ekker** a word used in some public schools to mean exercise

**floorer** an examination question you cannot answer

**groise** a swot or teacher's pet

**half** a term or half-term

**heidie** a Scottish term for a head teacher

**hookey** in the USA, to 'play hookey' is to play truant

**impot** an imposition

**mug** to study hard or swot

**schoolie** an Australian term that can mean both a school pupil or a school teacher

**skive** to play truant

**squish** a word used in some public schools to mean marmalade

**stinks** chemistry or science as a subject, or a teacher of this

**swot** a period of hard studying, or somebody who studies hard

**teacher's pet** a pupil who behaves obsequiously to a teacher in the hope of receiving privileged treatment

**tuck shop** a shop or area in a school where sweets or snacks are sold

**wag off** or **wag it** to play truant

**wedgie** a prank in which the victim's underpants are pulled up, causing uncomfortable constriction

## Campus slang

Like schools, universities are prolific generators of slang, as might be expected given their population of youths making the transition to adulthood, aware of the need to work hard for success as well as the urge to party while they can. While generations of its users come and go, much of this language sticks around and becomes traditional, while new terms are frequently coined and often disappear. Some slang is peculiar to particular educational institutions and does not travel; other expressions, while they may be strictly confined to Oxbridge, do become more widely known through being perpetuated in fiction and drama and being common to the background of many who come to form 'the establishment'. Much of the slang used by students is common to a wider spectrum of youth outside the 'ivory tower' of tertiary education and may be found under **Yoof slang**.

## *Glossary*

**bajan** or **bejant** a first-year student at St Andrews University

**boatie** a rowing enthusiast

**co-ed** a US term for a girl at a mixed-sex college

**cow college** a college in a remote rural area of the United States

**Desmond** a lower second-class honours degree (a pun on the name of Desmond Tutu, the South African archbishop, and '2:2', the common name for this class of degree)

**dig** a North American term for a hard-working student

**Douglas Hurd** a third-class honours degree (rhyming slang for a 'third', from the name of the former cabinet minister)

**flunk** to fail a course or examination

**flunk out** a student who 'flunks out' is dismissed from their college or university on the grounds of low academic achievement

**frat** a fraternity, an all-male college association in the USA

**frat house** a lodging house for fraternity members

**fresher** a first-year university or college student

**gapper** a student taking a year out (a 'gap year') from formal education

**Geoff Hurst** a first-class honours degree (rhyming slang for a 'first', from the name of the English footballer)

**grad** a graduate

**grad school** a US name for a university department offering advanced studies for graduates

**long** an old name for the long summer vacation

**medic** a medical student

**mods** the first public examination for a BA degree at Oxford University

**oak** at Oxford and Cambridge, to 'sport your oak' means to keep your outer door shut when you do not want visitors

**old college try** in the USA,

to give something 'the old college try' is to make a brave, spirited effort at something difficult to accomplish

**plough** to fail a student in an examination

**pluck** to fail a student in an examination

**poll** an old term used at Cambridge University to refer to the body of students who did not seek or obtain honours

**postdoc** a person engaged in postdoctoral research

**postgrad** a postgraduate student

**prelims** preliminary or entrance examinations

**premed** premedical studies (ie studies taken in preparation for professional medical training) or a premedical student

**prex** a US term for a president of a college

**prog** a proctor, an official who imposes university regulations

**rag day** or **week** the particular day or week during which students take part in processions, stunts, etc to raise money for charity

**smug** an industrious student who does not take part in social activities

**tosher** a non-collegiate student

**townee** or **townie** an inhabitant of a university town who has no connection with the university

**Trevor Nunn** an upper second-class honours degree (rhyming slang for a '2:1', from the name of the theatre director)

**undergrad** an undergraduate

**undergraduette** a female undergraduate

**uni** university

**vac** a university vacation

**varsity** university

**wonk** a US term for an excessively serious or studious person

# *Computer and Internet users' slang*

At one time the world of computers was that of white-coated scientists conducting unfathomable research using machines the size of small buildings. With the advent of the PC and the Internet, computers came into daily use by most people, and the slang generated by these activities has grown and spread. People sitting at home (many, no doubt in danger of becoming 'mouse potatoes') are now able to do things on their computers that a previous generation would have regarded as belonging to the realm of science fiction. While you don't have to be a total 'geek' to understand enough computerese to make the best use of your PC, 'geekspeak' itself may be a closed book (or file) to you. There is a particular jargon that the real 'techies' use to communicate with one another, allowing them to constitute a kind of illuminati (or 'digerati'), which excludes humble civilians. Much of it relates to the nuts and bolts, techniques and 'kludges', or wares both soft and hard (and otherwise), but much is about the people involved, with their characteristic attitudes and obsessions. Just as technical developments in this field are taking place daily and rapidly, so the language used to document it has to change constantly to keep up, and many terms quickly become as obsolescent as last year's model of PC.

## Glossary

**abandonware** software that is no longer distributed by its original publisher

**alphasort** to sort into alphabetical order

**beat-'em-up** a computer game in which an unarmed character has to fight against several enemies

**bells and whistles** additional, largely decorative rather than functional features

**bloatware** software with more facilities than most users need, making correspondingly large demands on the system's resources

**blog** a journal published on the Internet (a shortened form of 'weblog')

**blogger** a person who writes a blog

**blogosphere** the part of the World Wide Web that contains blogs

**bot** a computer program designed to perform routine tasks, such as searching the Internet, with some autonomy

**bug** a defect or fault in a computer system or program

**careware** software that is made available in exchange for making a donation of one's services, money, etc to a charity

**clickstream** a path used in navigating cyberspace

**crippleware** software that has been partly disabled to provide a limited demonstration of its use

**cuspy** a computer program that is well-written and easy to use may be described as 'cuspy' (from commonly *used system program*)

**cybernaut** a person who uses the Internet

**cyberslacking** the use of computers for recreational purposes when you are supposed to be working

**cybersquatting** the purchasing of an Internet domain name, usually one of a famous person, with the intention of selling it on at a profit

**dead tree edition** a paper version of material that is also available electronically

**deathmatch** in computer games, a mode of play in which players deliberately attempt to eliminate each other

**defrag** to defragment files (ie to rearrange them on a hard disk so that each occupies consecutive sectors without blanks between them)

**digerati** the body of people with expertise in or knowledge of computers and the Internet

**Easter egg** an undocumented sequence of code that is activated by a specific set of keystrokes, intended as a kind of practical joke

**finger** to 'finger' another computer user is to locate him or her by means of a special program

**firmware** software or similar instructions forming a more or less permanent and unerasable part of a computer's memory

**flame** an insulting, rude, or controversial e-mail message

**flame war** an acrimonious exchange of e-mail messages

**freeware** a program that can be copied without charge but not sold

**gamer** a dedicated player of computer games

**geek** someone who is

obsessively enthusiastic about computers

**geekspeak** the jargon used by 'geeks'

**GIGO** garbage in, garbage out (the axiom that incorrect input results in incorrect output)

**glitch** a sudden, usually brief, malfunction

**groupware** software that supports group activity

**hacker** a skilled and enthusiastic computer operator, especially one who uses his or her skills to break into commercial or government computer or other electronic systems

**jack in** to connect electronically

**keypal** a person who is only or mainly known to someone as an e-mail correspondent

**kludge** a botched or makeshift device or program which is unreliable or inadequate in function

**liveware** the people who work with a computer system, as distinct from its hardware or software

**lurk** to use the Internet only to read, not to send, messages

**meatspace** the physical world, as opposed to cyberspace

**micro** a microcomputer or microprocessor

**mouse potato** a person who spends a great deal of time using a computer, especially for leisure

**munge** if someone 'munges' data, it is altered so as to be useless or incapable of automatic manipulation

**nethead** an Internet enthusiast, especially one who spends a lot of time online

**netiquette** agreed standards for polite online behaviour

**netizen** a competent and enthusiastic user of the Internet

**Netspeak** the style of language characteristically used on the Internet, disregarding many of the conventions of traditional grammar and making frequent use of abbreviations and acronyms

**number-cruncher** a computer designed to carry out large quantities of complex numerical calculations, or someone who operates one of these

**onliner** a person who uses the Internet

**pharming** the covert redirection of computer users from legitimate websites to counterfeit sites in order to gain confidential information about them

**phishing** the practice of sending counterfeit e-mail messages in an attempt to get the recipients to divulge confidential information, such as details of bank accounts

**phreaking** the activity of hacking into a telephone system in order to make free calls

**pling** an exclamation mark

**POTS** Plain Old Telephone System

**rogue dialler** a program that redirects an attempt to access a dial-up Internet connection to a premium-rate phone number

**script kiddie** a computer hacker with limited knowledge and skill

**shareware** software available on free trial, often with restricted features or for a limited time, after which a fee must be paid if regular use is to continue

**shoot-'em-up** a computer game involving scenes of violent action, gunfights, etc

**shovelware** data, especially originating from traditional media, published in electronic form without appropriate adaptation to the new format

**silver surfer** an older person who enjoys using the Internet

**smart** making use of advanced technology, usually in combinations such as 'smart house' (one that is electronically controlled) and 'smart bomb' (one that is computer-guided)

**spam** electronic junk mail

**spammer** someone guilty of sending spam

**splash page** a page incorporating highly decorative or arresting graphics, displayed as the introduction to a website

**splog** an automatically generated and maintained blog, usually offering products for sale

**spyware** software that gathers information about the user and transmits it to another computer

**sticky** a 'sticky' website is one that attracts visitors and retains their attention

**stiffware** software that is no longer flexible, having been customized or having incomplete documentation or an obscure function and therefore being difficult to modify or remove without risk to other programs

**techie** a devotee of or expert in computer technology

**technobabble** or **technospeak** technical jargon, specialized words, acronyms and abbreviations used to describe computer hardware and software

**technofear** fear and dislike of computer technology

**technojunkie** someone who is obsessed with computer technology

**Trojan** or **Trojan horse** a concealed insertion of disruptive coded material within a program, coded to function at a preset time or on a preset condition

**troll** to provoke controversy or disagreement on the Internet

**vapourware** software or hardware that is loudly heralded but not yet (and possibly never to be) available

**webhead** an enthusiastic user of the World Wide Web

**wetware** the living human brain

**wired** connected to the Internet

## *Hip-hop slang*

The hip-hop movement arose in the USA in the 1980s, closely associated with rap music, breakdancing and graffiti. It developed its own characteristic style of dress (including baggy clothing and flashy training shoes) and accessories, all of which, along with its musical style, soon crossed over into the youth mainstream. The same was true of its slang, which, largely through the medium of song lyrics, reflected the movement's preoccupation with gang membership, violence, drug abuse and sexuality (often expressed in a controversially misogynistic way). Many of the terms in this list, although they may have originated in the world of hip-hop, will feature in the vocabularies of other youth groups.

## *Glossary*

**badonkadonk** shapely female buttocks (from the imaginary onomatopoeic sound made by these as they wiggle by)

**baller** someone with money, especially one who spends it conspicuously

**bammer** something (especially marijuana) that is described as 'bammer' is of inferior quality

**biter** someone who steals other people's tunes, song lyrics or dance moves

**bling** jewellery, especially of a large and conspicuous style

**booty** a person's buttocks, which rap performers habitually adjure their listeners to shake

**booty call** a date, especially with a view to sex, or a phone call made to arrange this

**bootylicious** sexually attractive

**chickenhead** a promiscuous woman

**chronic** a potent form of marijuana

**cream** money

**crib** someone's home

**crunk** a type of hip-hop music

**crunked** in a state of excitement, exhilaration or intoxication

**dawg** a US term for a close male friend

**def** excellent

**dime** a very attractive woman

**dope** excellent

**dun** a male friend

**five-oh** the police, or a police officer (from *Hawaii Five-O*, a popular US television cop show first broadcast in 1968)

**floss** to show off your wealth, clothes or possessions ostentatiously

**flow** to perform a rap smoothly and impressively

**fly** stylish or fashionable

**fo sho** or **fo shizzle** for sure

**gangsta** 'gangsta' is a style of rap music with aggressive and often misogynistic lyrics; a 'gangsta' is a performer of this style of music, or a member of a criminal gang

**gully** excellent or admirable

**hater** someone who is jealous of another's success

**ho** a disrespectful term for a woman

**homeboy** or **homegirl** an acquaintance from someone's own neighbourhood, especially a fellow member of a street gang (often shortened to **homie**)

**hood** or **'hood** neighbourhood

**iced** someone who is 'iced out' is wearing a lot of diamond jewellery

**krunk** same as **crunk**

**massive** a 'massive' is a gang, or a group of friends

**off the hook** excellent or highly attractive

**one-time** the police, or a police officer

**phat** excellent

**player** or **playa** a hip-hop artist, especially a successful one

**player hater** same as **hater**

**po-po** the police, or a police officer

**posse** a gang, or a group of friends

**props** to 'give someone their props' is to show them the proper respect

**represent** to act in a positive or assertive way

**scrub** an insignificant person, especially an inferior hip-hop artist

**shout-out** an acknowledgement or greeting

**skeet** to ejaculate

**stunt** to show off

**thick** a 'thick' woman is one who is sexually attractive

**trick** a male who is exploited by a female

**wanksta** a derogatory term for a would-be 'gangsta'

**what it is** a phrase used, mostly in the USA, as a greeting

**what's up** a phrase that can be used on its own as a greeting, or to introduce a request for information, as in 'This new software … what's up with that?'

**whip** a car

**word** or **word up** an expression used to show agreement or emphasize that something is true; also used as a greeting

## Gay slang

Much of gay slang arose when homosexual activities were against the law, even between consenting adults. It reflected a need for secret codewords to protect those involved with 'the love that dare not speak its name' from unwanted attention, harassment and persecution. This slang continues to flourish in these days of 'gay pride' more as the expression of, and a mark of belonging to, a recognized subculture, and the reclamation of the word 'queer' by gay people themselves is a prime example of a change in attitudes.

## Glossary

**abigail** a conservative, older homosexual man

**ace queen** a male who adopts a markedly womanly appearance

**agate** a small penis

**agatha** a gossip

**A-gay** or **A-list gay** belonging to a homosexual elite

**aggie** a homosexual sailor

**air express** sexual intercourse with a male air steward

**alamo** an interjection expressing sexual interest in another

**ambidextrous** bisexual

**amy** an ampoule of amyl nitrate

**angel** a male homosexual, especially a man who supports a younger lover

**angel food** a homosexual member of an air force

**angelina** a young male homosexual

**angel with a dirty face** a male homosexual who has yet to 'come out'

**ass pro** or **aspro** a homosexual male prostitute

**assy** a US term meaning bitchy or nasty

**Athenian** a paedophile

**auntie** an elderly homosexual male

**baby dyke** a lesbian who is young and inexperienced

**bagpiping** the practice of stimulating a partner's penis in one's armpit

**basket** a man's genitals, especially when observed as a bulge in his clothing

**bear** a hairy man

**belle** an effeminate young male homosexual

**breeder** a heterosexual

**butch** the more masculine partner in a homosexual relationship

**chicken** a sexual partner who is under age

**chickenhawk** a male homosexual who seeks out

under-age partners

**closet** 'the closet' is a hypothetical hiding place for a person who does not want to reveal their homosexuality

**closet queen** a male homosexual who is 'in the closet'

**come out** to declare openly one's homosexuality (short for 'come out of the closet')

**cottaging** the activity of soliciting in a public lavatory (a **cottage**)

**drag king** a female who dresses like a male

**fag hag** a heterosexual woman who enjoys the company of homosexual men

**femme** the more feminine partner in a homosexual relationship

**friend of Dorothy** a homosexual (from the character of Dorothy in *The Wizard of Oz*, as played by Judy Garland, a gay icon)

**fruit fly** same as **fag hag**

**gaydar** the supposed ability of a person, especially a homosexual, to sense whether or not someone else is homosexual

**gold star** a lesbian who has never had sex with a man

**government-inspected meat** a gay member of the US armed forces

**guppie** a gay yuppie

**hasbian** a woman who has had lesbian sexual experiences in the past but now lives a heterosexual life

**kiki** a homosexual, especially one who is equally comfortable with a passive or active role

**lavender marriage** a marriage of convenience used to disguise the homosexuality of one or both of the partners

**lemon** a lesbian

**lily law** the police

**lipstick lesbian** a lesbian with a conventionally feminine appearance

**mary** a male homosexual

**muscle Mary** a homosexual male bodybuilder

**out** to 'out' someone is to make their homosexuality public without their permission

**pink** relating to homosexuals, often used in expressions such as 'the pink pound' (the spending power attributed to the gay community)

**queer** homosexual (once a derogatory term applied to

homosexuals by heterosexuals, but now claimed by gay people for themselves)

**rice queen** a male homosexual particularly attracted to Asian partners

**rough trade** violent or sadistic male prostitutes or sexual encounters

**snow queen** a black male homosexual particularly attracted to white partners

**tbh** abbreviation for 'to be had', used to denote an active homosexual

**tea room** a public lavatory

**trade** a person that a male homosexual has sex with, especially a male prostitute

**troll** to wander the streets looking for a sexual partner

**twink** or **twinkie** an attractive young male homosexual

**yestergay** a person who has had homosexual experiences in the past but now lives a heterosexual life

# ACTIVITIES

## General sporting slang

The twentieth century saw a massive increase among the general public in interest and participation in sport. Increased leisure time made sport in a myriad of forms available to many, and widespread coverage in the press and on the broadcast media brought it to a wider audience than ever. Sport had always generated its own slang, but instead of being confined to the circles of players and aficionados, it now began to be widely disseminated by the large numbers of journalists and broadcasters who found they could make a living by writing or talking about it. The following list is a selection of terms that tend to be applied to sport as a whole; readers interested in vocabulary associated with a particular sport should look under the more specialized sections that follow.

### Glossary

**ace** an excellent player

**air shot** a stroke that fails to connect with the ball

**bench-warmer** a reserve player

**blinder** a spectacular performance

**boilover** an Australian term for a surprising result

**bridesmaid** a team or individual that is always runner-up or never quite makes it to the top

**champ** a champion

**charley horse** a US term for muscle strain caused by strenuous exercise

**decider** a game or score that decides the winner

**donkey-lick** in Australia, to 'donkey-lick' an opponent is to defeat them convincingly

**dynamo** a particularly energetic performer

**flier** a flying start

**grandstand** a player who 'grandstands' shows off to the crowd

**hammer** to defeat heavily

**in the zone** in a mental state that enables you to perform at the height of your abilities

**jock** a US term for a male athlete or sportsman

**jogger's nipple** painful inflammation of a runner's nipple caused by friction against clothing

**laugher** an easily won game

**letterman** a US student who has won distinction representing his or her college or university in a sport

**long shot** a player or team with only a remote chance of success

**nightcap** the last event of the day

**nightmare** to 'have a nightmare' means to perform particularly badly (often shortened to **mare**)

**park** a sports pitch or stadium

**physio** a physiotherapist

**pot** a trophy, especially a cup

**ref** a referee

**result** to 'get a result' means to win

**roids** short for anabolic steroids, drugs used to increase the build-up of body tissue, especially muscle, illegally used by some athletes

**scrapper** a player who is indefatigable and highly competitive

**shamateur** a sportsperson retaining amateur status while receiving payment for playing or competing

**shoo-in** a US term for an apparently certain winner

**showboat** a player who 'showboats' shows off to the crowd

**silverware** sporting trophies

**spank** to defeat heavily

**throw** to 'throw' a contest is to lose it deliberately, especially in return for a bribe

**ump** an umpire

**walk home** or **walk it** to win easily

**walkover** an easy victory

# Football slang

In the twentieth century Association Football, or soccer, became the most popular sport in the world, with its four-yearly World Cups drawing in ever-greater worldwide TV audiences. The great Liverpool FC manager Bill Shankly said that the game wasn't a matter of life and death – it was much more serious than that; others have explained it as a substitute for war. Certainly, without football, pub conversations would be unimaginably different and a lot less animated. Football terminology is learned young, during primary-school playground kickabouts, and is retained by many, along with devotion to the game, throughout their lives. With foreign millionaires owning Premier League clubs and famous British teams fielding eleven players who were all born outside the United Kingdom, is football still 'the people's game'? This is a question that continues to spark debate, but from a slang point of view it does look as if the sport is still holding on to its populist roots. Football slang continues to flourish, among the fans, whether they are armchair pundits or 'groundhoppers', as well as the commentators and journalists.

## Glossary

**aerial ping-pong** a disapproving term for a passage of play in which both sides head the ball back and forth without any attempt to control it on the ground

**afters** retaliation by a player who has been fouled

**beautiful game** football is often referred to as 'the beautiful game' – sometimes more in hope than veracity

**carpet** the turf on which football is played

**clean sheet** a goalkeeper or team 'keeps a clean sheet' when they do not let in any goals

**clogger** a player who is notorious for committing fouls

**close down** to 'close down' a player is to mark him tightly

**custodian** the goalkeeper

**derby** a game between two sides from the same area

**dig** a shot at goal

**dive** to fall over, pretending to have been fouled, in order to deceive the referee into awarding a free kick or penalty

**donkey** a slow and clumsy player

**early bath** the destination of a player who has been sent off

**early doors** at an early stage in the game

**engine** a player who has a 'good engine' has plenty of stamina

**exhibition football** or **stuff** play of such a high standard that it could serve as a demonstration of how the game should be played

**footie** or **footer** the game of football

**game on!** an expression popular among football commentators, used to mark an event that is adjudged to have made a relatively uninteresting contest spring into life, such as the scoring of a goal

**goalie** the goalkeeper

**go in hard** to tackle with authority

**groundhopper** a supporter who travels to see games at as many different stadiums as possible

**handbags** 'handbags' or 'handbags at ten paces' is sometimes used by commentators to describe incidents between players that involve pushing and threatening language but without much in the way of serious fisticuffs (implying that the confrontation is rather effeminate and not a proper man's fight)

**hat-trick** the individual feat of scoring three goals in one game

**hole** 'the hole' is the space on the pitch between the midfielders and the forwards

**hug the touchline** to play as near to the sidelines of the pitch as possible

**hungry** a team that is described as 'hungry' is eager to win

**keepie-uppie** the practice of juggling the ball with feet, knees, chest and even (if the player is appearing in a commercial for a soft-drink or sportswear manufacturer) the shoulders and the back of the neck

**magic sponge** a sponge soaked in water, applied to an injured player's limb by a trainer or physiotherapist, to which wonderfully curative effects are proverbially attributed

**man on!** a cry to a teammate to warn of an approaching defender

**midfield dynamo** a particularly energetic midfield player

**midfield general** a midfield player who controls a team's pattern of play

**net** to 'net' is to score a goal

**nutmeg** to beat an opposing player by playing the ball through the gap between his legs (often accompanied by a triumphant cry of 'nutmegs!')

**one-two** a move in which a player passes to a teammate then moves forward to receive the ball back immediately

**onion bag** the net behind the goals

**physical** a 'physical' player is one who relishes making tough challenges

**poacher** a player who lurks around the opposing team's penalty area in the hope of scoring an opportunist goal

**professional foul** a deliberate foul intended to prevent the opposition from scoring

**reducer** a strong challenge made with the intention of impairing the mobility of a dangerous opponent

**route one** a simplistic method of playing, based on kicking the ball long and hard into the opponents' half

**sitter** to 'miss a sitter' is to fail to score when it would have been easy to do so

**sky** to 'sky' the ball is to kick it high into the air, usually unintentionally

**soccer** association football (originally public-school slang, to distinguish it from rugby football, but now most commonly heard in the USA, to distinguish it from American football)

**stall** a team that 'sets its stall out' establishes the pattern of play it wants to pursue

**sticks** the goalposts

**stiffs** 'the stiffs' is a derogatory name for a club's reserve team

**take out** to 'take a player out of the play' is to bring him down by fouling him

**tapping** the practice (by a representative of a club) of making a covert approach to a player of another team about a possible transfer

**wall** a line of defending players who position themselves in front of an opponent taking a free kick in order to prevent a clear shot at goal

**wall pass** same as **one-two**

**woodwork** to 'hit the woodwork' is to strike the ball against a goalpost or the crossbar

## Rugby slang

There are, of course, two codes of rugby – union and league – and each can claim legions of devotees, but much of the jargon involved is common to both. There are differences, however. For example, in rugby league the move known in rugby union as the 'garryowen' tends to be more prosaically called an 'up-and-under'. (Readers of a certain age may recall the latter term being popularized in the 1970s by the famous league TV commentator Eddie Waring.) Rugby is renowned for being a very social game, with teams and supporters leaving their rivalry aside after a match to share beer, song and slang in pubs and clubhouses. Some people – especially soccer fans – claim to find its rules impenetrable, but at least in the list below they may find explanations for some of its language.

### Glossary

**bomb** a high kick

**fifteen-man game** rugby union, in which teams have fifteen players, as opposed to rugby league; the term is also used to refer to a running style of play in which backs and forwards contribute equally

**garryowen** a very high kick, after which the kicker and his teammates rush to catch the ball or tackle the catcher

**gas** if a player 'turns on the gas', he puts on a turn of speed

**girls** a term used by forwards to denote backs

**grubber** a kick which sends the ball low along the ground

**hard yards** the 'hard yards' are those made in carrying the ball forward against strong opposition

**hoof** to kick the ball powerfully

**hospital pass** a pass to a teammate who is about to be tackled and may thereby sustain an injury

**loose** when the ball is 'in the loose' it is not in the control of either side

**pill** 'the pill' is the ball

**ping** to 'ping' a player is to penalize him

**round-ball game** a rugby fan's term for Association Football

**rugger** rugby

**rugger bugger** an enthusiastic rugby supporter or player, often considered boorish

**scrum pox** impetigo spread by rugby players' faces rubbing together in the scrum

**shepherding** the illegal ploy of running in front of an opponent to shield the ball carrier

**sin-bin** an enclosure to which a player is sent for a statutory length of time when suspended from a game for an infringement or unruly behaviour

**spear tackle** the action (usually carried out by two players) of tackling an opponent, lifting him up by the legs and forcing him headfirst to the ground

**ten-man rugby** a style of play relying on the dominance of the forwards and kicking by either the scrum-half or the fly-half, rather than supplying possession to the backs

**third half** the drinking following a game

**thirteen-man game** rugby league, in which teams have thirteen players, as opposed to rugby union

**truck and trailer** a form of obstruction in which players run ahead of the ball-carrier when he is not bound on to them

**Twickers** Twickenham, where England plays its home games

**uglies** a term used by backs to denote forwards

**up-and-under** same as **garryowen**

**up the jumper** a style of play involving the advance of the ball through the forwards, with little passing and much mauling and driving

## Cricket slang

Cricket is sometimes criticized for being a game in which nothing much seems to happen for extended periods, possessed of rules that are a mystery to the uninitiated onlooker. It's no surprise that its slang is similarly mystifying, but it certainly gives the impression of a lot more going on than meets the uneducated eye. Many of the multitude of ways in which to deliver or repel the ball are given strange, colourful names, almost as if to deepen the mystery of how they are effected. What is someone new to the game to make of a 'beamer' or a 'jaffa', a 'cow shot' or a 'slog'? Perhaps it would be more agreeable to help a 'leggy' who's bagged a 'Michelle' celebrate in the 'hutch'. Cricket's image as a gentleman's game has long been belied by the on-pitch activities of 'chin music' and 'sledging', but crowd trouble has never featured amongst its supporters. Sometimes considered as being quintessentially English (symbolized by the thwack of wood on willow on the village green), cricket is of course an international game, and its slang reflects this, with terms from many countries.

## Glossary

**agricultural** an 'agricultural' shot is a vigorous but unskilled swipe at the ball by a batsman

**baggy green** any of the caps won by a cricketer playing for Australia

**beamer** a fast head-high ball that does not bounce

**blob** a score of nought (so called because it is round)

**bosie** an Australian term for a googly, ie a ball that spins in the opposite direction to the bowler's usual delivery

**bumper** a ball that bounces up sharply from the pitch

**bunny** same as **rabbit**

**bunsen** a wicket on which the ball spins a long way after pitching (shortened from 'Bunsen burner', rhyming slang for a 'turner')

**cherry** a new ball

**Chinaman** a ball bowled by a left-arm bowler that spins in the opposite direction to the bowler's usual delivery

**chin music** the bowling of balls that bounce up close to the batsman's head

**coffin** a case used to carry a player's equipment and clothing

**corridor of uncertainty** the area outside a batsman's off stump, where he is unsure whether to play a stroke or not

**cow corner** the area of the outfield in front of the wicket on the leg side, to which 'cow shots' are hit

**cow shot** an aggressive but technically incorrect shot to the leg side

**daisy-cutter** a ball bowled along the ground that keeps low on pitching

**dig** an innings

**dolly** an easy catch

**duck** a score of nought

**gardening** a batsman is said to be 'gardening' when he prods down loose areas of the pitch with the end of his bat

**gazunder** a low ball (so called because it 'goes under' the bat)

**gloveman** a wicketkeeper

**four ball** a poorly bowled ball that can be easily hit to the boundary for four runs

**gaper** an easy catch

**golden duck** a batsman who scores a 'golden duck' is dismissed by the first ball of his innings

**good areas** if a bowler is said to be putting the ball in 'good areas', he is bowling in such a way that the batsman is not able to score easily

**hat-trick** the feat of taking of three wickets with consecutive balls

**hutch** the pavilion, especially when considered as the destination of a batsman who is out

**jaffa** an exceptionally good ball that is difficult to play and is likely to take a wicket

**knock** a spell at batting

**leggy** a bowler of leg-breaks, balls that spin away from a right-handed batsman

**maker's name** to 'show the maker's name' is to play a forward defensive stroke with exaggerated correctness

**Michelle** a haul of five wickets by a bowler (a pun on the name of Michelle Pfeiffer, the American actress, and 'five for [so-many runs]', the common way of reporting a bowler's performance)

**nelson** the score of 111, believed by English players to be unlucky (said to originate from the widely but erroneously held belief that Lord Nelson had one eye, one arm and one leg)

**nightwatchman** a relatively unskilled batsman who is sent in to bat towards the end of the day's play in order to prevent a more skilled batsman from having to go in

**nine, ten, jack** the last three

batsmen in a team's batting order (numbers nine, ten and eleven)

**nurdle** if a batsman 'nurdles', he scores runs by gently pushing or deflecting the ball with the bat rather than hitting it hard

**pair** a 'pair' or 'pair of spectacles' is a score of nought in both innings of a game

**peg** a stump

**pie chucker** a pejorative term for a bowler whose deliveries pose little threat to the batsman

**plumb** unquestionably leg before wicket

**pyjama cricket** cricket played in coloured clothing rather than the traditional whites

**quickie** a fast bowler

**rabbit** an inferior batsman

**sandshoe crusher** an Australian term for a ball that pitches on the batsman's boots

**shooter** a delivery that keeps abnormally low after pitching

**sit on the splice** to bat defensively, making no attempt to score runs

**skier** a ball hit high into the air

**skittle out** if a team is 'skittled out', they are dismissed for a low score

**sledging** offensive, sometimes humorous, remarks made to a batsman in order to disturb his concentration

**slog** an aggressive but technically incorrect stroke

**stick** a stump

**sticky dog** a pitch that has been affected by rain and so is difficult to bat on

**stonewall** to bat extremely defensively

**tail** the weaker batsmen at the end of a team's batting order

**timbers** the stumps

**ton** a score of one hundred runs

**track** the pitch

**turn your arm over** to bowl, especially said of someone who is not a recognized bowler

**twirler** a spin bowler

**whites** the white clothes traditionally worn for playing cricket

**Windies** the West Indies cricket team

**wrong 'un** a googly

**yahoo** an exuberant attempt to hit the ball hard, often with disappointing results

## Boxing slang

Boxing is often described as 'the noble art' or 'the noble science', but to the uninitiated it can look like a brutal and bloody business. While in the past it may have been a pastime indulged in by gentlemen keen to learn self-defence and happy to abide by the Marquess of Queensberry's rules, professional boxing is an activity in which fortunes in prize money (not to mention betting) can be made, and escapes from the gutter are available to the talented (or lucky) few. For every Joe Louis or Muhammad Ali there are thousands of 'pugs' and 'palookas' who may well end up 'punchy' and with 'cauliflower ears'. So popular has boxing been as a spectator sport that many of its slang terms have crossed over into mainstream use, such as 'champ', 'pull your punches' and 'out for the count'. While women's boxing appears to be becoming increasingly popular, this aspect of the fight game does not yet seem to have generated much in the way of its own particular slang.

### Glossary

**bleeder** a boxer who is susceptible to being cut

**canvas** the floor of a boxing ring

**cauliflower ear** an ear permanently swollen and misshapen through being punched too often

**champ** a champion

**claret** blood (which is similar in colour to the wine)

**connect** to hit a target with a punch

**dive** if a boxer 'takes a dive', he pretends to have been knocked out in order to 'throw' a fight

**fight** in the USA, 'the fights' means a programme of boxing matches

**glass chin** or **jaw** a chin or jaw that is exceptionally vulnerable to a hard punch

**ham** an inexpert boxer

**ham-and-egger** an inferior boxer, useful only as a sparring partner

**haymaker** a wild swinging punch

**hit the canvas** to be knocked down

**kayo** or **ko** a knockout

**mill** 'a mill' is an old-fashioned term for a boxing-match

**mitts** a boxer's gloves or fists

**noble art** or **science** boxing is traditionally known as 'the noble art' or 'the noble science'

**one-two** a blow with one fist followed by a blow with the other

**out for the count** a boxer who is 'out for the count' is unable to rise and resume the fight during a count of ten by the referee

**palooka** a clumsy or stupid boxer

**prop** a boxer's extended arm

**pug** a boxer

**pull your punches** to hold back from hitting as hard as possible

**punch-drunk** or **punchy** having a form of cerebral concussion from past blows

**put out to grass** if a fighter is 'put out to grass', he is knocked down

**rabbit punch** a blow to the back of the neck

**rope-a-dope** the tactic of pretending to be trapped against the ropes, encouraging an opponent to tire himself out in throwing punches that are well-defended

**roundhouse** a wild swinging punch or style of punching

**ruby** blood

**saved by the bell** a boxer who is 'saved by the bell' has only avoided being knocked out by the fact that the bell to signal the end of the round rang before the referee could finish counting to ten

**slap-happy** same as **punch-drunk**

**slugfest** a match characterized by heavy blows

**slugger** a boxer, especially one who punches heavily

**southpaw** a boxer who leads with his right hand

**sucker punch** a punch that takes the recipient by surprise

**Sunday punch** a US term for a powerful punch intended to knock out an opponent

**sweet science** the art of boxing

**throw** if a boxer 'throws' a fight, he loses it deliberately, usually for money

**tomato can** an inferior boxer

**wind** the part of the body covering the stomach, a blow on which causes winding

# *Golf slang*

People who don't like golf are apt to dismiss it as 'a good walk spoiled'. However, the game has millions of devotees around the world, whether they are hacking round their local course with a sizeable handicap while dreaming of a hole in one, sinking a putt to head the leader board at the Masters or the Open, or simply watching a tournament on television. Perhaps it is the fact of being played out in the open country that leads golf to adopt animal imagery; in addition to standard terms such as 'eagle' and 'albatross', golf slang features 'tiger lines' and 'rabbits'. The game certainly brings players into intimate contact with nature in the form of vegetation, whether as 'cabbage', 'spinach' or (heavens forfend!) 'jungle'. However, a thought should probably be spared for all of those 'golf widows' who can't seem to extricate their husbands from the 'nineteenth hole'.

## *Glossary*

**ace** a hole in one

**afraid of the dark** a phrase used to describe a ball that seems reluctant to go into a hole

**air shot** a stroke that fails to connect with the ball

**Arthur Scargill** a shot that is hit well but leaves the ball in an unfavourable position (named after the union leader, because it is 'a great strike with a poor result')

**back door** if a putt goes in 'by the back door', it falls into the hole by slowly dropping in from one side

**bail out** if a player 'bails out', he or she plays safe, for example by aiming short of a green which has bunkers guarding it

**bandit** an amateur player who has a higher handicap than his skill merits, thus giving him or her an advantage in competitions

**cabbage** deep, thick rough

**carpet** 'the carpet' is the green

**dance floor** the green (so called because it is flat and smooth)

**dribbler** a shot that fails to travel very far

**egg** 'the egg' is any golf ball

**fried egg** a situation in which a ball has landed in soft sand in a bunker and sits in a circular hollow

**gimme** a short putt that an opponent is sportingly excused from playing, there being little likelihood of missing it

**golf widow** a woman whose husband spends a lot of time away from her, playing golf

**hacker** a poor amateur player

**heavy artillery** the driver (ie the club used to hit the ball a long distance)

**jail** if a ball is described as being 'in jail', this means that it has ended up in a spot from which it will be difficult to extricate it

**jungle** tall rough, bushes or trees, from which it is difficult to hit the ball

**legs** if a shot, usually a putt, 'has legs', it will run for a long distance

**lip out** if a ball 'lips out', it hits the rim of the hole but does not fall in

**member's bounce** a favourable bounce that takes the ball on to the fairway or green (so called because it always seems to be the member rather than a visitor who benefits from these)

**mulligan** a free extra shot sometimes allowed to a player to recover from an errant shot

**never up, never in** a comment made by or to a frustrated putter when he or she has hit the ball too softly

**nineteenth hole** the clubhouse bar (the natural destination after completing a round of eighteen holes)

**out of the screws** if a player hits a shot 'out of the screws', it is hit perfectly

**plug** a ball that 'plugs' becomes embedded in wet ground or sand

**shoot the pill** to 'shoot the pill' is to play golf

**rabbit** a poor amateur player

**reload** if a player reloads, he or she takes a second tee shot because the first may be lost or out of bounds

**Sally Gunnell** a mishit shot that nevertheless sends the ball a long way along the grass (named after the British athlete, because it is 'not pretty but a good runner')

**sclaff** to make a poor swing so that the sole of the club strikes the ground before striking the ball

**scratch** a 'scratch' player has a handicap of zero

**shank** to mistakenly strike the ball close to the heel of the club so that it makes contact with the shaft socket, causing the ball to fly to the right (for a right-handed player)

**short stuff** the fairway, where the grass is short

**spinach** same as **cabbage**

**stick** any golf club

**stiff** same as **stone dead**

**stone dead** a golf ball is 'stone dead' if it is so close to the hole as to make a putt a mere formality

**Texas wedge** a putter, when it is used from off the green (so called because the ground is hard and dry in Texas and so such shots are common there)

**tiger country** same as **jungle**

**tiger line** the most direct, and hence risky, line for a drive or approach shot

**up-and-down** an 'up-and-down' is an act of completing a hole from a position off the green by using one lofted shot and one putt

**watery grave** the fate of a shot hit into water

**whiff** same as **air shot**

**worker** a shot, especially a putt, that keeps running towards the hole for a long distance

**yips** 'the yips' refers to a nervous twitching before making a shot, caused by tension

## Horse-racing slang

Many sporting events can be the focus of betting, but horse-racing is probably the most popular for this activity. For this reason, much of the slang connected with horse-racing is also used by bookies and punters, and some of these terms will be found in the section on **Bookmakers' slang**.

The owning, breeding and racing of horses has long been the preserve of the wealthy, and not for nothing is horse-racing known as 'the sport of kings'. A 'day at the races' is a traditional day out for many, not just for the toffs sporting their often outrageous best at Royal Ascot, and the sight of a field of thoroughbreds pounding around a course is indeed a spectacle. However, where gambling and large amounts of prize money are involved, criminality is never far away, and a certain air of loucheness seems to remain inseparable from the sport, with its talk of 'ringers', 'nobbling' horses, and jockeys 'pulling' their mounts.

## *Glossary*

**also-ran** an 'also-ran' is a horse that *also ran* in a race but did not get a 'place'

**birdcage** the paddock at a racecourse

**bute** short for phenylbutazone, a drug illegally used in horse-doping

**card** the programme of races at a meeting

**course specialist** a horse that regularly performs well over a particular course

**gee-gees** horses

**impost** the weight carried by a horse in a handicap race

**jolly** 'the jolly' is the favourite in a race

**milk shake** a stimulating preparation containing sodium bicarbonate, given to a racehorse before a race

**morning glory** a horse that runs faster in morning training than in the actual race

**mudder** or **mudlark** a horse that responds well to muddy conditions

**neddy** an Australian term for a racehorse

**nightcap** the last race of the day

**nobble** to 'nobble' a racehorse is to injure or drug it to prevent it from winning

**pinhooker** a speculator who buys up foals, hoping to make a profit when selling them as yearlings for racing

**place** a position among the leading finishers (usually the first three) in a race

**pull** if a jockey 'pulls' a horse, he restrains it deliberately to prevent it from winning

**raider** a horse owned by a foreign owner

**ringer** a horse raced under the name of another horse

**scrub** if a jockey is said to be

'scrubbing', he is making a rapid to-and-fro movement with his arms over the horse's neck to urge it forward

**seller** a race the winning horse of which must be put up for auction at a price previously fixed

**shoo** in the USA, to 'shoo' a race is to fix it so that a particular horse wins

**shoo-in** a horse that is allowed to win a fixed race

**sport of kings** horse-racing is traditionally known as 'the sport of kings'

**sticks** the hurdles in steeplechasing

**turf** 'the turf' means the racecourse, horse-racing or the racing world

**whipper-in** the horse in last place at any moment in a race

## Motor-sport slang

Do small boys still want to be racing drivers when they grow up? Or have dreams of being a high-earning football player or an Internet millionaire taken over? Whatever the answer, motor-sport still exudes a type of glamour along with the aroma of spent fuel and burning rubber. More of us are car drivers than ever before, and it is not difficult to imagine being behind the wheel of a racing car at Le Mans or Indianapolis. Racing drivers, especially in Formula One, are still heroes to many, and the late Ayrton Senna has even been immortalized in rhyming slang (as you will read later in this book). While we can all 'drop the hammer' or 'put the pedal to the metal', most of us are unlikely ever to 'take the chequered flag' or hang out with 'pit babes'.

### Glossary

**banger** a stock car used in a race in which drivers deliberately crash into one another

**binders** brakes

**bottoming** the action of a car's chassis hitting the road surface

**clean air** air that has not been made turbulent by the passage of other cars and therefore does not have an adverse effect on a car's aerodynamics

**dirty air** air that has been made turbulent by the passage of other cars, and therefore has an adverse effect on a car's aerodynamics

**drop the hammer** when a driver 'drops the hammer', he or she depresses the accelerator fully

**flat spot** an area on a tyre that is more worn than other parts of the tyre

**groove** the best route around a course or track

**Indy 500** the Indianapolis 500, an annual motor race in Indiana, USA

**lollipop** a sign held up to communicate something to a driver

**off** an 'off' is an accident in which the car leaves the track

**paddles** a pair of levers on the steering wheel of a Formula One car, used by the driver to change gears

**pit babe** an attractive young woman employed by a team to adorn its pit area and promote the team

**pushing and shoving** contact made between cars in a race

**put the pedal to the metal** to accelerate fully

**race face** the expression of determination on the face of a driver about to enter a race

**shakedown** a test run of a car which has had a new part fitted

**shunt** an accident in which one car crashes into another

**shut the door** if one driver 'shuts the door' on another one, he moves over sharply to prevent a passing move

**skid lid** a crash helmet

**slicks** smooth tyres used in dry conditions

**splash and dash** a brief pit stop towards the end of a race, in which the car's fuel is topped up to ensure that it has enough to finish

**take the chequered flag** to win a race (the flag in question is the black-and-white variety shown to the winner and subsequent finishers in a race)

**traffic** cars that are further back in the field and moving more slowly than the leading cars

**wets** grooved tyres used in wet conditions

## American football slang

Until relatively recently, American football was precisely that
(neighbouring Canada had its own version), but the game is now also
played professionally in Europe as well. Through this development,
and the worldwide television transmission of showpiece games like
the annual Super Bowl, much of the sport's slang and jargon has
become familiar to the general public, not only to its aficionados. Like
baseball, the sport is central to American life, and many of its terms
are used as metaphors in everyday situations. For example, an 'end
run' is often used to mean any kind of evasive manoeuvre, a 'game
plan' can be applied to any planned undertaking, anyone who
criticizes from the vantage point of hindsight may be called a
'Monday-morning quarterback', and to 'run interference' can mean to
protect someone from those who seek to prevent him or her from
carrying out a task.

### Glossary

**birdcage** the facemask worn
by a lineman

**bomb** a pass thrown deep
downfield

**bullet** a fast, accurate pass

**chain gang** the members of
the officiating team concerned
with measuring the ten yards
required to retain possession

**cheap shot** a deliberate foul
on an unsuspecting opponent

**circus catch** a spectacular or
acrobatic catch

**climb the ladder** to jump
extremely high in order to
catch the ball

**cut** to 'cut' a player is to
remove him from the team

**end run** a play in which the
player with the ball tries to
run around the end of the line
of players opposing him

**freeze** to 'freeze' the ball is to
keep possession of it without
trying to score

**game plan** the strategy or
tactics used by a team

**gridiron** a football field, or
the game itself

**hail Mary** a high pass thrown
into the end zone at the end
of a half

**laundry** penalty flags thrown
by officials

**Monday-morning quarterback** someone who expresses opinions about strategic decisions after the outcome of a game is known

**North–South runner** a ball-carrier who tends to run straight ahead rather than elude tacklers

**on the numbers** if a pass is thrown 'on the numbers', it is thrown accurately, reaching the receiver at chest height and allowing an easy catch to be made

**pigskin** the football

**prayer** a desperate pass thrown in spite of the fact that no receiver is obviously in a position to catch it

**run interference** to block opposing players who are trying to tackle the player on your own side who is carrying the ball

**sack** to 'sack' a quarterback is to tackle him behind the line of scrimmage and before he can pass the ball

**spearing** the illegal move of striking an opponent with the crown of your helmet

**spike** to 'spike' the ball is to throw it vigorously to the ground, often to emphatically celebrate a touchdown

**takeaway** the act by a defence of forcing the attacking side to fumble, and then taking control of the ball

**taxi squad** a group of players who train with a team but do not play in games

**thread the needle** to pass the ball into a small gap between two defenders

**traffic** if a quarterback passes into 'traffic', there are a lot of players in the area where the ball is thrown

**trenches** the offensive and defensive lines, regarded as the site of strenuous and unappreciated effort

**wobbly duck** a badly thrown pass that travels with an eccentric motion

**X's and O's** the tactical manoeuvres formulated by coaches and traditionally explained to players through diagrams on which offensive players are marked with an X and defensive players with an O

**zebra** a member of the officiating team (from the black-and-white striped shirts worn by officials)

## Baseball slang

Like its English counterpart, cricket, the game of baseball delights in a wealth of jargon. The relatively slow pace and compartmentalized nature of the game of baseball makes it conducive to detailed analysis, and this has probably helped to foster this use of colourful language by players and commentators. Jargon terms abound in all aspects of the game, but especially when describing the game's climactic moments: a home run can be a 'homer', a 'tater', a 'dinger', a 'round-tripper' or a 'long ball', and more spectacular specimens may even be accorded the status of a 'moon shot' or a 'tape-measure shot'; when a pitcher strikes out a batter, he can be said to 'punch out' or 'fan' the batter, while the batter is said to 'whiff'.

An interesting aspect of baseball slang is how the jargon associated with 'America's pastime' can sometimes reflect wider elements of American culture: an easy catch is sometimes called 'a can of corn', harking back to the times when a storekeeper would knock down canned goods from the top shelf with a pole so that they dropped gently into his hand; while the two-digit system for numbering America's interstate highways means that a player whose batting average remains below .100 is said to be 'on the interstate'.

## Glossary

**aboard** if a batter is 'aboard', he has reached first base successfully

**bag** any of the bases

**bandbox** a small ballpark that makes it easy to hit home runs

**blast** a home run

**bush league** a minor league

**can of corn** an easy catch for a fielder

**chin music** a pitch that passes close to the batter's head

**crooked number** any number other than 0 or 1 recorded on a baseball scoreboard

**dinger** a home run

**dish** the home plate

**double header** two games played on the same day

**fan** if a pitcher 'fans' a batter, he strikes him out

**filthy** if a pitch is described as 'filthy', it breaks so sharply that it is almost impossible to hit

**flash the leather** to make a skilful defensive play

**frozen rope** a hit or throw that sends the ball on a fast, level trajectory

**gapper** a ball hit into the gap between two outfielders

**golden sombrero** a notional award given to a batter who strikes out four times in a game

**go yard** to hit a home run

**grand salami** a grand slam home run (ie one hit when there are runners at all the bases)

**heat** if a pitcher 'throws heat' or 'brings the heat', he has a powerful fastball

**high cheese** or **high heat** a pitcher's fastball thrown at the top of or above the strike zone

**homer** a home run

**hot corner** the position of third baseman (where the fielder has least time to react to balls hit in his direction)

**interstate** if a batter is 'on the interstate', he has a batting average below .100 (from the fact that American interstate highways all have two-digit numbers)

**K** a strikeout

**long ball** a home run

**Mendoza line** a batting average of .200, considered the lower limit of respectability for a professional hitter (named after a notoriously weak-hitting player)

**moon shot** a home run that travels a very long distance beyond the field of play

**paint the black** if a pitcher 'paints the black', he throws the ball right over the edge of the plate

**Punch-and-Judy hitter** a batter who is not capable of hitting the ball with great power

**punch out** to strike out a batter

**round-tripper** a home run (which allows the batter to perform a circuit of all the bases)

**slugger** a powerful batter, capable of hitting home runs

**table-setter** a batter whose job is to reach base so that the team's more powerful hitters can help him to score

**tape-measure shot** a home run that travels a very long

distance beyond the field of play

**tater** a home run

**Texas Leaguer** a gently hit ball that drops between the infield and the outfield

**tools of ignorance** the protective equipment worn by the catcher

**twin killing** a double play, where the fielding team puts out two members of the batting side

**Uncle Charlie** a curveball

**wheelhouse** if a pitch is thrown in a hitter's 'wheelhouse', the hitter is able to make a powerful swing at the ball

**whiff** if a batter 'whiffs', he strikes out

**yakker** a curveball

## *Basketball slang*

Basketball is a relatively young sport, having been invented in the United States in the late 19th century. Its popularity grew throughout the 20th century (especially among the very tall), and it spread throughout the world, helped by its appearance in Olympic Games and the highly entertaining exhibition matches played by the famous Harlem Globetrotters. Part of its appeal is that it can be played almost anywhere as long as a ball and a net are available. Players can even get together in the street to 'shoot a few hoops'. As with other sports, some of its terminology has passed into more general language usage; for example, a 'slam dunk' is now used to mean a dramatic and unqualified success in almost any context.

### *Glossary*

**air** the distance between the ground and the feet of a player who is shooting or jumping for the ball

**air ball** a shot that misses the basket

**alley oop** a pass that sets up a teammate for a slam dunk

**baller** a high-scoring player

**bank shot** a shot that hits the backboard before going through the basket

**b-ball** basketball

**board** an instance of the ball rebounding from the backboard

**brick** an inaccurate and poorly thrown shot

**bucket** the basket

**buzzer-beater** a basket scored just before the end of a period of play

**charity stripe** the foul line

**charity toss** a free throw

**deuce** a two-point field goal

**dish** to pass the ball

**downtown** the area of a basketball court beyond the three-point line (from which baskets count as three rather than two points)

**drain** to shoot the ball cleanly through the basket

**dunk** to jump up and push the ball down through the basket

**flop** a player who 'flops' tries to earn a foul against an opposing player by falling down when little actual contact has been made

**glass** the backboard

**hack** a foul

**hoops** the game of basketball

**hops** the ability to jump high in the air

**jam** same as **slam dunk**

**jumper** a shot made by a player jumping into the air

**old-fashioned way** making a three-point play 'the old-fashioned way' refers to scoring a two-point basket followed by a free throw (rather than scoring from beyond the three-point line)

**paint** the key-shaped area close to the net enclosed by the foul lines (so called because it is usually painted a different colour)

**prayer** a hopeful long-range shot, especially one made when time is running out at the end of a period of play

**reject** to block a shot

**rock** 'the rock' is the ball

**shake'n'bake** showy play, involving fast changes of direction and dexterous handling of the ball

**shoot hoops** to play basketball

**slam dunk** an act of jumping up and pushing the ball forcibly down through the basket

**strip** to 'strip' a player is to deprive him or her of possession of the ball

**stroke** to shoot the ball smoothly

**T** a technical foul

**trey** a three-point field goal

# Climbers' slang

Climbers are a special breed. They have fun doing things that most other people would regard as insanely dangerous, and the most cogent explanation they can come up with for scaling some terrifyingly lowering peak is 'because it's there'. In common with people involved in other highly risky activities, a black and self-deprecating humour runs through climbers' use of slang. It is as if dangers can be minimized by laughing at them. In this way, a life-protecting helmet becomes a 'brain bucket' and uncontrollable jerking of overtired limbs is labelled as 'death wobbles' or 'sewing-machine legs'. Much of the slang is concerned with that most vital element of any climb: holds. In their varying degree of size or usefulness, they can be as big as a 'party ledge', as deep as a 'jug', or as small and precarious as a 'mono' or 'nubbin'. Whatever the level of security they afford, above all they must not be 'manky'.

## Glossary

**barn door** the tendency of the body to swing away from the rock face when unsecured

**beta** knowledge of a climbing route, such as key protection placements and sequences of moves

**big wall** an extensive area that should take more than one day to climb

**bivvy** a bivouac, a makeshift camp without tents

**bivvy bag** a sleeping bag for use in a bivouac

**bobpoint** an ascent claimed but not actually made

**bomber** an adjective used to describe anything excellent, especially a protection device or belay

**bouldering** climbing on large boulders close to the ground without ropes

**brain bucket** a climbing helmet

**buildering** the practice of climbing buildings

**bumper belay** a belay secured to a motor vehicle

**chicken wings** the phenomenon of a climber's elbows rising unintentionally, caused by tiredness

**chickhead** a projection often

found in granite that provides good holds

**crater** to 'crater' is to fall and hit the ground

**crimp** a small, narrow hold held with the finger ends

**death wobbles** same as **sewing-machine leg**

**deck out** to hit the ground

**dyno** a move in which momentum has to be generated to reach the next hold

**edge** a hold that is too narrow to stand on

**Egyptian** a manoeuvre made with the body side-on to a steep rock face

**Elvis** to 'Elvis' is to experience a leg that jerks uncontrollably through tension

**flamed** exhausted and unable to climb any farther

**forearm pump** temporary weakness in the forearms resulting from build-up of lactic acid

**hang-dogging** the practice of lingering on a rope or safe hold

**jam** an improvised hold created by cramming part of the body into a crack

**jug** a large deep hold

**manky** used to describe any hold that is not dependable or a climbing aid that is not securely fixed

**moat** a US term for the area between snow and ice on a rock wall

**mono** a small hole, large enough to admit only one finger

**munge** dirt and debris found in holes

**nubbin** a very small hold

**party ledge** a wide ledge on which more than one climber may rest

**redpoint** to climb a route from bottom to top in a single attempt (after a period of practice)

**roof** an almost horizontal overhang

**sewing-machine leg** a leg that jerks uncontrollably through tension

**sharp end** the end of the rope to which the lead climber is attached

**slap** if a climber can touch a handhold but not grasp it, he or she is said to 'slap' it

**smear** to 'smear' is to gain purchase on a smooth rock face only by the friction of the climber's footwear

**vegetable garden** an area on a climb where the surface is covered with grass or lichen

# Surfers' slang

Surfing seems to have originated in Hawaii, but it was not until the 1960s that enthusiasm for the activity spread beyond a small coterie of devotees. Particularly in California, with its many beaches and seemingly perpetual sunshine, the sport grew into a craze among young people and soon spawned a subculture. The Beach Boys were the quintessential surfers' band and their hit songs helped introduce many surfing terms into wider use. The beach lifestyle was attractive to many who would never actually 'catch a wave', and 'beach bunnies' and 'hodads' were as much part of the scene as actual surfers. Surfers' clothes became fashionable too, and Hawaiian shirts and 'baggies' were soon sported on city streets as well as at the beach. Surfing was taken up in other parts of the world, of course, especially in Australia, and even in the cooler climes of the United Kingdom, and these countries added terms to the surfing lexicon. The characteristic slang was given a boost in the 1980s through its use by the heroes of the children's cartoon show *Teenage Mutant Ninja Turtles*, who were responsible for bringing the exclamation 'Cowabunga!' back into mainstream use. Much of the surfers' attitudes, language and clothing styles later found echoes in skateboarding culture.

## Glossary

**air** an 'air' is any move in which the surfer is in the air

**baggies** baggy, loose-fitting shorts

**bail out** to jump off your board to avoid a 'wipe-out'

**beach bunny** a young woman who spends a lot of time at the beach, associating with surfers

**beaver tail** a wetsuit with a crotch-piece that can be detached at the front and left hanging at the back

**blue juice** a particularly powerful wave

**bombora** in Australia, a large wave that breaks outside the normal surf line

**boogie board** a short surfboard on which the surfer lies

**catch a wave** to ride a wave that is breaking

**cowabunga!** a cry of triumph or approval

**cruncher** a wave that breaks too powerfully to be ridden

**deck** the top surface of the surfboard

**ding** a damaged area on a surfboard

**dumper** a wave that crashes suddenly downwards with great force, causing surfers to fall

**glasshouse** the area inside a wave

**gnarly** treacherous or dangerous

**goofy foot** if a surfer rides 'goofy foot', he or she surfs with his or her right foot in front of the left

**green room** same as **glasshouse**

**grommet** a derogatory term for a young surfer

**hang five** to ride a surfboard with the toes of one foot extended beyond the leading edge

**hang ten** to ride a surfboard with the toes of both feet extended beyond the leading edge

**hodad** someone who likes to frequent the company of surfers but is not a surfer

**honker** a very large wave

**hot-dog** a person who performs showy manoeuvres, such as spins and turns, while surfing

**kook** an inexperienced or inept surfer

**mondo** very

**nailed** a surfer who 'gets nailed' suffers a 'wipe-out'

**point break** an area where waves break around a promontory of land

**shark biscuit** a novice surfer

**shoot the tube** or **curl** to ride inside the tube of a wave

**shred** to surf in an impressive way

**sidewalk surfing** skateboarding

**soup** the foam left by a breaking wave

**stick** a surfboard

**tube** the concave leading edge of a wave, below the crest

**tubular** a wave that develops a significant 'tube' is said to be 'tubular'

**wipe-out** a fall from a surfboard after losing control or being knocked off by a wave

**woodie** a station wagon with wood panelling on the sides

## Skateboarding slang

The obvious comparison to be made about skateboarding is that it is like surfing on land, riding on wheels instead of waves, and, indeed, in surfers' slang skateboarders are called 'sidewalk surfers'. Other similarities between the activities include the all-embracing devotion shown by the true enthusiasts and the fact that particular subcultures were generated by them. Like surfers, 'skaterboys' and 'skatergirls' have their own styles of dress, which are much imitated by others who never take an active part in the sport itself. Similarly, the slang is full of terms for particular stunts or moves, from an 'aerial' to a 'nollie', and for the various surfaces on which to perform, from 'half-pipes' to 'vert ramps'. One difference between surfing and skateboarding is that the latter is much more prevalent. No beach with the proper waves is needed by 'skate rats', who are very much an urban breed. While the activity may have declined since its peak in the 1990s, the roaring and clacking of wheels and boards is still a familiar background noise in certain parts of city centres all over the world.

### Glossary

**aerial** an 'aerial' is a jump made into the air

**air** to 'catch air' is to perform an 'aerial'

**deck** the platform of a skateboard

**grind** to move along a rail (such as a handrail or a specially-designed structure) with only the bottom of the board in contact with the rail

**grind rail** or **grinding rail** a long narrow bar raised above the ground, on which stunts are performed

**grip tape** adhesive-backed tape applied to the 'deck' of a skateboard in order to provide more grip for the feet or for decorative purposes

**half-pipe** a U-shaped structure made of concrete, used in performing stunts

**kicker** a small ramp

**kick turn** a turn through 180 degrees

**mini ramp** a **half-pipe** in which one side is higher than the other, but not as high as in a **vert ramp**

**mongo foot** the front foot, especially when this is used for pushing (most skateboarders push with the back foot)

**nollie** a variation of the **ollie** in which the nose of the board is pushed down

**nose grind** a grinding manoeuvre in which only the front part of the board is in contact with the rail

**ollie** a jump into the air with the feet still touching the board, performed by pushing the tail of the board down with the back foot

**pipe** a large concrete tube inside which skateboarders perform stunts

**quarter-pipe** a variety of **half-pipe** with lower sides

**roll-in** a specially built slope down which skateboarders can gain the momentum needed for a stunt

**sidewalk surfing** skateboarding

**skatepark** an area set aside for skateboarding, including specially designed ramps, obstacles, etc

**skate rat** a skateboarding enthusiast

**skaterboy** or **skatergirl** a devotee of skateboarding, or sometimes simply a youth who adopts the clothing style associated with skateboarding

**snakeboard** a form of skateboard with pivoting footplates at either end

**truck** a steerable axle on a skateboard

**vert ramp** a type of **half-pipe** in which one side is extended almost vertically upwards

## *Hunting slang*

Hunting, especially fox-hunting, has been a traditional activity in Britain throughout the centuries, surviving even Oscar Wilde's famous description of an English gentleman galloping after a fox as 'the unspeakable in full pursuit of the uneatable'. Many of its peculiar expressions have become part of everyday speech, with 'tally ho' being adopted as a universal cry of encouragement, novices being initiated into various forms of activity being said to be 'blooded', and anyone involved in a vigorous pursuit being described as 'in full cry'. However, in the last decades of the 20th century, hunts were regularly disrupted by 'sabs' (anti-bloodsports campaigners), and in 2002 hunting with hounds was banned in Scotland, with England following suit in 2005, despite massive protests from not only the huntin', shootin' and fishin' fraternity, but also many ordinary country dwellers. It is still legal to stage 'drag' hunts, but whether or not the sport will survive without the ultimate goal of 'bowling over Charlie' remains to be seen.

## Glossary

**accounted for** used to describe a fox that has been killed

**anti** a hunt saboteur

**babble** if a hound is said to be 'babbling', it is making a noise to no purpose

**blank** a 'blank' covert is one that yields no quarry

**blood** to 'blood' a hunting novice is to smear his or her face with the blood of a quarry

**bolt** to 'bolt' a fox is to chase it from an earth using terriers

**bowled over** same as **accounted for**

**break up** if hounds 'break up' a fox, they eat it

**bruise** to ride recklessly along

**brush** the tail of a dead fox

**cap** a collection of money taken at a fox hunt, to be given to hunt servants or good causes

**cast** to 'cast' hounds is to direct them over ground where their quarry may have passed

**Charlie** a nickname for a fox being hunted

**check** when a pack of hounds loses the scent, it is said to 'check'

**chop** if a pack of hounds 'chop' a quarry, this means they kill it immediately, before it has had a chance to run

**cry** a 'cry' is a pack of hounds

**cubbing** the hunting of fox cubs

**drag** an artificial scent dragged along the ground for hounds to follow

**given best** a fox is 'given best' if it is allowed to get away

**given law** a fox is 'given

law' when it is allowed to run before the hounds are released to chase it

**hacking gear** same as **rat-catcher**

**in full cry** hounds in full pursuit of a quarry are said to be 'in full cry'

**lawn meet** a hunt meeting that takes place at the home of one of the members

**line** the track along which a quarry has travelled

**mask** a fox or other animal's face or head

**Mr Todd** a nickname for a fox

**own the line** when hounds find the scent of the quarry, they are said to 'own the line'

**pads** the paws of a dead fox

**pink** a scarlet hunting coat, or its wearer

**puss** a hare

**put up** a quarry is 'put up' when it is discovered by the hounds and runs away from them

**rat-catcher** unconventional hunting garb

**riot** when hounds chase quarry other than the desired animal, they are said to 'riot'

**rolled over** same as **accounted for**

**sab** a hunt saboteur, an opponent of blood sports who tries to sabotage hunting activities

**speak** hounds yelping when on the track of a quarry are said to 'speak'

**tufter** a hound that drives deer out of cover

**warrantable** used to describe any quarry that is of sufficient age to be hunted

**whipper-in** a huntsman's assistant, who controls the hounds

# Poker slang

The game of poker is one of the most famous and widely played of card games. Its specific origins are not absolutely clear, but it was certainly popularized in 19th-century America. It is the gambling game par excellence, and large sums of money are won and lost, particularly by professional players (or 'rounders'), who take part in a worldwide circuit of tournaments. Like any activity, it has evolved its own terminology and jargon. Even those who have never held a 'royal flush' in their clammy fingers or 'drawn dead' will be familiar with many poker expressions from movies and television dramas. For some reason (perhaps simple popularity), more than any other card game it has lent slang terms to the English language in general. For example, most of us know that 'a poker face' means an inscrutable one, an asset to a poker player concerned with not revealing the quality of his or her hand. Similarly, any decisive but hidden advantage can be called an 'ace in the hole', any activity that is considered insignificant may be described as being 'penny-ante', a 'busted flush' is often applied as a label for any failed project, and to 'cash in your chips' is to die.

## Glossary

**all-in** a player who is 'all-in' is staking all of his chips or money

**Anna Kournikova** a hand consisting of an ace and a king (named after the Russian tennis player, because it 'looks good but rarely actually wins anything')

**ante** or **ante up** to stake a bet

**bad beat** a particularly disappointing loss, such as when a good hand is beaten by a lucky one

**big slick** a dealt hand that contains an ace and a king

**blank** a card that is of no use to a player

**bullet** an ace

**busted flush** a potential flush that is never completed

**call** to demand the playing of (an exposed card)

**cowboy** a king

**dead man's hand** a hand with a pair of aces and a pair of eights (as held by Wild Bill Hickok when he was killed)

**draw** to 'draw' a card is to take one from the dealer

**draw dead** to draw cards to a hand that cannot win

**fold** a player who 'folds' withdraws from a hand

**freeze-out** a game played until only one player is left

**Harry Potter** a hand consisting of a jack and a king (a play on the initials of Harry

Potter's creator, *JK* Rowling)

**hole card** in stud poker, the card dealt face down in the first round

**kicker** a card not matched by any others in a hand

**monster** a hand that seems likely to win

**muck** to 'muck' a hand is to discard it

**nuts** a hand that can't be beaten is called 'the nuts'

**open card** a card dealt face up

**penny ante** a variety of poker in which only modest stakes are allowed

**quads** a hand with four cards of the same designation

**rounder** a professional player who enters many tournaments

**royal flush** a straight flush headed by the ace

**see** to meet and accept another's bet by staking a similar sum

**short stack** the lowest amount of chips held by any player at the table

**straight flush** a sequence of five cards of the same suit

**tell** an involuntary gesture that an experienced opponent may use to make deductions about a player's hand

## Bingo slang

Bingo is a game that seems to go in and out of fashion. Its heyday was probably in the postwar era, before television became available to most homes, when a visit to the bingo represented a good night out. Bingo halls and parlours (many of them converted from former cinemas) continue to flourish, but the Internet has led to the growth of online bingo – to a point where most players never actually leave home to play. One of the major areas of slang use in bingo is, of course, the descriptive terms employed by callers to designate the numbers as they appear. Most of these are rhyming slang (such as 'knock at the door' for four), or a near-approximation to a rhyme (as in 'clickety-click' for sixty-six). Many are traditional, containing references traceable back to the Edwardian music-hall (such as 'Kelly's eye' for number one, seemingly from an anecdote about a one-eyed person called Kelly); others change with the times, the prime example being number ten, which is eternally associated in the British mind with the Prime Minister's official residence at 10 Downing Street, and is currently known as 'Tony's den' when once it would have been 'Eden's den'. Other variations are regional rather than temporal, and the sheer number of these means that the list below could never hope to be complete.

## Glossary

**all the threes** thirty-three

**bang on the drum** seventy-one

**blackout** a version of the game in which all numbers on a card must be scored out to win

**buckle my shoe** thirty-two

**clickety-click** sixty-six

**Danny La Rue** fifty-two

**dauber** an ink marker used to cancel numbers on a card

**half a century** fifty

**Heinz varieties** fifty-seven

**house** an exclamation made by the first player to finish

**housey-housey** an old name for the game of bingo

**Kelly's eye** number one

**key of the door** twenty-one

**knock at the door** number four

**legs eleven** number eleven

**lucky seven** number seven

**old-age pension** sixty-five

**on** a player who is 'on' is waiting for only one more number

**snakes alive** fifty-five

**steps** thirty-nine

**sweet sixteen** sixteen

**three score and ten** seventy

**Tony's den** number ten

**top of the shop** ninety

**two fat ladies** eighty-eight

**two little ducks** twenty-two

**unlucky for some** number thirteen

**Winnie the Pooh** forty-two

# Part Two

# Slang in Areas of Everyday Life

## Booze

Drugs may come and drugs may go, but despite the vagaries of fashion and the advances of the pharmaceutical industry, the drug of choice for the majority of the world's population remains alcohol. Humankind's first discovery of how to brew or distil is as yet undocumented, but language describing, celebrating or bemoaning the effects of alcohol has been around since time immemorial. Perhaps it is the universality of the experience of drinking that makes it so productive of vocabulary. Social class is no barrier to 'the demon drink' and the toff in his country house may be no more or less 'blotto' on his 'champers' than the down-and-out on his park bench with his 'red biddy'.

Moderation in drink is of course to be admired, but it is the extremes of consumption, strength and inebriation that tend to generate slang. There is no need to be stuck for a word for 'drunk' when you can choose from a range stretching the full gamut of the alphabet, from 'arseholed' to 'zonked'. Your favourite tipple may be anything from 'amber fluid' to 'mothers' ruin' to 'vino collapso'. The list below does not attempt to cover everything in this particularly fecund field, but it ranges across the centuries and continents to present a glimpse of the world of booze, albeit through a glass, darkly.

## Glossary

**alkie** or **alky** an alcoholic

**amber fluid** or **nectar** beer

**arseholed** very drunk

**barfly** a drinker who spends a lot of time in bars

**bat** a drunken spree

**bender** a drunken spree

**bend the elbow** to drink alcohol, especially to excess

**bevvied** drunk

**bevvy** an alcoholic drink or a drinking session

**bladdered** very drunk

**blasted** thoroughly intoxicated by drink

**blind-drunk** so drunk as to be like a blind person

**blitzed** highly intoxicated by drink

**blootered** a Scottish term for drunk

**blotto** helplessly drunk

**blue ruin** gin

**boilermaker** a drink of whisky taken along with a drink of beer

**bombo** an Australian term for cheap wine

**booze** any kind of intoxicating liquor

**booze cruise** a foreign excursion for the purpose of buying cheap alcohol

**boozer** a person who boozes, or a pub

**booze-up** a drinking session

**bottle** 'the bottle' is alcoholic drink

**Brahms and Liszt** drunk (rhyming slang for 'pissed')

**brewski** a US term for a drink of beer

**Britney Spears** beers (rhyming slang)

**bubbly** champagne

**canned** drunk

**Cape smoke** locally made South African brandy

**chain lightning** a strong or harsh-tasting whisky

**champers** champagne

**chaser** a drink of a different type drunk immediately after another

**cockeyed** tipsy

**corked** an old term for drunk

**cratur** 'the cratur' is a term for whisky used in Scotland and Ireland

**crocked** a North American term for drunk

**dead men** empty bottles after a party or drinking bout (in the USA these are sometimes called **dead marines**)

**demon drink** 'the demon drink' is a name given to alcohol when considered as an evil influence

**dingbats** in Australia and New Zealand, someone who has 'the dingbats' is suffering from delirium tremens

**doctor** an old term for brown sherry

**drink with the flies** in Australia, to 'drink with the flies' is to drink on your own

**DTs** someone who has 'the DTs' is suffering from delirium tremens

**elevated** slightly drunk

**eye-opener** an alcoholic drink taken in the morning

**firewater** strong alcoholic spirits

**fizz** if you are offered a glass of 'fizz', it may be champagne, but then again it may be something less expensive

**froth-blower** a beer drinker

**full** drunk

**gnat's piss** any alcoholic drink considered to be unacceptably weak or tasteless

**grog** an Australian and New Zealand term for alcoholic drink, especially beer

**grog-on** or **grog-up** an Australian and New Zealand term for a drinking party or drinking session

**growler** a US term for a container of beer

**gutrot** rough, cheap alcohol

**half-cut** drunk

**half-seas-over** half-drunk

**hammered** very drunk

**happy** slightly drunk

**hard stuff** 'the hard stuff' means strong alcoholic spirits

**hit the bottle** to drink excessively

**hooch** whisky or any other strong liquor

**hophead** an Australian and New Zealand term for a drunkard

**inky** in Australia, someone who is 'inky' is drunk

**it** Italian vermouth, as in 'gin and it'

**jar** a drink of beer

**jarred** drunk

**jimjams** someone who has 'the jimjams' is suffering from delirium tremens

**Jimmy Woodser** an Australian and New Zealand term for a solitary drinker or a drink taken on your own

**Joe Blakes** in Australia, if you have 'the Joe Blakes', you have delirium tremens ('Joe Blakes' is rhyming slang for 'shakes')

**juice** a US term for alcoholic drink

**juiced** drunk

**jungle juice** alcoholic liquor, especially if very strong, of poor quality or home-made

**lager lout** a youth noted for his boorish, aggressive and unruly behaviour brought on by excessive drinking

**lashed** drunk

**legless** very drunk

**leg-opener** an alcoholic drink offered by a man to a woman to get her drunk with a view to seducing her

**liquid lunch** an instance of drinking alcohol at lunch-time instead of eating food

**liquored up** drunk

**load** to 'have a load on' is to be drunk

**loaded** drunk

**lock-in** a period of drinking in a pub after it has officially closed for the night

**lubricate** to 'lubricate' a person is to supply them with alcoholic drink

**lush** this can mean either drink itself or someone who drinks too much

**maggoty** very drunk

**Mick Jagger** lager (Scottish rhyming slang)

**middy** an Australian term for a glass of beer, varying in capacity from place to place

**moon-eyed** a US term for drunk

**moonshine** illicitly distilled or smuggled spirits

**moonshiner** someone who distils or smuggles illicit spirits

**mortal** very drunk

**mother's ruin** gin

**mountain dew** whisky, especially when illicitly distilled

**mullered** or **mullahed** drunk

**needle** in the USA, to 'needle' an alcoholic drink is to add more alcohol to it

**on the batter** someone who is 'on the batter' is on a drinking spree (such a person might also be described as being **on the lash**, **on the piss** or **on the razz**)

**on the wagon** abstaining from alcohol

**out of your skull** extremely drunk

**paralytic** helplessly drunk

**pickled** drunk

**pie-eyed** drunk

**pissed** drunk (a state in which a person can be compared to the most unlikely of imbibers, such as being 'pissed as a fart' or 'pissed as a newt')

**piss artist** or **pisshead** a heavy drinker

**piss-up** a bout of heavy drinking

**pixilated** a US term for drunk

**plastered** drunk

**plonko** an Australian term for an alcoholic

**quickie** an alcoholic drink to be rapidly consumed

**rat-arsed** or **ratted** drunk

**red biddy** a drink made of red wine and methylated spirits

**red-eye** a name applied in the US to poor-quality whisky, but in Canada to a drink of beer and tomato juice

**red ned** an old Australian term for cheap red wine

**ripped** drunk

**rosy** an old slang word for wine

**rubbidy** a pub (shortened from rhyming slang 'rub-a-dub-dub')

**rummy** a US term for a drunkard

**sauce** 'the sauce' is alcoholic drink

**sesh** a drinking session

**shampoo** champagne

**sheep-dip** inferior liquor

**sherbet** a term used in Australia for beer

**shicker** in Australia and New Zealand, 'shicker' can mean either strong drink or a drunkard

**shitfaced** a term for drunk, used mainly in North America

**shooter** a small drink of spirits

**short** a drink of spirits

**shot** a drink of spirits, often drunk in a small glass called a 'shot glass'

**shout** to 'shout' someone a drink is to buy one for them

**skinful** as much alcoholic drink as someone can hold

**slammer** a fizzy cocktail, usually made with tequila, imbibed in a single swift motion shortly after the glass has been slammed against a table or similar surface

**slaughtered** very drunk

**slewed** or **slued** drunk

**sloshed** drunk

**smashed** drunk

**smile** in old slang, to 'smile' was to take a drink, especially of whisky

**snakebite** a drink made of cider and lager in equal measures

**snifter** a small drink of spirits

**snootful** enough alcohol to make someone drunk

**snort** a quick drink

**soak** a heavy or habitual drinker

**sozzled** drunk

**spike** to 'spike' a drink is to make it stronger by adding spirits or other alcohol, whether or not the drinker is aware of this

**sponge** a drunkard

**sprung** tipsy

**squiffy** tipsy

**steaming** in an advanced state of inebriation

**stewed** drunk

**stiffener** a strong alcoholic drink

**stinko** drunk

**stonkered** or **stonkers** drunk

**suck the monkey** in old slang, to 'suck the monkey' meant to drink from a cask through an inserted tube

**suds** a North American term for beer

**swipes** weak, bad or spoilt beer

**swizzle** to excess

**tanked up** to 'get tanked up' is to drink heavily

**tape** alcoholic drink

**three sheets in the wind** somewhat drunk

**tiddly** or **tiddled** slightly drunk

**tie one on** to get drunk

**tight** drunk

**tinny** in Australia and New Zealand, a 'tinny' is a can of beer

**toot** a North American term for a drinking binge

**trashed** drunk

**tube** an Australian term for a can or bottle of beer

**twankay** gin

**twist** a mixed drink

**two-pot screamer** a disparaging term used by Australians to stigmatize someone who gets drunk on a comparatively small amount of alcohol

**under the table** hopelessly drunk; to 'drink someone under the table' is to outdo them in consuming alcohol while retaining a spark of consciousness

**under the weather** drunk

**up the pole** drunk

**usual** a pub customer who orders 'the usual' is asking for his habitual favourite drink

**vino** a generic term for wine

**vino collapso** wine that is guaranteed to have an intoxicating effect

**voddy** vodka

**wallop** beer

**watering hole** a pub

**well away** drunk

**wet** given to drinking, or tipsy

**wet your whistle** to have an alcoholic drink

**what's your poison?** or **what's yours?** what would you like to drink?

**whiffled** drunk

**whistled** drunk

**white lady** Australian slang for methylated spirits as a drink

**white lightning** illicitly distilled spirits

**widow** 'the widow' is a name for a proprietary brand of champagne produced by Veuve Clicquot (*veuve* being French for 'widow')

**wino** someone, especially a down-and-out, addicted to cheap wine

**wrecked** rendered incapable by drink

**zonked** drunk

# Food

Few things are more central to human existence than the food which
gives us sustenance – 'our daily bread' or 'the staff of life', to use a
couple of biblical expressions. We all need to eat, whether we are
'veggies' or unabashed meat-eaters, whether we are 'foodies' who
cultivate a delicate palate or omnivores who simply require a 'slap-up'
meal that they can 'wolf down'.

This vital element of daily life offers a rich crop of slang terms. Many
of these celebrate the enjoyment of our victuals: terms of relish, such
as 'hog it', 'scarf down' and 'scoff', easily outnumber those which
suggest a more measured approach. Also notable among food-
related slang are some colourful terms for local delicacies, such as the
American 'sloppy joe', the antipodean 'steamer' and the Londoner's
'wolly'.

Note that the list below also contains items relating to drink of the
non-alcoholic variety (the other kind being considered under **Booze**).

## Glossary

**afters** in a meal, the dessert or
   other course following a main
   course
**banger** a sausage (from the
   crackling sound made by
   sausages frying in a pan)
**barbie** a barbecue
**beanery** a US term for a
   cheap restaurant
**beano** a feast or party
**biccy** a biscuit
**blow-out** a lavish meal
**brekkie** or **brekky** breakfast
**brew** a drink of tea or coffee

**caff** a café or cafeteria
**char** tea
**chewie** chewing gum
**Chinese** a Chinese restaurant,
   or a meal bought from one
**chipper** an Irish term for a
   chip shop
**chippy** or **chippie** a chip
   shop, or a meal bought from
   one
**chop** a West African term for
   food
**chuck** food
**chuck wagon** a wagon

carrying food, cooking apparatus, etc, especially for cattle herders in the USA

**cuppa** a cup of tea

**dead men** the poisonous parts of a crab or other edible shellfish

**decaff** decaffeinated coffee

**deli** a delicatessen

**dig in** to begin eating

**dodger** food, especially bread

**doorstep** a thick slice of bread

**easy over** eggs cooked 'easy over' have been fried on both sides

**eatery** a restaurant

**eating irons** knife, fork and spoon

**eats** food

**elevenses** a snack taken at eleven in the morning

**feed** a plentiful meal

**feed your face** to eat heartily

**foodie** or **foody** a person who is greatly (even excessively) interested in the preparation and consumption of good food

**Frankenstein food** or **Frankenfood** food made or derived from genetically modified plants or animals

**fry-up** a meal consisting of various fried foods

**get outside of** to eat or drink (something)

**goosegog** a gooseberry

**greasies** in Australia and New Zealand, 'greasies' are fish and chips

**greasy** in Australia and New Zealand, a 'greasy' is a camp-cook in the outback

**greasy spoon** a cheap, shabby, often grubby café

**grub** food

**guts** to eat greedily

**hash house** an American term for a cheap restaurant

**hash slinger** someone who works in a **hash house**

**heart attack on a plate** a fry-up, considered as being unhealthy

**hen fruit** eggs

**hog it** to eat greedily

**Indian** an Indian restaurant, or a meal bought from one

**java** coffee (the island of Java being a famous source of coffee)

**jemmy** a baked sheep's head

**joe** a US term for coffee

**loop-the-loop** soup (rhyming slang)

**mash** mashed potato

**Milton Keynes** beans (rhyming slang)

**mousetrap** any cheese of indifferent quality

**muffin-fight** a tea-party

**mulligan** a stew made from various scraps of food

**murphies** potatoes (traditionally seen as the staple food of the Irish)

**nosebag** food

**nosh** food

**noshery** a café or restaurant

**nosh-up** a meal, especially a large one

**nuke** to cook or heat food in a microwave oven

**peck** to eat

**perk** to 'perk' coffee is to percolate it

**pig out** to overeat

**pop** any fizzy drink

**prog** provisions for a journey

**pud** pudding

**rabbit food** a non-vegetarian view of salad

**rasps** raspberries

**Rosie Lee** tea (rhyming slang)

**Ruby Murray** curry (rhyming slang)

**salt-junk** salt beef

**Sammy** a noodle

**sarnie** a sandwich

**satin and silk** milk (rhyming slang)

**scarf down** to devour greedily

**scoff** to devour

**scran** food or provisions

**scrumptious** delicious

**seconds** a second course or second helping

**shift** to swallow or consume

**sinker** a US term for a doughnut

**slap-up** a 'slap-up' meal is a sumptuous one

**sloppy joe** in the USA, a runny mixture of minced beef and sauce served on a half-roll

**snarf** to eat greedily

**soldier** a narrow strip of bread and butter or toast

**soul food** in the USA, food such as chitterlings, cornbread, etc traditionally eaten by African-Americans in the southern states

**spag bol** spaghetti bolognese

**spud** a potato

**square** a square meal, as in 'three squares a day'

**steamer** in Australian cuisine, kangaroo flavoured with pork

**sunny side up** eggs cooked 'sunny side up' have been fried on one side only and are served with the yolk showing

**tater** a potato

**tea fight** a tea-party

**tightener** a heavy meal

**toastie** a toasted sandwich

**tuck** food

**tucker** an Australian and New Zealand term for food

**two-eyed steak** a bloater

**veg** vegetables

**veggie** vegetarian

**veggies** vegetables

**wad** a sandwich, cake or bun

**weenie** a wiener sausage

**wire** to 'wire into' food is to eat it vigorously and assiduously

**wolf** to 'wolf' or 'wolf down' food is to devour it

**wolly** a Cockney term for a pickled olive or cucumber

## *Money*

If money makes the world go round, then money-related slang oils the wheels of monetary transactions. Ever since our ancient ancestors first advanced beyond the idea of trading one thing for another as the only way to do business, money (or the lack of it) has been a constant in all of our lives. Some of us may be comparatively well off ('flush', 'loaded', 'rolling in it'), while others find themselves without ('boracic', 'busted', 'skint', 'strapped for cash'), leaving a lot to be said for being 'comfortable'. The wealthy are often envied, and the resentment sometimes involved in this is shown by the use of such expressions to describe them as 'filthy rich' or 'stinking rich', as if there were something inherently disgusting about having a lot of disposable income. But then, surely no-one would settle for 'peanuts' when they could be 'raking it in'.

Why are there so many slang terms for amounts of money? After all, if you want to refer to a sum in pounds sterling ('nicker'), you can choose from a range going all the way from a 'oncer' through a 'fiver' and a 'tenner' to a 'big note' or even a 'monkey'; our American cousins can draw on any amount of 'folding green' from a 'fin' to a 'c-note' and beyond. It can't be just for familiarity or brevity's sake; it is almost as if bestowing a nickname on cash sums lends them a talismanic quality which might, through luck, attract them to us. There are always those to whom money and the material world are of at most secondary importance, but those of us who have to 'earn a crust' will always find ourselves trading in the slang of money.

---

## Glossary

**Ayrton Senna** a ten-pound note (rhyming slang for 'tenner')

**beer tokens** or **vouchers** money in notes

**big bucks** large amounts of money

**big note** a hundred-pound note

**bob** an old shilling

**bomb** a 'bomb' is a large amount of money

**boracic** or **brassic** having no money (a shortening of 'boracic lint', rhyming slang for 'skint')

**bouncer** a cheque that bounces through lack of funds in the account on which it is drawn

**broke** penniless

**buckshee** free

**busted** a US term meaning 'broke', having no money at all

**chickenfeed** a trifling sum of money

**c-note** a US hundred-dollar note

**comfortable** having enough money

**dead presidents** US banknotes (which feature portraits of former presidents)

**do-re-mi** money

**dosh** money

**double-bubble** 100% interest

**dough** money

**drink** a monetary inducement, bribe or reward

**earn a crust** to make a living

**exes** expenses

**filthy rich** very wealthy

**fin** a US five-dollar bill

**fiver** a five-pound note

**flush** well supplied with money

**folding green** or **folding money** a US term for paper money

**funny money** counterfeit money

**G** a thousand pounds or dollars (from **grand**)

**gelt** money

**go bust** to become bankrupt

**go for a song** to sell for a trifling amount

**grand** a 'grand' is a thousand pounds or dollars

**green** or **green stuff** a US

term for money, especially in notes (which are green for all denominations)

**greenback** a US dollar

**half a ton** fifty pounds

**hard up** having little money or none at all

**jack** a US term for money

**jitney** an old US term for a five-cent coin

**K** a thousand pounds (from 'kilo-' meaning a thousand)

**killing** a large financial gain

**kite** to 'kite' is to write a cheque before there is sufficient money in your account to cover it

**Lady Godiva** a five-pound note (rhyming slang for 'fiver')

**loaded** rich

**lolly** money

**max out** to 'max out' a credit card is to exhaust the limit of credit on it

**mazuma** money

**megabucks** large amounts of money

**monkey** five hundred pounds

**moola** money

**motser** or **motza** an Australian term for a large amount of money

**needful** 'the needful' is ready money

**never-never** 'the never-never'

is the system of buying goods on hire purchase

**nicker** a pound

**oncer** or **oner** a one-pound note

**on the knocker** on credit (similar expressions include **on the slate** and **on the nod**)

**on your uppers** or **beam ends** short of money

**oof** or **ooftish** money

**packet** a 'packet' is a large amount of money

**peanuts** a paltry sum of money

**plastic** credit or debit cards

**pony** twenty-five pounds

**poppy** money

**poultice** in Australia, a 'poultice' is a large sum of money

**quid** a pound

**raking it in** making substantial sums of money

**readies** ready money

**red cent** a very small amount of money (especially in the phrase 'not one red cent')

**rhino** an old term for money

**rolling in it** very wealthy

**rubber cheque** a cheque that bounces

**sawbuck** a US ten-dollar bill

**score** a 'score' is twenty pounds

**shekels** money
**shrapnel** loose change
**simoleon** an old US term for a dollar
**skint** without money
**smacker** in the UK, a pound; in the USA, a dollar
**smash** cash
**sov** a sovereign
**splash out** to spend a lot of money
**spondulicks** money
**square up** to settle a bill, debt, etc
**squid** a pound (a jocular variant of 'quid')
**stinking rich** very well off
**stony-broke** penniless, or nearly so
**stooze** to borrow money at a low rate of interest and invest it to make a profit
**strapped for cash** short of money
**strike it rich** to make a sudden large financial gain
**sub** a small loan
**tanner** an old sixpence
**teapot lid** a pound (rhyming slang for 'quid')
**telephone numbers** very large amounts of money
**tenner** a ten-pound note
**tick** credit
**tightwad** a skinflint or miser
**tin** money
**ton** one hundred pounds
**vowels** an IOU note
**wad** a large amount of money
**wonga** money
**yard** one hundred dollars

## Violence

Ever since Cain slew Abel, violence has been an unpleasant but ubiquitous element of the human condition. It is impossible to say when a human being first realized that a fist, as a 'bunch of fives', could be a weapon, but since time immemorial people have been using theirs to 'lamp', 'bop' and 'deck' one another. The development of weapons obviously made the infliction of violence more serious and telling, with 'chivs' being used to 'carve someone up' and 'coshes' employed to 'brain' a victim. Some people were obliged to improvise and stop drinking long enough to 'bottle' or 'glass' someone who had offended them. Advances in science and technology brought ever more deadly weapons in their wake, particularly firearms, equipping those of a violent cast of mind with a 'gat' or a 'barker' to 'plug' their foes, or even, if they could get their hands on a 'shooting iron' as deadly as a 'tommy gun', to 'fill them full of lead' or 'blow them away'.

It is equally revealing of the human intelligence that slang connected with violence shows the imagination at work, sometimes to lessen the ugliness of the acts with euphemism ('biffing' or 'boffing' don't seem all that bad, and 'happy slapping' sounds positively cheery), and sometimes to exaggerate their effects in threats. (Who could contemplate with equanimity being 'knocked into the middle of next week' or having their 'lights punched out'?) As long as 'man's inhumanity to man' has a role to play, there will be slang terms available for both the processes chosen and their effects.

## Glossary

**aggro** aggressive behaviour

**air rage** uncontrolled anger or aggression on an aeroplane

**barker** or **barking iron** a pistol

**belt** to give someone a sharp blow

**biff** to hit

**bitch slap** to slap someone across the face

**blow away** to kill or murder

**blue** an Australian and New Zealand term for an argument or fight

**boff** to hit

**bonk** to hit

**bop** to hit

**bottle** to attack someone using a bottle as a weapon

**bovver** violent behaviour, especially by street gangs

**brain** to hit someone hard on the head

**bruiser** a big, strong, aggressive person

**bump off** to kill or murder

**bunch of fives** a fist, especially when used to punch someone

**bundle** a brawl

**bust a cap** in US usage, to shoot a gun (gangstas seem to be continually threatening one another by offering to 'bust a cap in your ass')

**carve up** to injure someone by slashing them with a knife or razor

**cat-fight** an unseemly fight, especially between women, involving slapping and scratching

**cement overshoes** what a victim of American gangster assassination is said to get when his feet are encased in cement and he is sunk in a river

**chiv** a knife

**chopper** a submachine-gun

**clean someone's clock** to beat someone up

**clobber** to attack or strike very hard

**clock** to hit

**coldcock** in the USA, to 'coldcock' someone is to hit them hard over the head, often knocking them unconscious

**conk** to strike on the head

**cosh** a bludgeon, truncheon, lead-pipe or piece of flexible tubing filled with metal or the like, used as a weapon

**croak** to kill

**crown** to hit on the head

**deck** to knock to the ground

**deep-six** in the USA, to 'deep-six' someone is to kill them

**do** to 'do' or 'do over' a person is to beat up, thrash or assault them

**donder** in South Africa, to 'donder' someone is to beat them up

**drill** to 'drill' someone is to shoot them

**drive-by** a shooting committed from a moving vehicle

**duff up** to give someone a beating

**duke it out** to engage in a fist-fight

**dukes** the fists

**dust** to 'dust someone's jacket' is to give them a beating

**eat lead** to be shot

**equalizer** a US term for a gun, especially a pistol

**facer** a severe blow on the face

**fill in** to beat someone up or even kill them

**flatten** to knock someone out

**floorer** a knock-down blow

**fourpenny one** an old term for a blow or punch

**gat** a gun

**GBH** grievous bodily harm, or any violent assault

**glass** to attack someone with a broken glass or bottle

**go ballistic** to become violently angry

**going-over** a beating

**happy slapping** the practice of physically attacking an unsuspecting victim while an accomplice records the incident on a camera-equipped mobile phone

**hatchet man** a man paid to use violence on others

**heater** a gun

**hiding** a thrashing

**hit** a murder by a criminal or criminals

**hitman** a person employed to kill or attack others

**ice** to 'ice' a person is to kill them

**iron** a pistol or revolver

**job** in Australia, to 'job' someone is to punch them

**kicking** a violent attack

**knock** to 'knock someone into the middle of next week' or 'knock seven bells out of' someone is to give them a severe thrashing

**lamp** to punch or thump

**lander** a heavy blow

**larrup** to flog or thrash

**lather** to thrash

**lead** bullets, especially in the phrase 'fill someone full of lead', meaning to shoot them several times

**lead towel** an old term for a bullet (perhaps based on an earlier form 'oaken towel', meaning a cudgel, which perhaps makes more sense)

**leather** to thrash

**light into** to attack

**marmelize** or **marmalize** to thrash

**mess up** to subject someone to a violent physical attack

**mix it** to fight forcefully

**mouse** a black eye

**mug** to attack someone with the intention of robbing them

**mugger** someone who mugs people

**muller** or **mullah** to beat someone severely or even murder them

**nut** to butt with the head

**oner** a heavy blow

**open a can of whoop-ass** in the USA, to 'open a can of whoop-ass' on someone is to give them a beating

**paddy-whack** a blow or a beating

**pasting** a thrashing

**physical** to 'get physical' is to use physical force

**plug** to punch or shoot someone

**plump** to strike or shoot

**plunk** in North America, to strike someone with a sudden blow

**postal** in the USA, to 'go postal' is to become violently angry (from the sudden bouts of violence recorded among US postal workers)

**punch out** to 'punch someone out' or 'punch someone's lights out' is to beat them up

**queer-bashing** the practice of making gratuitous attacks on homosexuals

**rattler** a telling blow

**road rage** uncontrolled anger or aggression between road users, often involving violence and injury

**rough up** to treat someone violently

**ruck** a fight

**rumble** a gang fight

**Saturday night special** a US term for a small, inexpensive handgun

**scrap** a fight

**scrape** a fight

**seeing-to** if you give someone 'a good seeing-to', you beat them severely

**shiner** a black eye

**shiv** a knife (a variant of **chiv**)

**shooter** a gun

**shooting iron** a firearm, especially a revolver

**slosh** to hit

**slug** a bullet

**snuff out** to 'snuff someone out' is to kill them

**soak** to beat or pummel

**sock** to hit someone hard

**sockdolager** a US term for a hard, decisive blow

**sort** to 'sort someone out' is to beat them up, especially as a punishment

**stiff** to murder

**stonker** in Australia, to 'stonker' someone is to kill them

**stop a bullet** to be shot

**Sunday punch** a US term for a powerful punch intended to knock out an opponent

**take out** to 'take someone out' is to kill them

**tommy gun** a Thompson submachine-gun

**top** to kill

**towel** to thrash or cudgel

**warm** to 'warm' someone is to beat them

**whop** or **whup** to beat someone soundly or severely

**work over** to beat up or thrash

**yike** an Australian term for a fight

## Oaths

When moved by strong emotion, shock or surprise, people often say the strangest things. (Why would anyone ask to be 'blown down' or aspire to be 'a monkey's uncle'?) Sometimes they are trying to avoid actually swearing and giving offence, as in 'by George' or 'jeepers creepers'; at other times they are using expressions known only to a select few, as in 'by the Great Cham's beard'. As all of the expressions below can be used to express a similar range of emotions from shock to delight, there is no point in defining them; however, their origins are explained as far as this is possible. Many are euphemisms, allowing the speaker to draw back from the brink of out-and-out blasphemy or dodge any bad luck that naming the real thing might incur. Harmless, and often in themselves meaningless, words and phrases are substituted. (How, for example, is one supposed to be 'hornswoggled', and by whom?) These types of 'soft-pedalled' expressions are quaintly called 'minced oaths' (as in 'mincing one's words'). Through perusing such a list of colourful exclamations, perhaps those whose inevitable reaction to anything from the slightest surprise (pleasant or otherwise) to the end of the known universe is 'oh my God!' might learn something of the art of elegant variation.

### Glossary

**as I live and breathe** implying that something is as true as the speaker's own existence

**blimey** a corruption of 'God blind me'

**blow me (down)** perhaps, given the reference to wind, of a nautical origin

**by George** a euphemism for 'by God'

**by gum** a euphemism for 'by God' (people from the north of England, especially Yorkshire, are often caricatured as continually saying 'Eeh, by gum')

**by heck** a euphemism for 'by hell'

**by jiminy** perhaps a euphemism for 'by Jesus', but it has been suggested that 'jiminy' is related to 'Gemini'

**by jingo** 'jingo' here is not

a euphemism for 'Jesus', but seems to derive from a piece of stage conjurers' double-talk

**by Jove** the supreme god of the Romans is evoked here (**by Jupiter** is a variant of this)

**by the Great Cham's beard** the 'Great Cham' is an old-fashioned way of referring to the Great Khan, or emperor of the Mongols

**by the Lord Harry** probably not an invocation of a particular peer of that name, but a euphemism for 'by the Lord'

**cor** a shortening of 'cor blimey', which is a variant of **gorblimey**

**crikey** a euphemism for 'Christ'

**cripes** a euphemism for 'Christ'

**crivens** or **crivvens** a stereotypical Scottish oath (perhaps from 'Christ' combined with 'heavens')

**crumbs** a euphemism for 'Christ'

**drat** a corruption of 'God rot' (readers of a certain age may recall the cartoon character Dick Dastardly's more elaborate version, **drat and double drat**)

**for goodness' sake** probably a euphemism for 'for God's sake'

**for Pete's sake** probably not an invocation of the apostle Peter, but a variant of 'for pity's sake'

**for the love of Mike** probably a euphemism for 'for the love of Christ'

**gee whiz** probably a euphemism for 'Jesus'

**God help us** originally a plea for divine aid

**golly** a euphemism for 'God'

**good heavens** essentially meaningless, but the mention of heavens gives it a religious flavour

**good lord** a reference to God

**goodness**, **goodness gracious** or **goodness me** probably a euphemism for 'God'

**gorblimey** a Cockney corruption of 'God blind me'

**gosh** like 'golly', a euphemism for 'God' (some people profligately go so far as to use both at once)

**heavens above** similar to **good heavens**

**hell's bells** the idea that hell is equipped with bells is also found in the rather cynical soldiers' song of World War I, 'The bells of hell go ting-a-ling-a-ling, for you but not for me'

**holy smoke** probably a euphemism for 'holy Christ' (variants include **holy moly** and **holy shit**)

**I declare** irretrievably associated with Southern belles, this is shortened from a longer statement actually declaring something

**I'll be a monkey's uncle** one of the more elaborate euphemisms for 'I'll be damned' (another is **I'll be hornswoggled**)

**I'll go to the foot of our stairs** a northern English expression, perhaps hinting at a need to be alone and think about what has happened, or perhaps simply an ironic refusal to be impressed

**jeepers creepers** a meaningless euphemism for 'Jesus Christ'

**jiminy cricket** probably a euphemism for 'Jesus Christ' (but see also **by jiminy**)

**jings** a stereotypical Scottish oath (a euphemism for 'Jesus')

**jumping Jehoshaphat** probably a euphemism for 'Jesus or Jehovah', helped by the fact that the name of the Old Testament personage in question has a fine ring to it

**lord (bless us and) save us** based on a plea for God's mercy

**my goodness** probably a euphemism for 'my God'

**my word** originally a promise that a statement is true

**oh my God** an all-purpose exclamation so commonly used that its original religious content has been utterly devalued

**shiver my timbers** a stock nautical expression perhaps originating on stage rather than in seafaring actuality ('timbers' refers to the planks making up a wooden ship)

**snakes alive** the origin of this apparently meaningless expression is unknown

**starve the bardies** an Australian expression (bardies are a kind of insect grub)

**stone me** or **stone the crows** this has no known explanation, but it has been suggested that 'the crows' may have originally been 'the cross'

**strewth** a corruption of 'God's truth'

**well I never** probably

shortened from a longer expression along the lines of 'well, I never heard the like before'

**would you believe it** originally intended to cast doubt on the likelihood of what has happened

**ye gods (and little fishes)** probably originating in drama, the invocation of the classical pantheon is clear enough, but the optional second element is more obscure

**you wouldn't read about it** an Australian expression suggesting, perhaps, that the phenomenon being commented upon is too outrageous even to be committed to fiction

## *Euphemisms*

The avoidance of mentioning unpleasant or offensive things by substituting something milder is a daily word-juggling feat that most of us are bound to undertake, whether we do so through mere good manners, sensitivity to the feelings of others or fear of disapproval. Also, since the latter decades of the 20th century, the concept of political correctness has exerted a powerful influence on public behaviour, making it all but obligatory to choose our words carefully to avoid giving offence to sections of society that are perceived as being discriminated against or disadvantaged. While many find this linguistic self-censorship admirable, others dismiss it as 'weasel words' (evasive language using words whose meaning has been sucked from them like eggs emptied by a weasel). Governments, with their beloved spin doctors, are second to none in their devotion to euphemism, in thrall as they are to popularity polls. It would never do to alarm the lieges by confronting them with the often unpleasant stark realities.

While the days of spinster aunts forever trembling on the brink of being shocked are long gone, there does still seem to be a general tendency in society to reach for a euphemism rather than call a spade a spade. The big taboos are still in place, even if they are seen as less scary than before. The media still report sexual intercourse in terms of 'sleeping with' one another, even though we all know that precious little sleep may have figured in an encounter between two people 'as nature intended'. We still prefer to call the toilet 'the bathroom' and talk about 'spending a penny' even though inflation has long since seen to it that a visit to 'inspect the facilities' costs rather more than that nostalgic sum. Death, they say, is the last taboo, and judging by the number of ways to pussyfoot around the subject (from 'pushing up daisies' to 'dropping off the perch' or 'popping your clogs') it still remains such 'an awfully big adventure' that most of us prefer not to confront it in plain words.

One common use of euphemism is in mild swearing, and examples of this may be found under **Oaths**.

## *Glossary*

**a fate worse than death** rape

**as nature intended** naked

**bally** used in mild oaths instead of 'bloody'

**bathroom** to 'go to the bathroom' means to go to the toilet; similarly, 'bathroom tissue' is toilet paper

**be helping the police with their inquiries** to be under arrest

**behind** your 'behind' is your buttocks

**be intimate with** to have sexual intercourse with

**bend the elbow** to drink alcohol, especially to excess

**big C** 'the big C' is a euphemism for cancer

**bit on the side** a person's partner in extramarital sexual relations

**bleeding** a euphemism for 'bloody'

**boobs** or **boobies** a woman's breasts

**cash in your chips** to die

**-challenged** this suffix is highly generative of euphemisms, including 'vertically-challenged' meaning short in stature, 'follically-challenged' meaning bald, and 'intellectually-challenged' meaning not very intelligent

**collateral damage** a military euphemism for

civilian casualties or damage
to property that was not a
military target

**comfort station** a US term
for a toilet

**correctional facility** a US
term for a prison

**curse** 'the curse' is a
euphemism for menstruation
or a menstrual period

**cut the cheese** a US term
meaning to break wind from
the anus

**differently-abled** disabled

**drop off the perch** or **twig**
to die

**economy** something
described as 'economy' is
cheap

**eventide home** a home for
elderly people

**exchange this life for a
better one** to die

**exotic dancer** a stripper

**fall off the back of a lorry**
goods that are described as
having 'fallen off the back
of a lorry' have actually been
stolen

**fall off the perch** or **twig**
to die

**feck** an Irish euphemism for
'fuck'

**feeling no pain** drunk

**finance** beloved particularly

of car salesmen, this actually
means a loan, as in to 'provide
finance' or 'zero-percent
finance'

**friendly fire** a military
euphemism for accidental
firing on your own side instead
of the enemy

**front bottom** the vagina

**full and frank exchange of
views** a bitter argument

**full-figured** overweight

**gardening leave** compulsory
paid leave to be taken in
the time preceding the
formal termination date of
employment

**generously proportioned**
overweight

**glamour** involving nudity, eg
a 'glamour model' is a woman
who poses for photographs
naked or scantily dressed, and
'glamour photography' is the
production of nude pin-ups

**go to meet your maker**
to die

**guest of Her Majesty**
someone serving a prison
sentence

**have a bun in the oven**
to be pregnant (a woman
might equally **have a
watermelon on the vine**)

**have a screw loose** to be

slightly mentally deranged (a variation of this is **have a slate loose**)

**have cash-flow problems** to be penniless

**have issues** a phrase that can mean anything from displaying a readiness to take offence to being seriously mentally disturbed

**how's your father** amorous frolicking or sexual intercourse

**indulge** to drink alcohol

**inspect the facilities** to go to the toilet

**in the family way** expecting a baby

**in your birthday suit** naked

**join the choir invisible** to die

**join the majority** to die

**kick the bucket** or **kick it** to die

**lad** a man's 'lad' is his penis

**lady of the night** a prostitute

**lead poisoning** death by shooting

**let go** to 'let someone go' is to sack them from a job

**let off** to break wind from the anus

**liquidate** to kill

**low-budget** cheap

**monthlies** menstruation or a menstrual period

**move your bowels** to defecate

**negatively privileged** underprivileged, ie not enjoying normal social and economic rights

**no better than she should be** to describe a woman in these terms is to suggest that she has loose morals

**no oil painting** unattractive

**not a happy bunny** highly displeased

**not playing with a full deck** not having all your mental faculties intact

**not the sharpest knife in the drawer** not very intelligent

**number one** and **number two** expressions used especially to and by children to refer to urination and defecation respectively

**nymph of darkness** a prostitute

**on the rag** a woman who is 'on the rag' is menstruating

**overindulge** to drink too much alcohol

**painters** a woman who 'has the painters in' is menstruating

**pardon** or **excuse my**

**French** pardon my bad language

**pass away** or **on** to die

**pavement pizza** a puddle of vomit in the street

**pay a call** or **visit** to go to the toilet

**pink oboe** the penis

**play away (from home)** to be sexually unfaithful to your partner

**play for the other team** to be homosexual

**play the field** to be sexually promiscuous

**point Percy at the porcelain** to urinate

**pop your clogs** to die

**powder room** a ladies' toilet

**powder your nose** a woman who says she is going to 'powder her nose' is actually going to the toilet

**pre-owned** second-hand

**pushing up daisies** dead and buried

**put to sleep** if an animal, particularly a pet, is 'put to sleep', it is painlessly killed

**refreshment** an alcoholic drink

**resting** what out-of-work actors are said to be doing

**rest room** a toilet

**roll in the hay** a sexual encounter

**secure accommodation** prison

**see a man about a dog** to urinate

**see you next Thursday** if you say a person is 'a see you next Thursday' you mean you dislike them intensely (the expression is a play on beginning to spell out 'cunt' – C.U. – then substituting the last two words instead of the letters N and T)

**sex worker** a prostitute

**shuffle off this mortal coil** to die

**sleep with** to have sexual intercourse with

**something for the weekend** a packet of condoms

**sow your wild oats** to indulge in youthful dissipation or excess

**spend a penny** to go to the toilet

**strain the spuds** to urinate

**streetwalker** a prostitute

**technicolour yawn** vomit

**term of endearment among sailors** a euphemism for 'bugger'

**the lift** (or **elevator**)

**doesn't go all the way to the top floor** this person is not of normal intelligence

**the lights are on but nobody's home** this person is not of normal intelligence

**tired and emotional** drunk

**underachieve** to fail

**under the weather** suffering from a hangover

**visibly moved** in tears

**we need to talk** I want to end our relationship

**wooden overcoat** a coffin

**working girl** a prostitute

## Insults

'Sticks and stones will break my bones, but names will never hurt me.' So goes the old adage. However, the gentle reader should be warned that this section contains material that, far from being politically correct, may be extremely offensive to many. Human beings constitute a disputatious species and they love to exchange insults; some of these are even used as friendly banter between friends. While humour and even ingenuity can be displayed in an individual's choice of insults – who could take serious offence at being called a 'big girl's blouse'? – most of the human brain's inventiveness in this particular field seems to go into devising expressions that are ever more hurtful and vile. In more lawless times, an insult was something that a person might be seen as justified in avenging by deadly violence, and people were more likely to keep a bridle on their tongues. In our more civilized age, while respect is something that is demanded by everyone as soon as they are able to speak, individuals apparently feel free to bestow the grossest terms on one another with impunity.

The more common varieties of insult tend to fall into only a handful of categories: race, level of intelligence, sexual activity, and sexual orientation, each viewed from the perspective of 'the majority' towards the minority or outsider. Racial epithets, thus, are mostly directed at non-Anglo-Saxons, and include 'bogtrotter' for an Irish person, 'Chink' for a Chinese person, and a host of terms for a dark-skinned individual, from 'coon' to 'wog'. As far as intelligence is concerned, it is mostly those who are considered stupid that are picked upon, stigmatized as 'berks', 'bimbos', 'drongos' and 'meatballs'. Only rarely is a person insulted for being smart, as in the American use of 'poindexter'. In sexual matters, it doesn't do to be seen as too sexually active (especially for a woman), otherwise you risk being labelled a 'ho', 'scrubber' or 'slapper'. That particular gender imbalance aside, most of the vulgar words for the male and female private parts, as well as sexual acts, can be used as insults; so well known are they that there is little point in listing them here. The same is true for the excretory functions. Despite liberalization both in the law and societal attitudes in general, homosexuals continue to be the target for insults, with terms such as 'dyke', 'shirt-lifter' and 'bender' still being heard, while older examples like 'Nancy-boy' are replaced by less familiar terms like 'batty boy'. It might be regarded as progress, however, that while in the past one of the worst things one person could impute to another was illegitimate birth (as in 'by-blow'), nowadays, with fluid relationships and families composed of children from different marriages, this is no longer likely to hurt, let alone break any bones.

## Glossary

**arse bandit** a male homosexual

**batty boy** a West Indian term for a male homosexual

**bender** a male homosexual

**berk** a fool (perhaps some people would use this less insouciantly if they realized it is a shortening of 'Berkeley Hunt', a piece of rhyming slang)

**big girl's blouse** an effeminate or ineffectual male

**bimbo** a young woman who is physically attractive but dim, naïve or superficial

**bogtrotter** an Irish person (in Ireland itself the term is reserved for an uncultured rustic)

**bohunk** an American term for a person of Slavic origins

**bull dyke** a lesbian of masculine appearance

**bumsucker** a toady

**by-blow** an old term for an illegitimate child

**chav** a boorish uneducated person who appears to have access to money but not to taste

**cheese-eating surrender monkeys** a US term for the French

**Chink** or **Chinky** a Chinese person

**coffin-dodger** an old person

**conchy** or **conchie** a conscientious objector

**coon** a black person

**cow** an unpleasant woman

**cracker** in the USA, a poor white

**creeping Jesus** a cringingly sanctimonious person

**crinkly** an old person

**dago** a man of Spanish, Portuguese or Italian origin

**dickhead** an idiot

**dinge** a US term for a black person

**dipstick** a stupid person

**doofus** a US term for a stupid person

**drack** an Australian term for an unattractive woman (from 'Dracula's daughter')

**drongo** an Australian term for a stupid or worthless person

**droob** another Australian term for a stupid or worthless person

**dumbbell** a stupid person

**dweeb** a US term for a fool or **nerd**

**dyke** a lesbian

**Eyetie** an Italian

**face-ache** a name to call a person considered ugly or permanently displeased

**fag** or **faggot** a male homosexual

**fairy** a male homosexual

**fatso** a fat person

**fogy** or **fogey** an old person

**four by two** a Jew (rhyming slang)

**Frog** or **Froggie** a French person

**fruit** a homosexual

**galah** an Australian term for a fool

**geek** an intellectual person, especially one without social skills

**gippo** a Gypsy or Egyptian person

**git** a stupid or unpleasant person

**gobshite** a stupid person

**God-botherer** an excessively pious person

**gook** a member of an Asiatic race

**greaseball** or **greaser** a US term for a person of Latin racial origin

**gringo** an English-speaking person in Spanish-speaking America

**growl and grunt** a fool (rhyming slang for 'cunt')

**gub** in Australia, a 'gub' is a white person, as opposed to an Aboriginal

**guinea** a US term for a person of Italian descent

**hayseed** a town-dweller's derogatory term for a rustic, traditionally a stupid person

**hick** an unsophisticated country-dweller

**ho** an African-American form of 'whore', disrespectfully applied to any woman, except, presumably, the speaker's mother

**honky** an African-American term for a white person

**horse's hoof** a male homosexual (rhyming slang for 'poof')

**iron hoof** a male homosexual (rhyming slang for 'poof')

**jerk** a useless or stupid person (the implication being that masturbation plays too great a part in his life)

**jessie** a Scottish term for an effeminate male

**jungle bunny** a black person

**kike** a Jew

**klutz** an idiot

**louser** an Irish term for a contemptible person

**mare** a woman

**meatball** and **meathead** two US terms for a stupid person

**mong** a stupid person (shortened from 'mongol', an old term for a person afflicted with Down's syndrome)

**mopoke** in Australia, a dull-witted or boring person

**motherfucker** any objectionable or unpleasant person (a term much devalued of its original shock value by overuse; it is often shortened to **mother** or **mutha**)

**muntu** a South African term for a black person

**Nancy-boy** a homosexual or effeminate male

**nerd** a clumsy, foolish, socially inept, feeble, unathletic, irritating or unprepossessing person

**nigger** a black or dark-skinned person (**nig-nog** is a variant of this)

**no-mark** a person who

makes no impression, a nonentity

**numbnuts** a US term for a stupid person

**Paki** a Pakistani

**palooka** a US term for a stupid or clumsy person

**pansy** a male homosexual

**pikey** a Gypsy or traveller

**pillock** a stupid person

**plonker** an idiot

**poindexter** a US derogatory term for an intellectual person

**poof** a male homosexual (**pooftah** is a variant of this)

**pommy** an Australian term for a British person

**prat** a fool

**prune** a despised or silly person

**pussy** a man considered as weak or ineffectual

**putz** a US term for a stupid person

**raghead** an Arab

**ratbag** a despicable person

**redneck** a US term for a country-dweller, especially one considered stupid or extremely conservative

**reffo** an Australian term for a refugee

**sambo** a black person

**schmuck** a US term for a pitiful, stupid or obnoxious person (there are several similar American insults beginning with the letters 'sch-', all derived from Yiddish, including **schlemiel**, **schlep**, **schmo** and **schnook**)

**scrubber** an unattractive or promiscuous woman

**sheep-shagger** an urban person's derogatory term for a rural person

**shirt-lifter** a male homosexual

**shit-for-brains** a term used for a stupid person

**shithead** a contemptible, unpleasant person

**shower** a group of people the speaker disapproves of

**simp** a simpleton

**siwash** a derogatory term for a Native American of the north-western states

**slag** a promiscuous woman; also applied to any contemptible person

**slaphead** an involuntarily bald man

**slapper** a promiscuous woman

**sleaze** a person who behaves in an immoral or underhand way (also called a **sleazebag** or **sleazeball**)

**smartarse** or **smartass**

a would-be clever or witty person

**s.o.b.** an abbreviation of **sonofabitch**

**sod** an obnoxious person

**sonofabitch** an obnoxious or difficult person

**spade** a black person

**spag** an Australian term for an Italian person

**spastic** a useless or stupid person (often shortened to **spaz** or **spazzy**; formerly a term referring to a person with cerebral palsy)

**spic** a US term for a person of Hispanic descent

**squirt** an unimportant and irritatingly pretentious person

**strap** an Irish term for a sluttish woman

**stupe** a stupid person

**swish** a US term for a male homosexual, especially if effeminate

**Taig** a Northern Irish term for a Roman Catholic

**tail** a 'bit of tail' or 'piece of tail' is an offensive term for a woman

**teapot lid** a Jew (rhyming slang for 'Yid')

**thickhead** a stupid person (also called a **thickie** or **thicko**)

**thunderthighs** a disparaging name for someone who is overweight

**tightarse** a mean or miserly person (the US equivalents are **tightass** and **tightwad**)

**toerag** a despicable person (originally referring to a tramp with strips of cloth tied around his feet)

**tosser** an unpleasant or despicable person

**towelhead** a person who wears a turban or headcloth

**turd-burglar** a male homosexual

**village bike** in a small community, the 'village bike' is a local woman who seems to be sexually available to all comers (because 'anyone can ride her')

**wally** a stupid or otherwise despised person

**wanker** a worthless, contemptible person

**wog** a non-white foreigner

**woofter** a male homosexual

**wop** a member of a Mediterranean or Latin race, especially an Italian

**wrinkly** an old person

**wuss** a weak or timid person

**Yid** a Jew

**yo-yo** a fool

## Rhyming slang

Most people know a few items of rhyming slang, even if they may not be aware that a particular colourful turn of phrase in their vocabulary belongs in that category. Because many of these expressions are often shortened in daily use from a two-word term to the first element only (eg 'have a butcher's at this load of cobblers') the fact that they started out as rhyming slang may be lost. A particular case in point is 'Berkeley Hunt', which in its much-truncated version 'berk' is used without terribly offensive intent by many who would never allow the rhyming 'target' to pass their lips. Sometimes the phrase used to furnish the rhyme is chosen for its wit or specific relevance (as in 'daisy roots' for boots, which are hard to pull up, or 'Sweeney Todd' (the famous murderer) for the Flying Squad). At other times the choice of rhyme seems to be arbitrary and carries no added meaning. Occasionally the rhyme is, strictly speaking, no rhyme at all but assonance or near-rhyme, as in 'Kate Carney' for the army.

Rhyming slang seems to have come to prominence in the mid-19th century amongst the Cockneys of London. At first primarily used by market traders and the criminal fraternity, it is quintessentially the type of slang in which meanings are disguised, designed to prevent outsiders from knowing what is being spoken about. It is supposed to have been spread in the trenches in World War I among many conscripts who otherwise would probably not have encountered it. However it was disseminated, rhyming slang was soon not restricted to Cockneys. It became very popular in Australia, where 'Joe Blake' was used to mean a snake, and 'John Hop' a cop or policeman. A separate strand of Scottish rhyming slang developed, often with rhymes that only work if pronounced in a strong Scots accent (such as 'corned beef' for deaf , or 'Mick Jagger' for lager). Some say that the invention of rhyming slang is an outlet for those whose creativity may otherwise be denied; others maintain it is now just a piece of fun. Wherever the truth lies, new expressions are being coined continually, with more recent examples being 'Ayrton Senna', 'Britney Spears' and 'Pete Tong'.

## Glossary

**Adam and Eve** believe, especially in the phrase 'Would you Adam and Eve it?'

**apples and pears** stairs

**Ayrton Senna** a tenner, ie a ten-pound note (from Ayrton Senna, a Brazilian racing driver)

**babbling brook** a cook (used in Australia)

**Barnet Fair** the hair

**Barry White** shite (from Barry White, an American soul singer)

**Berkeley Hunt** a cunt (the origin of the insult 'berk')

**bird lime** time

**boat race** the face

**boracic lint** skint

**bottle and glass** the arse

**bowler hat** a rat (used in Ulster)

**Brahms and Liszt** pissed

**Bristol cities** titties

**Britney Spears** beers (from Britney Spears, an American singer)

**brown bread** dead

**bunsen burner** an earner, ie a profitable activity

**butcher's hook** a look

**Cain and Abel** a table

**Chalfont St Giles** piles, ie haemorrhoids (from the name of a village in Buckinghamshire)

**China plate** a mate

**cobbler's awls** balls

**corned beef** deaf (used in Scotland, where deaf is pronounced 'deef')

**cream crackered** knackered

**daisy roots** boots

**dicky-bird** a word

**dicky dirt** a shirt

**dustbin lids** kids

**Emma Freuds** haemorrhoids (from Emma Freud, an English broadcaster)

**Farmer Giles** piles

**four by two** a Jew

**frog and toad** a road

**God forbids** kids

**growl and grunt** a cunt

**gypsy's kiss** a piss

**half-inch** pinch, ie to steal

**Hampstead Heath** teeth

**Hampton Wick** the prick, ie the penis

**Hank Marvin** starving (from Hank Marvin, an English guitarist)

**horse's hoof** a poof

**iron hoof** a poof

**jam jar** a car

**jimmy riddle** a piddle, ie

an act of urination

**joanna** a piano (an unusual example of rhyming slang in that it consists of just a single word rather than a phrase)

**Joe Baxi** a taxi (from Joe Baksi, an American heavyweight boxer in the 1940s)

**Joe Blake** a snake (used in Australia, where 'the Joe Blakes' can also mean 'the shakes')

**John Hop** a cop, ie a policeman (used in Australia and New Zealand)

**Kate Carney** the army

**kipper and plaice** the face

**Lady Godiva** a fiver, ie a five-pound note

**linen draper** a newspaper

**Lionel Blairs** flares (from Lionel Blair, an English entertainer)

**loaf of bread** the head

**loop-the-loop** soup

**Melvyn Bragg** a flexible term which can mean either a 'shag', ie an act of sexual intercourse, a 'fag', ie a cigarette, or a 'slag', ie a promiscuous woman (from Melvyn Bragg, an English writer, broadcaster and, it would seem, magnet for

rhyming slang)

**Mickey Mouser** a Scouser, ie a Liverpudlian

**Mick Jagger** lager (used in Scotland, where this is a genuine rhyme)

**Milton Keynes** a term which can mean either 'baked beans' or 'jeans'

**mince pies** the eyes

**mutt and jeff** deaf

**nellie duff** puff, ie one's life

**north and south** the mouth

**old king cole** the dole, ie unemployment benefit

**Oxo cube** the Tube, ie the London Underground

**pen and ink** a stink

**Pete Tong** wrong (from Pete Tong, an English DJ and broadcaster)

**plates of meat** the feet

**pony and trap** crap, either meaning 'an act of defecation', or as an adjective meaning 'bad or inferior'

**pork pie** a lie (often shortened to **porky**)

**rabbit and pork** talk

**raspberry ripple** a term which can mean either 'cripple' or 'nipple'

**Richard the Third** a turd

**Rory O'More** a door

**Rosie Lee** tea

**round the houses** trousers (used in London, where this is a genuine rhyme)

**Ruby Murray** a curry (from Ruby Murray, a Northern Irish singer)

**satin and silk** milk

**sherbet dab** a (taxi) cab

**sherman tank** a term which can mean either 'Yank' or 'wank'

**Sweeney Todd** Flying Squad

**swiss roll** a hole, ie the anus (used in Ireland)

**syrup of fig** a wig

**taters in the mould** cold ('taters' means potatoes)

**tea leaf** a thief

**teapot lid** a term which can mean either 'Yid', 'kid' or 'quid'

**threepenny bits** a term which can mean either 'tits' or 'the shits', ie diarrhoea

**tin bath** a laugh (used in London, where this is a genuine rhyme)

**tit for tat** a hat (often shortened to **titfer**)

**Tod Sloan** own, especially in the phrase 'on your tod' (from Tod Sloan, a famous US jockey)

**Tom and Dick** sick

**tomfoolery** jewellery

**tom tit** a shit

**Tony Blairs** flares (from Tony Blair, British politician)

**toy dolls** balls, ie testicles (used in Ulster)

**trouble and strife** a wife

**turtle dove** a glove

**two and eight** a state

**Uncle Dick** sick

**whistle and flute** a suit

# *The weather*

What more perennial topic of conversation can there be than the weather? We are all affected by this everyday phenomenon and discussing it is proverbially a common means of breaking the ice between strangers. It is obvious from even the most cursory glance at the slang terms used in talking about the weather that commonplace, unremarkable meteorological conditions do not feature greatly. It seems that only the extremes of climate exercise our minds enough to generate slang. Most of us who live in the British Isles experience a greater amount of rain than natives of, say, California or the

Australian outback, and thus we have many ways of commenting on heavy rain, from 'coming down in buckets' to 'raining cats and dogs' and the even more elliptical 'nice weather for ducks'. Extremes of cold are also deemed worthy of remark, with 'cold snaps' that may even lead to 'brass monkey' weather. This is not to say that we never see the sun; British people do also encounter the odd 'sizzler' or 'scorcher'. Greater controls on atmospheric pollution may have made the famous 'pea-soupers' a thing of the past, but if those who detect a long-term change in seasonal weather due to global warming are proved right, we may have to contemplate a whole new range of slang terms for weather.

## Glossary

**baltic** very cold

**brass monkeys** used to describe extremely cold weather (from the more elaborate phrase 'cold enough to freeze the balls off a brass monkey')

**broiler** a very hot day

**bucket** very heavy rain is often said to be 'coming down in buckets' or to be 'bucketing down'

**buster** in Australia, a strong south wind

**chuck it down** to rain heavily

**cold snap** a sudden cold spell

**doctor** a strong wind believed to blow away germs (such as the Cape Doctor in South Africa or the Fremantle Doctor in Western Australia)

**frog-strangler** a US term for a torrential downpour of rain

**liquid sunshine** an ironic term for rain

**monkey's wedding** a South African term for simultaneous sunshine and light rain

**nice weather for ducks** wet weather

**nip** if there is 'a nip in the air', the weather is cold or frosty

**parky** chilly

**pea-souper** an old term for a thick yellow heavy-smelling fog

**perishing** very cold

**piss down** or **pee down** to rain heavily

**plump** especially in Scotland, a 'plump' is a sudden heavy fall of rain

**rain cats and dogs** to rain very heavily

**rain like a cow pissing on a flat rock** to rain particularly heavily

**ripsnorter** a gale

**scorcher** a very hot sunny day

**Scotch mist** a fine rain

**sheet** if rain is 'sheeting down', it is falling fast and heavily, or 'coming down in sheets'

**sizzler** a very hot day

**snow-eater** in the USA, a warm dry wind blowing down the eastern side of the Rocky Mountains

**socked in** in North America, a place, such as an airport, is 'socked in' if a weather condition, such as heavy snow or fog, cuts it off from normal traffic

**spitting** raining in scattered drops

**split the trees** if the sun is 'splitting the trees', the weather is fine and sunny

**stair rods** very heavy rain

**sunshower** simultaneous sunshine and light rain

**tip (it) down** to rain heavily

**twister** a tornado

**wet** in Australia, 'the wet' is the rainy season

# *Work*

Most of us have to work for a living. Some are fortunate enough to derive great satisfaction from their jobs and may consider themselves adequately reimbursed for their labour (on the 'gravy train' or on a 'nice little earner', for example). Generally, though, we'd rather be doing something else, even if it's only having a 'sickie' or 'duvet day'. One of the ways in which many people keep at bay the tedium or unpleasantness they are faced with daily in having to 'earn a crust' is to use slang terms in the workplace. Some of the vocabulary used is concerned with the type of work itself, and certain jobs attract slang titles which often play wittily on aspects of the work involved, such as 'chippy' for a carpenter, 'spark' for an electrician or 'greasy' for a sheep-shearer. Other terms are less than complimentary and represent a rather disrespectful assessment of people in other lines of work.

For example, an accountant may be dismissed by those with a more cavalier attitude to finances as a mere 'bean counter', or someone who works exclusively inside an office may be viewed by those in the field as a 'desk jockey' or 'paper pusher'.

The flipside of having to work for a living is, of course, being out of work, and terms relating to this may be found in the following section, which is concerned with **Unemployment**.

## *Glossary*

**admin** administration

**axeman** a ruthless cutter of costs

**bean counter** an accountant

**boss cocky** an Australian term for a boss

**brickie** a bricklayer

**canteen culture** a system of behaviour said to exist in certain, usually male-dominated, organizations, promoting loyalty to the group and discriminating against outsiders

**car-hop** a North American term for a waiter or waitress at a drive-in restaurant

**carny** a North American term for someone who works in a carnival

**chippy** a carpenter (**chips** is a variant of this)

**chucker-out** someone whose job is to expel undesirable people from a public house, meeting, etc

**crimper** a hairdresser

**desk jockey** a US term for a clerk

**duvet day** an unofficial day off work taken by an employee for no better reason than unwillingness to get out of bed

**earlies** early shifts

**earn a crust** to make a living

**earner** something that brings a good income or profit, often in the phrase 'a nice little earner'

**fast-track** to 'fast-track' an employee is to promote them speedily

**foreigner** a job done privately by an employee without the employer's knowledge

**free-rider** someone who enjoys benefits obtained for

workers by a trade union without being a member of that union

**gaffer** a boss

**gandy dancer** a US term for a labourer, especially one on a railway line

**garbo** an Australian term for a garbage collector

**ghostbuster** an employee of the Inland Revenue responsible for detecting and pursuing people who have not paid tax on their incomes

**gig** an engagement or job, especially for a musician

**glass ceiling** an unofficial yet unmistakable barrier on the career ladder, through which certain categories of employees (usually women) find they can see but not progress

**gofer** a junior employee who is given errands to run by other members of the staff (from 'go for')

**goldbrick** in the USA, to 'goldbrick' is to shirk your duties or responsibilities

**golden handcuffs** a substantial personal financial incentive or stake specifically designed by a company to induce a valued employee to remain on its staff

**golden hello** a large sum given to a much-wanted new employee on joining a firm

**graft** to work hard

**grauncher** a clumsy, incompetent mechanic

**graveyard shift** a shift starting at midnight or during the night

**gravy train** a job or scheme which offers high rewards for little effort

**grease monkey** a mechanic

**greasy** an Australian and New Zealand term for a sheep-shearer or a camp-cook in the outback

**grip** an Australian term for a job or occupation

**hack** a journalist

**hackette** a female journalist

**higher-ups** people in superior positions

**holy Joe** a parson

**homer** a job done at home or away from the usual workplace

**honcho** a boss, leader or manager

**humper** someone who carries heavy loads, such as a porter in a market

**ink-slinger** a professional author or journalist

**jackaroo** in Australia, a newcomer, or other person gaining experience on a sheep or cattle station

**jawboning** in the USA, governmental urging of industry to restrict wage increases, accept restraints, etc

**jillaroo** a female **jackaroo**

**jobsworth** a minor official who regards the rigid enforcement of petty rules as more important than providing a service to the public (from such a person's typical excuse for being unhelpful: 'It's more than my job's worth to …')

**josser** an old Australian term for a clergyman

**journo** a journalist

**kick upstairs** to 'kick someone upstairs' is to promote them to a less active or less powerful position

**knock off** to stop work

**legal eagle** a lawyer

**lollipop man, woman** or **lady** a crossing-warden carrying a pole with a disc on the end

**matlo** or **matlow** a seaman or sailor

**medico** a medical practitioner or student

**milko** an Australian term for a milkman

**munchkin** a US term for a low-level employee

**navvy** a labourer, originally one on a 'navigation' or canal

**nixer** an Irish term for a job, especially a spare-time or irregular one, the earnings of which are not declared for tax purposes by the worker

**on the sick** a worker who is 'on the sick' has been certified as medically unfit for work (**on the club** is an old-fashioned variant of this)

**paper-pusher** a clerk, especially one in a humble or humdrum position

**paper-stainer** a poor author or hack writer

**pen-** or **pencil-pusher** a clerk who does boring, routine work

**Philistine** a bailiff

**pill** a doctor

**pink ceiling** an unofficial yet unmistakable barrier on the career ladder, through which gay people find they can see but not progress (modelled on **glass ceiling**)

**postie** a postman

**quack** a doctor

**racket** a job or occupation

**rag-out** an unofficial strike

**rainmaker** a high-powered employee who generates a great deal of income for his or her employers

**rat** someone who works for less than the agreed standard wage for a job; also used to mean a strike-breaker

**scab** a worker who continues to work during a strike, or takes the place of a striking worker

**screw** salary or wages

**sickie** a day's sick leave

**skivvy** 'a skivvy' is a drudge or servant, usually female; to 'skivvy' is to work as a skivvy

**sling ink** to write for the press

**slog your guts out** to work extremely hard

**snapper** a photographer

**soda jerk** in North America, someone whose job is to serve soft drinks, ice cream, etc at a shop or counter

**spark** or **sparks** an electrician

**start** to 'give someone a start' is to give them a job, especially a manual job

**sub** or **subbie** a subcontractor

**suit** a derogatory term for a bureaucratic functionary or administrative official

**swindle-sheet** an expense account

**totem pole** a hierarchical system in a place of work

**wharfie** an Australian and New Zealand term for a wharf labourer

## Unemployment

If the world of work has an opposite, it is surely the world of unemployment. They say that in the 21st century there is no longer any such thing as the 'job for life' that to previous generations seemed to be within the grasp of many. Spells of being out of work are a common experience and being unemployed no longer has quite the social stigma that it once attracted. However, while some employers may prefer to euphemize dismissal from a job as 'gardening leave', most people know perfectly well when they are being given 'the boot', 'the bullet' or 'the chop'. Since the creation of the welfare state, being 'on the beach' or 'on the street' has not meant utter poverty or starvation. While it is not (and is not intended to be) a replacement for a decent wage, 'the dole' (unemployment benefit, or Jobseeker's Allowance to give it its proper current designation) serves to keep the wolf from the door for many. There are always some who seem to prefer being unemployed to having to graft for a living, and are content to live off benefits (supplemented in some cases by earnings from the black economy) but as the slang terms for such 'doleys' or 'dole-bludgers' show, they do not garner much respect in wider society.

## *Glossary*

**axe** to 'get the axe' is to be dismissed from a job

**bludge** in Australia and New Zealand, to 'bludge' means to live off the state rather than work

**boot** to 'get the boot' is to be dismissed from a job

**bullet** to 'get the bullet' is to be dismissed from a job

**bum** a tramp or sponger

**chop** to 'get the chop' is to be dismissed from a job

**compo** an Australian term for redundancy pay

**deadbeat** a down-and-out

**dole** 'the dole' is a payment made by the state to unemployed people

**dole-bludger** an Australian and New Zealand term for someone who would rather live off state

benefits than work

**doley** or **dole-ite** someone who is **on the dole**

**dosser** a vagrant

**gardening leave** compulsory paid leave to be taken in the time preceding the formal termination date of employment

**giro** a social-security payment by giro cheque

**golden handshake** a large sum of money, or some equivalent, given to an employee who retires or is otherwise forced to leave

**golden parachute** an unusually lavish cash payment to a senior member of a firm on their dismissal following a takeover

**heave** someone who is given 'the heave' or 'the heave-ho' is

dismissed from their job
**old king cole** the dole
(rhyming slang)
**on the beach** out of work
**on the dole** receiving state
benefits for being out of work
**on the street** out of work
**pink slip** in the USA, a notice
of dismissal given to an
employee
**put out to grass** someone
who is 'put out to grass'
retires from work (whether
voluntarily or otherwise)

**sign on** to register for
Jobseeker's Allowance
**social** 'the social' is social
security
**supp ben** supplementary
benefit
**wallaby** in New Zealand,
someone who is 'on the
wallaby' or 'on the wallaby
track' is travelling through the
bush, especially looking for
work
**Weary Willie** a tramp or
workshy person

## Class and social concerns

Politicians like to pontificate about the seemingly universal goal
of a 'classless society'. Certainly, most developed countries in the
21st century are less stratified by class than ever before and more
characterized by what is known as 'social mobility'. That last phrase,
however, rather gives the game away. Perceptibly different levels
continue to exist in most societies, whether the criterion is wealth,
birth or, as is increasingly the case, celebrity (from 'A-list' down
through the pecking order); the only real difference is that now it is
relatively easier to move up (or down) the scale.

People's perception of themselves as being different from others
readily finds expression in slang. In the United Kingdom the 'green-
wellie' brigade are ranged against 'crusties', and the 'Sloane Rangers'
are figuratively, although maybe not literally, miles apart from the
'chavs'. In the USA, few would admit to representing 'Joe Sixpack'
or identify themselves as 'crackers'. Even an aggressively egalitarian
country like Australia stigmatizes some of its citizens as 'bogans'.

Whether we are 'Essex Girls' or 'Hooray Henrys', whatever we identify as the measure of success, we would all rather belong to the 'big league' than to the 'great unwashed'.

## Glossary

**A-list** celebrities, etc who are seen as belonging to the most important or famous group may be described as 'A-list'

**big league** someone or something categorized as being 'in the big league' is among the most important or powerful people or organizations

**big noise** an important person (**bigwig** means the same thing)

**B-list** celebrities, etc who are seen as not belonging to the most important or famous group may be described as 'B-list'

**blue rinse brigade** a collective name for well-groomed middle-class older women

**bogan** an Australian and New Zealand term for a low-class unrefined person

**boho** a bohemian

**buppy** a black urban professional (modelled on **yuppie**)

**chav** a boorish uneducated person who appears to have access to money but not to taste

**C-list** celebrities, etc who are seen as belonging to an insignificant or unadmired group may be described as 'C-list' (such pitiable folk may also be called **D-list**, **E-list**, etc, all the way down to **Z-list**, depending on the amount of derision being poured on them)

**cracker** a poor white person from the southern USA

**crusty** a person who appears fashionably unkempt, often with matted hair or dreadlocks, as part of an alternative lifestyle

**Essex Girl** an archetypal working-class female from south-east England with low-brow tastes and supposedly limited intelligence

**Essex Man** an archetypal working-class male from south-east England without cultural interests or good taste, but with a large disposable income which he spends freely, mainly on consumer goods and entertainment

**great unwashed** 'the great unwashed' is a contemptuous term for the general populace

**green-wellie** of, belonging to or relating to the British upper-class country-dwelling set (stereotypically represented as wearing a certain kind of heavy green wellington boots)

**hard hat** someone who works in a job in which protective headgear is required, usually seen as being obstinately conservative

**hayseed** a town-dweller's derogatory term for a rustic, traditionally a stupid person

**hick** an unsophisticated country-dweller

**high-hat** a person who puts on airs

**high muck-a-muck** an important, pompous person (originally from a term in the Chinook jargon used among traders and Native Americans in the north-western USA, meaning literally 'plenty of food')

**his nibs** or **her nibs** a mock title for an important person

**Hooray Henry** a young middle- or upper-class man with an affectedly ebullient manner

**Joe Sixpack** the average man in the street (rather snootily seen as interested mainly in consuming cans of beer)

**la-di-da** affectedly elegant or superior, especially in speech or bearing

**Nimby** someone who is willing for something to happen so long as it does not affect them or take place in their locality (from the initial letters of 'not in my back yard')

**non-U** not belonging to the upper class of society (see **U**)

**oik** a boor or lout

**prole** a member of the labouring class (shortened from 'proletarian')

**redneck** a US term for a country-dweller, especially one considered stupid or extremely conservative

**schemie** a Scottish term for a person who lives on a council estate (from 'housing scheme')

**Sharon** a disparaging term for a young working-class woman

(because the name is believed to be common among that group)

**sheep-shagger** an urban person's derogatory term for a rural person

**silvertail** an Australian term for a wealthy socialite or social climber

**sleb** a celebrity

**Sloane Ranger** a young person, typically upper-class or upper-middle-class and female, who favours expensive casual clothing suggestive of rural pursuits, speaks in distinctively clipped tones, evinces certain predictable enthusiasms and prejudices, and is resident (during the week) in the Sloane Square area of London or a comparable part (often shortened to **Sloane**)

**square** boringly traditional or orthodox

**stuffed shirt** a pompous, unbendingly correct person, especially one who is of no real importance

**swell** a dandy, a fashionable or finely dressed person

**top-drawer** belonging to or typical of the upper class

**Tracey** same as **Sharon**

**trailer trash** in the USA, poor and uneducated people, typically living in trailer parks

**U** short for 'upper-class', used to describe words, behaviour, etc as used by or found among that echelon of society (the opposite of this is **non-U**)

**upper crust** the upper class or aristocracy

**yuppie** a '*young urban professional*'

# *Politics*

Politics does not enjoy much of a reputation these days. Voting turnouts tend to be low as more and more people perceive that their votes seem to change nothing and it is a challenge to politicians to 'get out the vote'. Increasing numbers would rather watch *The West Wing* on TV than make the journey to a polling station.

Cynicism also abounds in the slang of politics, with the people's representatives engaging in 'doughnutting' and being interested mainly in self-aggrandizement and securing 'jobs for the boys'. Individuality among politicians appears to be at an all-time low, with leaders and whips making sure that the rank and file are 'singing from the same hymn sheet' and staying strictly 'on-message'. Even in 'the world's greatest democracy', the USA, ordinary people are deeply suspicious of what goes on 'inside the Beltway'. The public looks on disgustedly, waiting for the next '-gate' scandal to break.

## *Glossary*

**another place** speakers in the House of Commons traditionally do not mention the House of Lords by name but refer to it as 'another place'

**bafflegab** the professional logorrhoea of many politicians, characterized by prolix abstract circumlocution, used as a means of persuasion, pacification or obfuscation (you get the idea)

**banana republic** any small country dependent on foreign investment (originally applied to any of the small republics in the tropics dependent on exports of fruit)

**Beltway** in the USA, the Washington Beltway (equivalent to a British 'ring road') surrounds Washington DC, and the area 'inside the Beltway' is often seen as an enclosed world where political intrigues are the order of the day

**carpetbagger** a person who uses a place or organization with which they have no previous connection for political ends

**commie** a derogatory term for a communist (in Australia, **commo** is also used)

**dark horse** a candidate not brought forward until the last moment

**diplomatese** the jargon or obscure language used by diplomats

**dog-whistle politics** a style of campaigning which aims to send subliminal messages to a certain group of voters without disturbing the wider electorate

**doughnutting** the surrounding of a speaker in parliament by other members to give an impression, especially to television viewers, of a packed house

**dove** a politician who advocates peace or conciliation

**dry** a 'dry' is a person who favours strict adherence to hardline right-wing conservative policies

**flag waver** a politician who makes a great show of patriotism

**-gate** a suffix attached to the name of a person or place to denote a scandal (from the 'Watergate' affair in 1970s America)

**get out the vote** to successfully encourage members of the public to turn out and vote in elections

**GOP** Grand Old Party, a nickname for the US Republican Party

**hawk** a politician who advocates war, aggressiveness or confrontation

**heeler** a US term for a faithful but unscrupulous follower of a party boss (also called a **ward heeler**)

**hot button** an emotive topic or sensitive issue

**jobs for the boys** jobs given to or created for friends and supporters

**kitchen cabinet** an informal, unelected group of advisers to a political office-holder

**leftie** a left-winger

**nat** a nationalist

**Number Ten** 10 Downing Street, the official residence of the British prime minister

**off-message** someone who is 'off-message' is departing from the party line

**on-message** someone who is 'on-message' is adhering to the party line

**pinko** a person who is something of a socialist but hardly a 'red'

**pipe-layer** a US term for someone who exercises unseen political influence

**pol** or **politico** a politician or political activist

**pork barrel** in the USA, a bill or policy promoting spending of federal or state money on projects undertaken because of their appeal to the electorate rather than their meeting a real need

**press the flesh** to go about
shaking hands with people,
especially potential supporters

**Prez** 'the Prez' is a nickname
for the president of the United
States

**red** a 'red' is a communist

**reds under the bed**
supposed communist
infiltrators

**retread** a member of
parliament who is re-elected
to the House of Commons
having previously lost their
seat

**singing from the same
hymn sheet** in broad
agreement

**spin doctor** someone (often
a public relations expert)
employed by a politician, etc

to influence public opinion,
especially by presenting
information to the public in
the most favourable light

**stalking horse** a candidate
in an election who stands
only to facilitate the success
of another as yet undeclared
candidate

**tanky** a hard-line communist
(perhaps from such a person's
not objecting to the former
Soviet Union's use of tanks
in quelling opposition in its
satellite states)

**tinpot dictator** the
autocratic ruler of a small state

**Trot** a Trotskyist

**veep** a US term for a vice-
president

**ward heeler** see **heeler**

**wet** moderately conservative

## Clothing and fashion

While we all (or most of us) tend to buy and wear clothes, we don't
all work in the fashion industry or have an insight into its peculiar
terminology. We might be able to recognize 'heroin chic' in the pages
of a glossy magazine, but we certainly wouldn't want to exemplify it.
However, most of us have used slang terms for the fashions we like to
sport or have worn in our time. In the 1980s we might have favoured
'boob tubes' or 'DMs' (or even both); those of an older generation
may even have been 'Teds' and remember when 'DAs' and 'drainpipes'
were 'all the go'.

Fashion is by its very nature transient, but the slang connected with it often survives long after the items in question have been consigned, like 'kipper ties' and 'brothel creepers', to the back-wardrobe of history. It is notoriously impossible for the printed word to keep up with trends, and in no time at all referring to 'bling' will become 'old hat'.

## Glossary

**all the go** or **all the rage** very fashionable

**bags** trousers

**basher** a straw hat

**beanie** a small, close-fitting hat

**beautiful people** 'the beautiful people' are the rich, attractive and fashionable members of a society

**beetle-crushers** big heavy boots

**best bib and tucker** someone wearing this combination is in their best clothes

**bling** or **bling bling** jewellery, especially of a large and conspicuous style

**body fascism** an ardent and obsessive belief in the importance of physical appearance over other personal characteristics

**boob tube** a woman's garment of stretch fabric covering the torso from midriff to armpit

**brothel creepers** men's soft, usually suede, shoes with thick crêpe soles

**bumbag** a small bag worn on a belt around the waist (in the USA this is called a **fanny pack**)

**bumfreezer** a jacket that reaches only to the waist

**cardi** a cardigan

**chuddies** underpants (from Hindi)

**clobber** clothes

**clodhopper** a heavy, clumsy shoe or boot

**clothes-horse** a person, usually a woman, who is perceived as a model for fashionable clothes

**coolhunter** a person who studies and advises on probable trends in fashion

**cossie** a swimming costume

**cut-offs** shorts made by

cutting off the legs of jeans just above the knee

**DA** an abbreviation for **duck's arse**

**daggy** an Australian and New Zealand term meaning 'unfashionable'

**daisy roots** boots (rhyming slang)

**daks** an Australian term for trousers (originally a trade name)

**dicky dirt** a shirt (rhyming slang)

**DJ** a dinner jacket

**DMs** Doc Martens®, a proprietary brand of lace-up leather boots with light, thick, resilient soles

**drainpipes** very narrow trousers

**duck's arse** or (US) **ass** a man's hairstyle in which the hair is swept back to a point on the neck resembling a duck's tail, especially worn by **Teddy boys** in the 1950s

**duds** clothes

**fanny pack** see **bumbag**

**fashionista** a follower or setter of fashion

**fashion victim** someone who slavishly follows the latest fashions

**fly** stylish or fashionable

**fogle** a silk handkerchief

**frillies** light and pretty underwear for women

**gay deceiver** a foam-padded brassiere

**gear** clothes, especially young people's fashionable clothes

**gimme cap** a US term for a peaked cap printed with a company logo or a trademark, distributed free among the public to promote the brand

**glad rags** your 'glad rags' are your best, or dress, clothes

**glitterati** the current fashionable set, ie famous, glamorous, rich and beautiful people

**go commando** to forgo the use of underpants

**groovy** up-to-date or in style (especially in the 1960s)

**gussy up** to smarten up

**hankie** a handkerchief

**heroin chic** a trend in the fashion industry in which models are used who portray a pale emaciated appearance thought to resemble that of heroin addicts

**hip** knowing, informed or well abreast of fashionable knowledge and taste

**hot** currently fashionable

**It Girl** a young woman who

is, or makes it her business to be, noted in fashionable circles for her charisma, beauty and wealth

**jammies** pyjamas

**jemimas** elastic-sided boots

**jiggy** someone who is 'jiggy with it' is abreast of the latest fashions

**kecks** or **keks** trousers

**kipper tie** a very wide, and often garish, necktie

**kit** clothes, especially in the phrase 'get your kit off'

**knicks** knickers

**Lionel Blairs** flared trousers (rhyming slang for 'flares')

**lippy** lipstick

**loons** or **loon-pants** trousers that flare widely from the knees, especially as worn by hippies

**Milton Keynes** jeans (rhyming slang)

**monkey suit** a man's evening suit

**muffin top** a roll of fatty flesh that spills out over the top of a pair of low-cut trousers

**number** an admired item of women's clothing, as in 'that little red number'

**penguin suit** a man's black dinner jacket and white shirt

**PJs** pyjamas

**raggery** clothes, especially women's clothes

**rag trade** the trade concerned with designing, making and selling clothes

**round the houses** trousers (London rhyming slang)

**Roy** an Australian term for a fashion-conscious young male

**scanties** underwear, especially women's brief panties

**schmutter** clothing (derived from Yiddish)

**scream** colours that clash acutely are said to 'scream'

**shades** sunglasses

**sharp** overly smart or fashionable in dress

**shimmy** a chemise

**skinny** a pullover or other garment that fits tightly may be described as 'skinny'

**skinny-rib** a sweater made of ribbed wool or similar fibre

**skivvies** a term used especially in North America for a man's undergarments

**skivvy** an Australian and New Zealand term for a knitted cotton polo-necked sweater

**sloppy joe** a large loose sweater

**snazzy** very attractive or fashionable

**snip** a tailor

**snotrag** a handkerchief

**spit curl** a curl of a person's hair pressed flat on the temple

**square** a person of boringly traditional outlook and opinions, especially in musical taste or dress

**strides** trousers

**suicide blonde** a blonde who has achieved her hair colour by bleaching and dyeing (a pun on the phrase 'dyed by her own hand')

**sundown** a US term for a woman's broad-brimmed hat

**sunnies** an Australian term for sunglasses

**superwaif** an extremely thin and childlike young fashion model

**sweats** a combination of sweatshirt and sweatpants

**swell** a fashionable or finely dressed person

**swinging** a word used to describe anything that is fashionable or anyone who is fully alive to, and appreciative of, the most recent trends and fashions (the term itself seems to go in and out of fashion)

**swish** smart or stylish

**tackies** a South African term for tennis shoes or plimsolls (perhaps from their rubber soles being slightly sticky)

**Ted** a **Teddy boy** or **Teddy girl**

**Teddy boy** an unruly adolescent, originally in the 1950s, affecting a dandyish style of dress (so called because their clothes were reminiscent of those worn during the reign of Edward VII)

**Teddy girl** the female equivalent of a **Teddy boy**

**teeny-bopper** a young teenager, especially a girl, who enthusiastically follows the latest trends in pop music, clothes, etc

**threads** clothes

**tile** a hat

**tippy** in the height of fashion

**titfer** a hat (from the rhyming slang 'tit for tat')

**togs** clothes

**Tony Blairs** flared trousers (rhyming slang for 'flares')

**trollies** underpants

**turtle dove** a glove (rhyming slang)

**tux** a tuxedo

**undies** underclothes

**unhip** square, not trendy

**wedgies** wedge-heeled shoes

**whale tail** if a woman is revealing the top of her thong

above her low-cut trousers, the shape of this leads her to being described as sporting a 'whale tail'

**whistle** a suit (shortened from the rhyming slang 'whistle and flute')

**wifebeater** a US term for a man's vest worn without a shirt over it

**winkle-pickers** shoes with long pointed toes

**with it** following current trends

**woolly** a woollen garment, especially a sweater

## Transport

We all need to get from A to B, whether by 'Shanks's pony', on public transport (such as 'the Tube'), or in one's 'wheels'. The level of private ownership of motor vehicles is higher than ever, and many of us have a love affair with our car, even if it is recognizably an old 'banger' rather than a 'Roller'. We each tend to think that we surpass our fellow motorists in driving skills: it is always the other driver who is a 'boy racer' bedecking his vehicle with 'go-faster stripes', and we would never admit to being an 'amber gambler' or 'tailgating' some innocent road user. Of course we need a four-wheel drive vehicle to nip down to the corner shop, but we would never countenance referring to it as a 'Chelsea tractor'. Certainly, we would never dream of 'hot-wiring' someone else's 'jam jar'. But whether your chosen motor is a 'beamer' or a 'Chevy', a 'hot hatch' or a 'runabout', if you have a 'prang' or a 'blow-out' you can always rely on a 'cabbie' to take you home in a 'Joe Baxi'.

### Glossary

**amber gambler** a reckless driver who speeds through a traffic light after it has changed from green to amber

**anchors** the brakes of a motor vehicle

**artic** an articulated lorry

**banger** a decrepit old car (from the sounds likely to come from its exhaust)

**beamer** a nickname for a BMW car

**biker** or **bikie** a motorbike rider

**blow-out** when a motor vehicle has a 'blow-out', one of its tyres bursts

**boneshaker** any vehicle of dubious reliability and comfort

**boy racer** a male driver who has a juvenile need to impress others with the speed and aggression of his driving

**bus** a pilot may often refer to an aircraft as a 'bus'

**cabbie** a taxi driver

**carb** a carburettor

**Chevy** a nickname for a Chevrolet car

**Chelsea tractor** a four-wheel drive vehicle that is never actually used off-road but is mainly driven around a fashionable inner-city area (such as Chelsea in London)

**chopper** a 'chopper' can mean either a helicopter or a type of motorcycle or bicycle with very high handlebars and a low saddle

**clock** the speedometer or mileometer on a vehicle

**clunker** a useless old car

**combi** an Australian term for a camper van

**copter** a helicopter

**crate** a decrepit aeroplane or car

**cut up** to 'cut up' another vehicle is to overtake it and then move dangerously close in front of it

**drag** a 'drag' can mean a car, lorry or wagon

**droop snoot** a cockpit section on an aircraft that can be lowered to provide downward visibility at low speeds

**egg beater** a helicopter

**el** in the USA, 'the el' is an elevated railway (this is also written as **L**)

**fender bender** a US term for a collision between motor vehicles in which little damage is done

**flivver** a dated term for a small cheap motor car

**Friday afternoon car** a new car with many faults in it (supposedly built on a Friday afternoon when workers' concentration is poor)

**gas-guzzler** a car that consumes large amounts of petrol

**go-faster stripes** a derogatory term for matching horizontal stripes painted along the sides of a car for sporty effect, which apparently give (especially young male) drivers of cars bearing them a sense of superior power and road skill

**greaser** a member of a gang of long-haired motorcyclists

**growler** a four-wheeled horse-drawn cab

**gun** to 'gun' an engine or 'give it the gun' is to press down on the accelerator, or to rev it up noisily

**hot hatch** a more powerful version of a standard hatchback car

**hot-wire** to 'hot-wire' a motor vehicle is to start its engine without a key by manipulating the wiring

**Jag** a nickname for a Jaguar car

**jam jar** a car (rhyming slang)

**Joe Baxi** a taxi (rhyming slang)

**joyrider** someone who drives for pleasure, especially someone who drives recklessly in a stolen car

**jump** to 'jump the lights' or 'jump a red light' is to drive through traffic lights when the red light is showing

**kangaroo** a motor vehicle is said to 'kangaroo' if it moves forward in jerks because of the driver's poor clutch control

**L** see **el**

**low rider** a customized car in which the suspension has been lowered

**meat wagon** a name used for various vehicles, particularly a police van for transporting prisoners, an ambulance or a hearse

**Merc** a nickname for a Mercedes car

**motorway madness** a term used in the media for reckless driving in bad conditions on motorways, especially in fog

**paint job** a motor vehicle's 'paint job' is the way in which it is painted, especially when customized

**petrolhead** a motor vehicle enthusiast

**pimp** to 'pimp someone's ride' is to customize their motor vehicle

**pipsqueak** a two-stroke motorcycle

**prang** to 'prang' a vehicle is to crash it

**ragtop** a folding canvas roof on a sports car, or a car with such a roof

**rat run** a minor road heavily used by traffic trying to avoid a congested major road

**reggo** an Australian term for the registration of a motor vehicle

**ride** a US term for a person's motor vehicle

**rig** an articulated lorry

**Roller** a nickname for a Rolls-Royce car

**runabout** a small car

**scorch** to drive very fast

**sewing machine** any small car, especially a foreign model

**Shanks's pony** if you go somewhere 'on Shanks's pony' or 'by Shanks's pony', you go on foot

**shunt** a car accident

**skid lid** a crash helmet

**sleeping policeman** a low transverse hump built into the surface of a road, intended to slow down traffic

**soup up** to 'soup up' a car is to increase the power of its engine

**speed cop** a policeman who watches out for motorists who are exceeding the speed limit

**speed freak** an enthusiast of fast driving

**speedo** a speedometer

**spy in the cab** a tachograph fitted in a lorry or truck

**stretch** a 'stretch' or 'stretch limo' is a luxurious custom-made limousine that has been lengthened to provide extra seating

**tacho** a tachograph or tachometer

**tailgate** to 'tailgate' another vehicle is to drive dangerously close behind it

**ton** to 'do a ton' is to make a vehicle travel at 100 miles per hour

**ton-up boy** a motorcyclist or driver who habitually travels at 100 miles per hour

**tootle** to travel casually along

**Tube** 'the Tube' is the London Underground

**uey** a U-turn

**vroom** to 'vroom' an engine is to rev it

**welly** to 'give it some welly' is to put your foot down heavily on the accelerator

**wheels** someone who has 'wheels' has their own car

**whirlybird** a helicopter

**winker** a direction indicator on a motor vehicle

One particular area of slang connected with transport is the terminology popularized by users of CB (Citizens' Band) radio in the

1970s and 1980s. Beginning among truck drivers in North America, who were avid to form 'convoys' and avoid the attentions of traffic police, this slang soon spread, helped by its use in films and television programmes, to the United Kingdom. Here is a selection of the most popular terms, some of which came to be used more widely:

**back door** the rear of a vehicle

**bear** a police officer (shortened from **smokey bear**)

**bear in the air** a police helicopter

**breaker** any CB user

**convoy** a group of vehicles travelling together, whether for fun and companionship or to present a daunting prospect to police officers

**front door** the lead vehicle in a convoy

**good buddy** a term of address for a fellow CB user

**handle** a nickname used by a driver to identify himself or herself in transmissions

**picture taker** a speed camera or radar gun, or a police officer using one of these

**polo mint** a roundabout

**seat cover** a woman

**smokey** or **smokey bear** a police officer (from Smokey the Bear, a cartoon bear used in the USA to promote fire safety, depicted wearing a hat similar to that of a Highway Patrol officer)

**smokey in a plain brown wrapper** an unmarked police car

**suicide jockey** the driver of a truck carrying a load of explosives

**twenty** someone's 'twenty' is their location (from the police radio code term '10-20')

# *Nationality*

Slang terms for people who belong to particular countries are found all over the world, not only in English. Some of this springs from the basic human need to identify with those we feel to be our own kind, the concomitant of which is categorizing other people as 'foreigners'.

While some of the slang terms for nationalities are fairly innocent
and harmless, or even friendly (such as 'Bajan' or 'Enzedder'), others
are undoubtedly hostile (like 'Froggie' or 'white settler') or speak of a
sense of superiority (as in 'bogtrotter' or 'guinea'), and in many cases
these terms are offensive.

It is not surprising that citizens of countries which have been at war
with one another should adopt derogatory names for their enemies.
After all, it helps to dehumanize them and makes their destruction
seem more impersonal. Terms like 'boche', 'Kraut' or 'Nip' are obvious
products of this process. Immigration, which leads to the presence
of visible outsiders in a community, is also generative of labels for
nationalities. 'Paki' in Britain, and 'bohunk' and 'Polack' in the United
States are examples of this; but, certainly in this list, Australia seems
to take the biscuit, dubbing, as it does, the British incomer as a
'choom', 'kipper', 'pommy', 'pongo' or 'woodbine' and the Italians as
'spags'.

Please note that a distinction is made here between nationality and
race (which can of course transcend nationality). Racial slang may be
found in the section immediately following this one.

## Glossary

**Argie** an Argentinian
**Aussie** an Australian
**Bajan** a native of Barbados
**Bim** an inhabitant of Barbados
**boche** a German
**bogtrotter** an Irish person
**bohunk** a North American
term for a person of Slavic
origins
**Brit** a British person
**Canuck** a Canadian (within

Canada, however, this term
refers specifically to a French-
Canadian)
**choom** an Australian term
for an English person (perhaps
reflecting a pronunciation of
'chum')
**Enzedder** a New Zealander
**Eyetie** an Italian
**Frog** or **Froggie** a French
person (because frogs' legs are

seen as a typical French dish)

**gippo** an Egyptian

**guinea** a US term for a person of Italian descent

**Hun** a German

**Heinie** a US term for a German

**Jap** a Japanese person

**Jerry** a German

**Jock** a Scotsman

**kipper** an Australian term for a British person

**Kiwi** a New Zealander

**Kraut** a German (from 'sauerkraut', seen as a typical German dish)

**limey** a US term for a British person (from the Royal Navy's use of lime juice to prevent scurvy)

**Mick** an Irishman (from 'Michael', seen as a typical Irish name)

**Nip** a Japanese person (from 'Nippon', a Japanese name for Japan)

**Ossi** a citizen of the former German Democratic Republic (East Germany) before reunification with the Federal Republic in 1990 (a German abbreviation of *Ostdeutsch*, meaning 'East German')

**Paddy** an Irishman (from 'Patrick', seen as a typical Irish name)

**Paki** a Pakistani

**parleyvoo** an old term for a French person (from the French phrase *parlez vous ...?* meaning 'do you speak ...?')

**Polack** a Polish person

**pommy** an Australian term for a British person, especially an Englishman (often shortened to **pom**)

**pongo** an Australian term for an English person

**Russki** or **Russky** a Russian

**Sandy** a Scotsman (a diminutive form of 'Alexander', seen as a typical Scottish name)

**Sawney** an old nickname for a Scotsman (from **Sandy**)

**sherman tank** an American (rhyming slang for 'Yank')

**spag** an Australian term for an Italian (from 'spaghetti', seen as a typical Italian dish)

**squarehead** an old term for a Scandinavian or German

**Taffy** a Welshman (from 'Dafydd', a Welsh form of 'David')

**Wessi** a citizen of the German Federal Republic (West Germany) before reunification in 1990 (a German abbreviation of *Westdeutsch*, meaning 'West German')

**white settler** a Scottish term

for an English person who
moves into a rural area and
makes no attempt to blend
sympathetically into the local
community

**woodbine** an Australian term
for an English person (from a
popular brand of cigarette)
**Yank** or **Yankee** an
American

## Race

Slang connected with race is related to, but not identical with,
the slang of nationalities, and some of the same concerns give rise
to these terms: the desire to identify with a common group, the
stigmatizing of some people as 'other', the need to perceive ourselves
and our kind as somehow intrinsically superior, and basic instinctive
hostility.

It should be borne in mind that when many of these terms were
first coined they were deliberately designed to be insulting, and
even if they were not, they often *are* offensive (some of them may
also be found in the section on **Insults**). The fact that such terms
are included here should not be taken by the reader as approval
for or agreement with them. But although racial slang may not be
condoned, it certainly does exist.

Racial epithets are used in most countries and in many languages,
but since this book is concerned with slang in English, most of
the terms here inevitably originate from the point of view of the
English-speaking majorities in their countries of origin. Thus, many
of the expressions focus on non-Western, non-English-speaking
characteristics (such as 'Chinky', 'gook' or 'towelhead') or on the non-
white colour of the target's skin (as in 'darkey', 'redskin' or 'nigger').
The fact that English-speaking people of other racial descent from
the 'WASP' majorities abound in countries such as the USA and South
Africa means that sometimes the boot is on the other foot (as in
'honky' or 'gub').

## Glossary

**Abo** an Australian name for an Aboriginal or Aborigine

**Anglo** a person of British extraction

**Balt** an Australian term for an immigrant from the Baltic region; also used loosely to mean any European immigrant

**Binghi** an Australian name for an Aboriginal or Aborigine (from an Aboriginal word meaning 'brother')

**Chinee**, **Chink** or **Chinky** a Chinese person

**chow** an old term used in Australia and New Zealand for a Chinese person

**coon** a black person

**darkey**, **darkie** or **darky** a black person

**dinge** a US term for a black person

**four by two** a Jew (rhyming slang)

**fuzzy-wuzzy** a dark-skinned native of various countries, especially a member of a race characterized by tightly curled hair

**geechee** in the rural south of the USA, a 'geechee' is a black person

**gippo** a Gypsy or Egyptian person

**gook** a member of an Asiatic race

**greaseball** or **greaser** a US term for a person of Latin racial origin

**gringo** an English-speaking person in Spanish-speaking America

**gub** in Australia, a 'gub' is a white person, as opposed to an Aboriginal

**Hebe** a Jew (shortened from 'Hebrew')

**honky** an African-American term for a white person

**Jacky** or **Jacky-Jacky** an Australian name for an Aboriginal

**Jim Crow** a US term for a black person

**jungle bunny** a black person

**Kaffir** a term used by white South Africans for a black person (from an Arabic word meaning 'unbeliever')

**kike** a Jew

**moke** a US term for a black person

**muntu** a South African term for a black person

**nigger** a black or dark-skinned

person (**nig-nog** is a variant of this)

**ofay** a term used by black Americans for a white person

**Paki** a Pakistani; also used loosely to mean any person of Asian ethnicity

**pikey** a Gypsy

**raghead** an Arab

**redskin** a Native American

**rooinek** an Afrikaans term for a British or English-speaking person (literally meaning 'red neck')

**sambo** a black person

**sheeny** a Jew

**shine** a US term for a black person

**siwash** a derogatory term for a Native American of the north-western states

**smouch** a South African term for a Jew

**spade** a black person

**spic** a US term for a person of Hispanic descent

**teapot lid** a Jew (rhyming slang for 'Yid')

**towelhead** a person who wears a turban or headcloth

**WASP** a white Anglo-Saxon Protestant

**wetback** a Mexican illegal immigrant to the USA (imagined as having swum or waded across the Rio Grande)

**wog** a non-white foreigner

**wop** a member of a Mediterranean or Latin race, especially an Italian

**Yid** a Jew

# Religion

Like the slang associated with race, the slang connected with religion can be derogatory or offensive, especially when it is a tenet of a particular faith or denomination that its believers have a monopoly on the true religion. This results in a tendency to pour scorn on other beliefs as 'mumbo-jumbo' and label their adherents with belittling or dismissive names, such as 'left-footer', 'pantile' or 'Moonie'. It is interesting to note that some names originally coined as derogatory terms, such as 'Quaker' and 'Shaker', ended up being embraced by the objects of derision and became established as the standard names of those particular faiths.

One strain of religious slang in the glossary below seems to reflect an overwhelming, if largely unspoken, British assumption that religious observance should be private, quiet and dignified. It is obviously not the done thing for members of the clergy to rant like a 'Bible-basher' or 'tub-thumper'; nor to be tedious (as in 'preachify'). Extremes of enthusiasm amongst worshippers are also to be deplored. To be a 'hot-gospeller' is not quite the thing, and to be 'happy-clappy' is apparently worse. Presumably a 'fundie' would be beyond the pale. In an increasingly secular age, at least in nominally Christian countries, it would perhaps behove religious people to concentrate more on common ground, such as a shared belief in 'the man upstairs'.

## *Glossary*

**Bible-basher** a vigorous, aggressive or dogmatic Christian preacher (such a person might also be called a **Bible-pounder** or **Bible-thumper**)

**broad-brim** a Quaker (from the broad-brimmed hats with which they were once identified)

**chapel** people described as 'chapel' belong to a Nonconformist church rather than to the established church

**church** people described as 'church' belong to the established church

**creeping Jesus** a cringingly sanctimonious person

**devil-dodger** a preacher, especially of the ranting kind; also used to mean someone who attends various churches to be on the safe side

**fundie** or **fundy** a religious fundamentalist

**get religion** to become religious

**God-botherer** a clergyman or any excessively pious person

**God squad** any religious group, especially an evangelical Christian one, considered overly zealous in moralizing and attempting to convert others

**goy** a term used by Jews for a non-Jew

**happy-clappy** a term used to denote any form of demonstratively enthusiastic Christian worship, especially involving chanting and hand-clapping

**Hebe** a Jew (shortened from 'Hebrew')

**holy Joe** a 'holy Joe' is a parson or a piously religious person

**holy Roller** a US term for a member of a Pentecostal church

**hot-gospeller** a loud, forceful proclaimer of a vigorously interactive kind of religious faith

**hot place** 'the hot place' is a euphemism for hell

**japan** to 'japan' a clergyman means to ordain him (from the idea of applying a coat of varnish)

**Jesus freak** a devout Christian

**left-footer** a Roman Catholic

**man upstairs** 'the man upstairs' is a jocular name for God

**mick** a Roman Catholic, especially in Australia (from the perception of most Catholics as being of Irish extraction)

**Moonie** a member of the Unification Church (after its founder Sun Myung Moon)

**mumbo-jumbo** any object of foolish worship or fear

**non-con** a Nonconformist

**Old Harry**, **Old Nick** and **Old Scratch** nicknames for the Devil

**oncer** someone who habitually goes to church once on a Sunday

**pantile** a word formerly used to denote Nonconformist churches or their congregations (because their chapels were often roofed with pantiles)

**patrico** a disreputable, vagrant or illiterate priest

**pi** obtrusively religious or sanctimonious

**pious fraud** a religious humbug

**preach** a sermon

**preachify** to preach, especially tediously

**Prod**, **Proddy** or **Proddie** a Protestant, especially in Ireland

**reverend** a member of the clergy

**rock chopper** an Australian term for a Roman Catholic (playing on the initials 'RC')

**Sally Army** the Salvation Army

**Salvo** an Australian term for a member of the Salvation Army

**sheeny** a Jew

**sky pilot** a military chaplain

**smouch** a South African term for a Jew

**swaddler** a Methodist, or any Protestant

**Taig** a Northern Irish term for a Roman Catholic

**tub-thumper** a ranting preacher

**twicer** someone who habitually goes to church twice on a Sunday

**tyke** an Australian and New Zealand term for a Roman Catholic

**Wee Free** a member of the minority of the Free Church of Scotland that refused to join with the United Presbyterian Church in 1900

**Yid** a Jew

# *Places*

Slang terms connected with places arise from two main origins: the desire to refer affectionately to our 'own patch' and the need to differentiate other places as being foreign or less desirable by comparison. Citizens of New York, Edinburgh and New Orleans are happy to use and propagate the terms 'the Big Apple', 'Auld Reekie' and 'the Big Easy'; New Zealanders and Australians boast of living in 'Godzone' or 'the Lucky Country'. However, who would be proud of hailing from 'beyond the black stump', a 'jerkwater' town, 'the Great Wen' or 'la-la land'? Being born 'on the wrong side of the tracks' is something you might admit to from the privileged position of having made a success of your life against the odds, but not while you are still a resident of that ill-omened locality. Anyone wishing to appear worldly or sophisticated is hardly likely to advertise the fact that they come from 'the boondocks'.

People from specific places are often given slang designations, and a selection of these appears in the list below. Once again, these names can be affectionate, redolent of a sense of identity and belonging, as in 'hoosier', 'tar heel' or 'Scouser'. On the other hand, no-one is likely to describe themselves with any enthusiasm as a 'banana-bender', 'jackeen' or 'weegie'. You may prefer the fresh air and tranquillity of a rural lifestyle, but would you ever willingly describe yourself as 'a hick from the sticks'?

## *Glossary*

**Auld Reekie** Edinburgh (literally meaning 'old smoky')

**banana-bender** a native of Queensland

**Bananaland** Queensland

**Big Apple** 'the Big Apple' is a nickname for New York City

**Big Easy** 'the Big Easy' is a nickname for New Orleans, Louisiana

**Big Smoke** 'the Big Smoke' or simply 'the Smoke' is a nickname for London, or any metropolitan area characterized by atmospheric pollution

**black stump** an Australian and New Zealand term for a mythical distance-marker on the edge of civilization, especially in the phrase 'beyond the black stump' meaning 'in the far outback'

**Blighty** Britain, especially when thought of as home by a soldier serving abroad

**blue nose** a person from Nova Scotia

**boondocks** 'the boondocks' is a North American term for any wild or remote area, or a dull, provincial place (often shortened to **the boonies**)

**Bris**, **Brissie** or **Brizzie** Brisbane, Australia

**Brum** Birmingham (shortened from the old form 'Brummagem')

**Brummie** a person from Birmingham

**buckeye** a person from Ohio

**burb** in the USA, 'the burbs' are the suburbs

**burg** a US term for a town

**Chiantishire** a facetious name for a part of Tuscany regarded as having been colonized by affluent British tourists

**Chi-town** Chicago

**dive** a disreputable place

**dorp** a South African term for a town that is considered as provincial and backward

**down-home** a US term referring to something that is characteristic of the southern states or of the countryside

**Emerald Isle** 'the Emerald Isle' is a nickname for Ireland

**Enzed** New Zealand

**Frisco** San Francisco

**Geordie** a person from Tyneside

**Gib** Gibraltar

**Godzone** a nickname used

by New Zealanders and Australians for their own country (a pun on 'God's own country')

**Gotham** New York City, probably most familiar to millions worldwide as the home of Batman (a nickname applied by Washington Irving, from the name of a village in Nottinghamshire connected with traditional stories of simpletons)

**Great Wen** 'the Great Wen' is a nickname for London (a 'wen' is a cyst)

**hick** a derogatory term for a person from the country

**hoosier** a person from Indiana

**jackeen** an Irish term for a Dubliner

**jerkwater** in the USA, a 'jerkwater' place is small and insignificant

**keelie** a Glaswegian

**la-la land** Los Angeles, connoting a lifestyle based around the entertainment industry, drug abuse and eccentric beliefs

**Londonistan** London, perceived as a haven for Islamic radicals

**Lucky Country** 'the Lucky Country' is a term used by Australians for Australia

**Manc** a person from Manchester

**Med** 'the Med' is the Mediterranean Sea

**Mickey Mouser** a person from Liverpool (rhyming slang for 'Scouser')

**Motown** or **Motor City** Detroit (from its being a centre of the automobile industry)

**Newfie** a person from Newfoundland

**Old Dart** an Australian term for Britain

**one-horse town** a town that is small, poor or lacking in amenities

**Oz** Australia

**Pompey** Portsmouth

**pond** 'the pond' is the Atlantic Ocean

**Roseland** the areas of south-east England outside London (from the initial letters of 'rest of south-east')

**Scouse** or **Scouser** a person from Liverpool

**slurb** an area combining the appearance and qualities of a slum and a suburb

**Smoke** see **Big Smoke**

**sticks** 'the sticks' is a term for the remote rural areas of a country

**tar heel** a person from North Carolina

**Tassie** Tasmania

**tenderloin** a US term for a district where bribes to the police and other forms of corruption are extremely common

**Tinseltown** Hollywood

**tuckahoe** a person from eastern Virginia

**Uncle Sam** the United States of America

**weegie** a Scottish term for a person from Glasgow

**Windy City** 'the Windy City' is a nickname for Chicago

**wrong side of the tracks** someone from a slum or other socially disadvantaged area may be said to come from 'the wrong side of the tracks'

**Yank** or **Yankee** outside of the USA a 'Yank' means an American, while within the USA it means a northerner, especially a New Englander

---

Each of the states of the USA has at least one official nickname. These names, which may arise from the state's history or geography or from the local flora and fauna, are an object of pride and can often be seen adorning vehicle registration plates. Here is a selection of some notable and intriguing examples:

**Aloha State** Hawaii
**Bay State** Massachusetts
**Badger State** Wisconsin
**Beaver State** Oregon
**Beehive State** Utah
**Buckeye State** Ohio
**Cornhusker State** Nebraska
**Empire State** New York
**Golden State** California
**Gopher State** Minnesota
**Granite State** New Hampshire

**Keystone State** Pennsylvania
**Lone Star State** Texas
**Nutmeg State** Connecticut
**Peach State** Georgia
**Pelican State** Louisiana
**Show Me State** Missouri
**Sooner State** Oklahoma
**Sunshine State** Florida
**Tar Heel State** North Carolina
**Volunteer State** Tennessee

## *Animals*

Among the many species that share the Earth, only *Homo sapiens* has acquired the power of true speech, and it is not surprising that, having distributed taxonomic designations to all other known members of creation, human beings also turn to slang to label the more familiar animals. There are many reasons for this. Some are the names we teach to children to help them identify, and lose any fear of, animals they will see daily, like 'bow-wow' or 'pussy'. They say that none of us are many generations away from ancestors who lived off the land, and many familiar terms for livestock remain instantly recognizable, from 'billy goat' to 'gee-gee' to 'woollyback'. Domestic animals have for centuries shared our lives as pets, and these 'companion animals', once the descendants of free-roaming predators, have long been reduced to being referred to as 'doggies' and 'moggies', with any hound that plainly lacks a pure pedigree being jocularly labelled a 'Heinz'. One can only wonder how the dachshund, once bred to hunt the formidable badger, might react (if it only knew) to the loss of dignity contained in the designation 'sausage dog'. Fiercer wild animals have also gathered slang names; perhaps it makes them seem less scary if you can think of an alligator as a 'gator', a crocodile as a 'croc' and a rattlesnake as a 'rattler'. Even creatures regarded by humankind as no better than pests can be referred to in ways that seem to diminish and contain them, such as 'blowie', 'cootie' or 'mossie'.

## *Glossary*

**beastie** a Scottish term for any small insect or other invertebrate

**billy goat** a male goat

**bitser** an Australian term for a mongrel dog (because it is made up of 'bits of this and bits of that')

**blowie** an Australian and New Zealand term for a blowfly

**bow-wow** a dog

**cat** an Australian term for any timid animal

**cootie** a North American and New Zealand term for a head or body louse

**crabs** crab-lice

**creepy-crawly** any creeping insect or invertebrate

**critter** an animal (from a US dialect pronunciation of 'creature')

**croc** a crocodile

**devil's darning-needle** a dragonfly or damselfly

**doggie** a dog

**gator** an alligator

**gee-gee** a horse, especially in terms of racing and betting

**Heinz** a mongrel dog (from the food manufacturer Heinz, whose proud boast in advertising was '57 varieties')

**hoss** a dialect or US version of 'horse'

**hound** any dog, irrespective of breed, may be referred to as a 'hound'

**Joe Blake** a snake (Australian rhyming slang)

**joey** a young kangaroo

**jumbuck** an Australian term for a sheep

**kitty** a cat, especially a kitten

**livestock** a facetious term for any domestic or body vermin

**lunker** a particularly large specimen of an animal, especially a fish

**midgie** or **midgy** a Scottish term for a midge

**mog**, **moggie** or **moggy** a cat

**moke** a donkey; in Australia and New Zealand this means a worn-out or inferior horse

**mollymawk** a New Zealand term for the fulmar

**mong** an Australian shortening of 'mongrel'

**monkey** an Australian term for a sheep

**mossie** or **mozzie** a mosquito

**mutt** a dog, especially a mongrel

**nag** a horse, especially an inferior one

**nellie** or **nelly** a large petrel

**peke** a Pekinese dog

**poddy** an Australian term for a young animal, especially a calf or lamb

**Polly** a parrot

**pooch** a dog, especially a mongrel

**prad** a horse

**puss** or **pussy** a cat

**rattler** a rattlesnake

**roach** a cockroach

**roger** a goose

**roo** a kangaroo

**ropable** or **ropeable** an Australian and New Zealand term applied to cattle or horses that are wild and unmanageable

**saddler** a US term for a saddle horse

**sausage dog** a dachshund

**sea lawyer** a shark

**skeeter** a US term for a mosquito

**spadger** a sparrow

**stripes** a 'stripes' is a tiger

**taddie** a Scottish and Australian term for a tadpole

**tiggywinkle** a hedgehog

**woolly** an Australian and US term for a sheep, especially before shearing

**woollyback** a sheep

**Yorkie** a Yorkshire terrier

## The human body

Slang is often created to deal with things that people know intimately, and what could be more directly familiar to most people than their own bodies? Slang terms for the body or parts of the body arise out of a desire to be light-hearted or humorous, to dispense with using unnecessarily formal terminology in everyday life, or even to avoid the embarrassment some people feel at having to name in public the most private parts of all. Given the racy nature of much slang and its preoccupations, it can be no surprise that bodily slang tends to focus on those areas that make the obvious differences between the sexes, from 'beaver' to 'twat', 'boobs' to 'titties' and 'chopper' to 'wedding tackle'. Some of the names for the sexual organs do double duty and are also listed under **Insults**.

Given the overtly sexual nature of some of this slang, readers may find elements of this list to be offensive.

## Glossary

**abs** the abdominal muscles

**badonkadonk** shapely female buttocks (from the imaginary onomatopoeic sound made by these as they wiggle by)

**baps** female breasts

**basket** a man's genitals, especially when observed as a bulge in his clothing

**batty** a West Indian term for the buttocks

**bazoo** a US term for the mouth

**beanpole** a skinny person

**bearded clam** the female genitals

**beaver** the female genitals or pubic area

**beef bayonet** the penis

**beetle-crushers** big heavy feet

**beezer** the nose

**behind** the buttocks

**big brown eyes** a US term for a woman's breasts

**bingo wings** flaps of skin that hang down from the upper arms (so called because they are often displayed by people raising a hand to claim victory in bingo)

**bingy** an Australian term for the stomach

**boat race** the face (rhyming slang)

**boko** the nose

**bollocks** the testicles

**boobs** or **boobies** the female breasts

**booty** a person's buttocks

**bottle and glass** the backside (rhyming slang for 'arse')

**box** the vagina

**breadbasket** the stomach

**Bristol cities** a woman's breasts (rhyming slang for 'titties')

**broad in the beam** wide-hipped

**bunghole** the anus

**buns** the buttocks

**bush** the pubic hair

**butt** the buttocks

**cake hole** the mouth

**can** a North American term for the buttocks

**chassis** a woman's body, especially when considered attractive, as in the phrase 'a classy chassis'

**chopper** the penis (not to be confused with the relatively innocent **choppers**)

**choppers** the teeth

**chrome dome** a bald head, or a person who has one

**claret** blood

**clock** the face

**cobblers** the testicles (shortened from 'cobbler's awls', rhyming slang for 'balls')

**cock** the penis

**coit** an Australian term for the buttocks

**cojones** a US term for the testicles (borrowed from Spanish)

**conk** the nose or the head

**cooze** a US term for the female genitals

**cornstalk** an Australian term for a tall thin person

**cory** the penis

**crack** the cleft of the buttocks, or the vagina

**crown jewels** the male genitals

**cunt** the female genitals (also called **cunny**)

**curves** the rounded contours of a woman's body

**delts** the deltoid muscles

**dial** the face

**dick** the penis

**dogs** the feet (someone complaining that their feet are sore may say, 'My dogs are barking')

**dome** the head

**dong** the penis

**duff** the buttocks or rump

**dukes** the fists

**Dutch pink** blood

**face-fungus** a moustache or beard

**family jewels** the male genitals

**fanny** a word that causes an element of Transatlantic confusion: in the UK this means the female genitals; in the USA it refers to the buttocks of either sex

**five-o'clock shadow** the new growth of hair that becomes noticeable on a man's shaven face in the late afternoon

**flab** excess body fat

**front bottom** the vagina

**gams** legs, especially shapely female ones

**gash** the vagina

**gazongas** a term used mainly in the USA for female breasts, especially when large

**glim** an eye

**gnashers** the teeth

**gob** the mouth

**goggle-eyed** having bulging or staring eyes

**gogglers** or **goggles** the eyes

**goolies** the testicles

**growler** the female genitals (probably shortened from 'growl and grunt', rhyming slang for 'cunt')

**grundle** a US term for the perineum, the area between the genitals and the anus

**gut** a paunch

**Hampstead Heath** teeth (rhyming slang)

**heinie** a US term for the buttocks

**hooter** the nose, especially a particularly large one

**hooters** a North American

term for a woman's breasts

**index** an old term for the nose

**ivories** teeth

**jacksie** or **jacksy** the backside or anus

**John Thomas** the penis

**jugs** a woman's breasts

**keister** a US term for the buttocks

**kipper** a person's face or mouth (shortened from 'kipper and plaice', rhyming slang for 'face')

**kisser** the mouth

**knackers** the testicles

**knob** the penis

**knockers** female breasts

**lamps** the eyes

**laughing gear** the mouth

**loaf** the head (originally the first part of 'loaf of bread', the Cockney rhyming slang for 'head')

**love handles** the deposit of fat sometimes found on either side of the back just below the waist

**love muscle** or **love truncheon** the penis

**lunchbox** the male genitals, especially when made prominent by tight clothing

**man-boobs** fleshy deposits of fat on the chest of an overweight male, seen as

resembling female breasts

**map** your 'map' is your face

**maulers** the hands

**meat and two veg** the penis and testicles

**mince pies** the eyes (rhyming slang)

**minge** the female genitals

**mitts** the hands

**muff** the female genitals

**mug** the face

**mush** the face

**nadgers** the testicles (probably derived from 'gonads', as is the equivalent term **nads**)

**nana** the head

**napper** the head

**naughty bits** the genitals

**noggin** the head

**noodle** a chiefly North American term for the head

**norks** an Australian term for a woman's breasts (perhaps from Norco Co-operative Ltd, a butter manufacturer)

**north and south** mouth (rhyming slang)

**nut** the head

**nuts** the testicles

**one-eyed trouser snake** the penis

**onion** the head

**pearly gates** the teeth (often shortened to **pearlies**)

**pecker** a US term for the penis
**pecs** the pectoral muscles
**peepers** the eyes
**peg** a leg
**peter** the penis
**phiz** or **phizog** the face (from 'physiognomy')
**pills** the testicles
**pink oboe** the penis
**pins** legs
**pisser** the penis
**plates of meat** feet (rhyming slang)
**plonker** the penis
**poontang** the female genitals
**pork sword** the penis
**pot-belly** a protuberant belly
**prat** the buttocks
**prick** the penis
**pubes** the pubic hair
**puppies** the female breasts
**puss** the face
**pussy** the female genitals
**putz** a US term for the penis
**quim** the female genitals
**rack** a US term for a woman's breasts
**raspberry ripple** nipple (rhyming slang)
**Red Lane** the throat or gullet
**ring** the anus
**rocks** the testicles
**rod** the penis
**roger** the penis

**schmuck** the penis
**schnozzle** the nose
**scone** an Australian term for the head
**scrag** the neck
**shaft** the penis
**shitter** the anus
**short and curlies** the pubic hair
**six-pack** a set of well-defined abdominal muscles
**slats** a US term for the ribs, often the target of a blow
**slit** the vagina
**snatch** the female genitals
**snitch** the nose
**snoot** the nose
**snout** the nose
**soup strainer** a moustache
**spare tyre** a roll of fat around the midriff
**swede** the head (from the shape of the vegetable)
**tackle** the male genitals
**tadger** same as **todger**
**tail** the female genitals
**threepenny bits** a woman's breasts (rhyming slang for 'tits')
**ticker** the heart
**tit** or **titty** a woman's breast
**todger** or **tadger** the penis
**tonk** an Australian term for the penis
**tool** the penis

**top bollocks** a woman's breasts

**trap** the mouth

**trilbies** the feet

**tush** or **tushie** a US term for the buttocks (from a Yiddish word)

**twat** the female genitals

**wang** or **whang** the penis

**wazoo** a US term for the anus

**weapon** the penis

**wedding tackle** the male genitals

**weeny** or **weenie** a US term for the penis

**whang** same as **wang**

**willy** the penis

## Bodily functions

Bodily functions are, by definition, common to everybody, and like many other intimately familiar daily experiences, they are enormously generative of slang designations. As with slang terms for the human body itself, many of these spring from attempts to euphemize or even disguise things that are felt to be too shameful to mention directly. How many of us these days would be truly offended by the direct naming of these natural processes? It is as if we are all in fear of upsetting the delicate sensibilities of some universal maiden aunt, a relic from the Victorian age. Some of these niceties of expression are taught to us in childhood, and we in turn pass them on to our own offspring (unless we are particularly liberated), including 'poo', 'pee' and 'blow off', not to mention the faintly militaristic 'number one' and 'number two'. Even in adulthood, we avoid calling a spade a spade; for instance, how many times during an evening out might a woman really need to 'powder her nose'? And is anyone still so sensitive as to need the protection of the delightfully circumlocutory 'see a man about a dog'? Also, it seems that we tend to minimize, or treat as humorous, the effects of bodily dysfunctions or extremes by application of slang names, like 'Aztec two-step', 'squits', 'skitters' or 'trots' for diarrhoea, or 'technicolour yawn' or 'talking on the porcelain telephone' for vomiting. We all know what it is; we just shy away from telling it like it is.

## Glossary

**Aztec two-step** diarrhoea (a variation on **Montezuma's revenge**)

**barf** to vomit

**bark** to cough

**blow chunks** to vomit

**blow off** to break wind from the anus

**bogy** or **bogey** a piece of nasal mucus

**burp** to belch

**cack** or **kack** excrement

**chuck up** to vomit

**chunder** an Australian term meaning to vomit

**crap** excrement

**curse** 'the curse' is a euphemism for menstruation or a menstrual period

**cut the cheese** a US term meaning to break wind from the anus

**Delhi belly** diarrhoea, especially as suffered by people visiting India and other developing countries

**dewdrop** a drop of mucus hanging from the end of the nose

**doo-doo** excrement

**doss** to sleep

**dump** to 'dump' or 'take a dump' is to defecate

**fart** to break wind from the anus

**fetch up** to vomit

**forty winks** a short nap

**gippy** or **gyppy tummy** diarrhoea, a severely upset stomach, thought of as a hazard of holidaying in hot countries

**go** to urinate

**gob** to spit

**goose bumps** gooseflesh, a knobbly condition of the skin due to cold, horror, etc

**greeny** or **greenie** a piece of nasal mucus

**honk** to vomit

**hurl** to vomit

**in the family way** expecting a baby

**jimmy riddle** an act of urination (rhyming slang for 'piddle')

**jobbie** a lump of excrement

**leak** to 'leak' or 'take a leak' is to urinate

**let off** to break wind from the anus

**let one go** to break wind from the anus

**lose your lunch** to vomit

**Montezuma's revenge** diarrhoea, especially caused by travelling in Mexico or eating Mexican food (after Montezuma, the last Aztec emperor of Mexico, who was deposed by the Spanish conquistadors)

**monthlies** menstruation or a menstrual period

**move your bowels** to defecate

**number one** and **number two** expressions used especially to and by children to refer to urination and defecation respectively

**on the rag** a woman who is 'on the rag' is menstruating

**painters** a woman who 'has the painters in' is menstruating

**pay a call** or **visit** to go to the toilet

**pee** to urinate

**pee-pee** urine

**piddle** to urinate

**piss** to urinate

**plop** to defecate

**point Percy at the porcelain** to urinate

**pony and trap** an act of defecation (rhyming slang for 'crap')

**poo** excrement

**poop** excrement

**powder your nose** a woman who says she is going to 'powder her nose' is actually going to the toilet

**puke** to vomit

**pump ship** to urinate

**Richard the Third** a lump of excrement (rhyming slang for 'turd')

**runs** 'the runs' is another name for diarrhoea

**see a man about a dog** to urinate

**shits** 'the shits' is another name for diarrhoea

**skitters** 'the skitters' is another name for diarrhoea

**slag** an Australian term meaning to spit

**slash** to urinate

**snot** nasal mucus

**spend a penny** to go to the toilet

**spew your ring** to vomit so violently that you seem in danger of bringing up your anus

**spunk** semen

**squits** or **squitters** 'the squits' and 'the squitters' are names for diarrhoea

**strain the spuds** to urinate

**talk on the porcelain telephone** to vomit into a toilet

**technicolour yawn** an act of vomiting

**threepenny bits** diarrhoea

(rhyming slang for 'shits')
**tinkle** an act of urinating
**tom tit** an act of defecating
   (rhyming slang for 'shit')

**trots** 'the trots' is another
   term for diarrhoea
**turd** a lump of excrement
**upchuck** to vomit

# Sex

If, as they say, prostitution is the oldest profession, then sex must
be the oldest obsession. The urge to procreate has been part of the
human experience since the dawn of time, and it shows no sign
of dying out in the 21st century. It seems that people are always
talking about sex (or thinking about it), and if slang is made for the
particularly racy and informal areas of language use, then it can be
no surprise that sex is so highly productive of slang expressions; so
much so, in fact, that the list below is by far the longest of all those
for the topics dealt with in this book (even though it omits many of
the synonyms for the genitals which are listed under **The human
body**). All areas of the sexual experience are covered, from the
act itself (from 'nooky' to 'rumpy-pumpy'), through variations (like
'doggy fashion', 'sixty-nine' or 'yodelling in the canyon'), and solitary
practices (such as 'beating your meat' or 'smacking the pony').

It has to be said that much of sexual slang smacks of misogyny. It is
as if males are ashamed and even resentful at being placed at the
mercy of the female sex by their most basic urges. Women are often
objectified (for example as 'a bit of skirt', 'poontang' or 'a piece of
tail') or scorned for too readily giving men what they want (as in
'floozie' or 'bike').

While there is some evidence of female reciprocation in this respect,
sexual slang remains overwhelmingly macho. Except for those trying
to start a family, procreation has been largely replaced by recreation
as the main driving force behind sex, and much sexual slang dwells
on the 'fun' aspects of the activity. If consenting adults want to 'fool

around' or have a bit of 'slap and tickle', then why should they not enjoy themselves? Though sex has its darker sides, it may be argued that the comic is often not very far away.

It should be noted that many sexual expressions are brutally frank, and some readers may find elements of this list to be offensive.

## Glossary

**a bit of all right** an attractive woman

**a bit of rough** a person, especially a man, whose unrefined manner is seen as sexually attractive

**a bit of skirt** a woman (alternatives to this include **a bit of muslin**)

**AC/DC** bisexual

**babe** an attractive woman

**bag off** to have a romantic or sexual encounter

**bagpiping** the practice of stimulating a partner's penis in one's armpit

**ball** to have sexual intercourse with

**bang** to have sexual intercourse with

**bareback** 'bareback sex' is sex without using a condom

**barrelhouse** a US term meaning to have sexual intercourse

**bash** to solicit as a prostitute

**beat** to 'beat off' or 'beat your meat' means to masturbate

**beefcake** very muscular men, considered attractive to women

**bi** bisexual

**bike** a promiscuous woman, especially in such phrases as 'the village bike'

**bishop** a man who 'bashes' or 'bangs the bishop' masturbates

**BJ** a **blowjob**

**blowjob** an act of fellatio

**boff** to have sexual intercourse with

**bone** to have sexual intercourse with

**boner** an erection of the penis

**bonk** to have sexual intercourse with

**booty call** a date, especially with a view to sex, or a phone call made to arrange this

**bootylicious** sexually attractive

**brewer's droop** inability to achieve an erection when drunk

**bring off** to 'bring someone off' is to induce an orgasm in them

**broad** a US term for a woman

**bull dyke** a masculine lesbian

**bum** to have anal intercourse with

**bump and grind** to dance erotically with exaggerated movements of the hips

**bump uglies** to have sexual intercourse

**carpet muncher** someone who engages in cunnilingus

**cathouse** a US term for a brothel

**cattle market** a place, such as a nightclub, where sexual partners are acquired without romance, sentiment or dignity

**cherry** virginity, or the hymen

**chung** sexually attractive

**cocksman** a sexually potent or active man

**cockteaser** a woman who deliberately provokes a man's sexual arousal, then refuses him sexual intercourse

**come** to 'come' or 'come off' is to experience orgasm

**come on to** to 'come on to' someone is to make sexual advances towards them

**come-to-bed eyes** eyes that seem to signal that the owner is sexually available

**cop off** to have a romantic or sexual encounter

**cottaging** the activity of soliciting in a public lavatory (a 'cottage')

**crackling** women as objects of sexual desire

**cream your jeans** to ejaculate or secrete sexual lubricants while fully dressed

**crib** a brothel

**cruise** to go round public places looking for a sexual partner

**crumpet** a woman or women collectively viewed as sexual objects (now also applied to men)

**cum** ejaculated semen

**dance the blanket hornpipe** to have sexual intercourse

**diddle** to have sexual intercourse with

**dip your wick** a man who 'dips his wick' has sexual intercourse

**do** to 'do' someone is to have sexual intercourse with them

**dogging** the activity of visiting isolated public places, usually at night, to engage in, or observe other people engaging in, sexual activity, especially in parked cars

**doggy fashion** when people have sex 'doggy fashion', the man penetrates the woman from behind

**dolly-mop** an old term for a slut or prostitute

**do the business** to have sexual intercourse

**do the horizontal mambo** to have sexual intercourse

**do the wild thing** to have sexual intercourse

**doxy** an old word for a mistress

**dyke** a lesbian

**eye** to 'give someone the eye' is to look at them in a sexually alluring way

**fanny batter** vaginal secretions

**feel** to 'feel' or 'feel up' someone is to caress their genitals

**felch** to 'felch' someone is to lick or suck ejaculated semen from their anus

**fem** or **femme** the more feminine partner in a homosexual relationship

**finger-fuck** to stimulate someone's vagina or anus using a finger

**fire blanks** a man who 'fires blanks' is infertile

**fist** or **fist-fuck** to stimulate someone's vagina or anus by inserting the whole hand into it

**flagrante delicto** in the act of sexual intercourse

**floozie** a prostitute or woman of doubtful sexual morals

**fool around** to have sexual intercourse, or indulge in sexual frolicking

**foxy** sexually attractive

**French** fellatio

**French kiss** a kiss in which the tongue is inserted into the partner's mouth

**French letter** a condom

**frig** to masturbate, or to have sex

**fruit** a homosexual

**fruity** salacious, saucy or smutty; also used to mean homosexual

**fuck** to 'fuck' is to have sexual intercourse; a 'fuck' is an act of sexual intercourse or a sexual partner

**fuck buddy** a person with whom one regularly has sexual intercourse without being in an emotional relationship

**fuck-me shoes** or **pumps** shoes considered as being sexually alluring

**gam** an act of oral sex (shortened from the French word *gamahuche* or *gamaruche*)

**gang bang** successive sexual intercourse with one female by a group of males

**gender bender** a person who for deliberate effect, publicity or amusement adopts a sexually ambiguous public image and style

**get into someone's knickers** or **pants** to seduce someone

**get it on** to 'get it on' with someone is to have sexual intercourse with them

**get it up** to achieve an erection of the penis

**get jiggy** to 'get jiggy with' someone is to have sexual intercourse with them

**get laid** to have sexual intercourse

**get off** to experience orgasm

**get off with** to 'get off with' someone is to gain their affection or have a sexual encounter with them

**get your ashes hauled** to have sexual intercourse (you might similarly **get your oats**, **get your end away** or **get your leg over**)

**get your kit off** to take off your clothes

**get your rocks off** to experience orgasm

**give head** to perform oral sex

**give one** to 'give someone one' is to have sexual intercourse with them

**glad eye** to 'give someone the glad eye' is to ogle them

**go all the way** to have full sexual intercourse

**gobble** to engage in fellatio

**go down on** to 'go down on' someone is to perform oral sex on them

**golden showers** urination on a sexual partner as a means of gratification

**gonk** a prostitute's client

**go off** to experience orgasm

**goose** to 'goose' someone is to prod them between the buttocks from behind

**Greek love** anal sex

**greens** sexual intercourse

**grind** to circle the hips erotically

**grope** to fondle someone for sexual pleasure

**handjob** an act of manually

stimulating the penis of another person

**hand relief** masturbation

**hard** 'a hard' or 'hard-on' is an erection of the penis

**have** to 'have' someone is to have sexual intercourse with them

**have it away** to have sexual intercourse

**have the hots for** to be sexually attracted to

**hickey** a US term for a lovebite, a red patch on the skin caused by a sucking kiss

**hit on** to 'hit on' someone is to make sexual advances towards them

**horn** an erection of the penis

**hornbag** an Australian term for a sexually attractive woman

**horny** sexually aroused or lustful

**hot** sexually aroused or sexually attractive

**hot pants** to 'have hot pants' for someone is to have sexual desire for them (**have the hots** means the same thing)

**hottie** a sexually attractive person

**how's your father** amorous frolicking or sexual intercourse

**hump** to have sexual

intercourse with

**hunk** a sexually attractive man

**hustler** a prostitute

**in flagrante delicto** same as **flagrante delicto**

**it** in a sexual context, 'it' can mean either sexual intercourse (as in 'do it' or 'have it') or sexual appeal

**jack off** to masturbate

**jazz** to 'jazz' someone is to have sexual intercourse with them

**jazz mag** a pornographic magazine

**jerk off** to masturbate (**jerk your peter** is a US variant of this)

**jiggy-jiggy** sexual intercourse

**jim hat** or **jimmy hat** a US term for a condom

**jism** or **jizz** semen

**johnny** a condom (see also **rubber**)

**jump** to 'jump' someone is to have sexual intercourse with them (**jump someone's bones** is a US variant of this)

**kink** an unusual sexual preference

**kinky** sexually perverted

**knee-trembler** an act of sexual intercourse in a standing position

**knob** to have sexual

intercourse with

**knock** to 'knock' or 'knock off' someone is to have sexual intercourse with them

**knocking shop** a brothel

**knock up** to 'knock up' a woman is to make her pregnant

**ladyboy** same as **shemale**

**lay** to 'lay' someone is to have sexual intercourse with them; a 'lay' is an act of sexual intercourse, or a sexual partner (as in 'a good lay')

**leg-man** a man for whom a woman's legs are her principal features of sexual attraction

**leg-over** an act of sexual intercourse

**love juice** vaginal secretions or semen

**make** to 'make' or 'make it with' someone is to have sexual intercourse with them

**make a move on** to make sexual advances to

**make out** a US term meaning to engage in lovemaking

**maneater** or **mantrap** a sexually voracious woman

**meat rack** a place where young male homosexual prostitutes gather

**muff diver** someone who engages in cunnilingus

**nail** to 'nail' someone is to have sexual intercourse with them

**naughty** an Australian and New Zealand term for an act of sexual intercourse

**nooky** or **nookie** sexual intercourse

**nympho** a nymphomaniac

**one-night stand** a sexual relationship lasting only one night

**on the pull** a person who is 'on the pull' is hoping to form a sexual relationship by frequenting places such as nightclubs or pubs

**party hat** a condom

**pick up** to 'pick someone up' is to meet and establish a sexual relationship with them

**pick-up joint** a club, bar, etc where people go meet sexual partners

**play away (from home)** to be sexually unfaithful to your partner

**play footsie** to rub your foot or leg against another person's, usually with amorous intentions

**play pocket billiards** to fondle your testicles with a hand in your trouser pocket

**play the pink oboe** to

engage in fellatio

**play with yourself** to masturbate

**poke** to have sexual intercourse with

**poontang** sexual intercourse, or women regarded sexually

**proposition** to invite someone to take part in sexual intercourse

**pudding** to 'pull your pudding' means to masturbate

**pull** to 'pull' someone is to succeed in forming a sexual relationship with them

**pussy** sexual intercourse, or a woman considered as a sexual object

**put out** someone, especially a woman, who 'puts out' is willing to grant sexual favours

**put the make on** to make sexual advances to

**quickie** a hurried act of sexual intercourse

**randy** sexually excited

**red-light district** an area where prostitutes work

**rent boy** a young male prostitute

**ride** to 'ride' someone is to have sex with them; a 'ride' is an act of sexual intercourse or a sexual partner (especially female)

**rim** to stimulate the anus, especially orally

**roasting** a form of group sexual activity in which a person is penetrated in more than one orifice at the same time

**roger** if a man 'rogers' a woman, he has sex with her

**roll** a North American term meaning to have sexual intercourse with

**roll in the hay** a charmingly rustic euphemism for a sexual encounter

**root** an Australian and New Zealand term meaning to have sexual intercourse

**rough trade** violent or sadistic male prostitutes or sexual encounters

**rubber** or **rubber johnny** a condom

**rumpy-pumpy** sexual intercourse, especially when casual or playful

**safe** a North American term for a condom

**S and M** sadomasochistic practices

**score** to succeed in finding a sexual partner

**screw** to have sexual intercourse with

**screw around** to have

many sexual partners

**scumbag** a US term for a condom

**sex kitten** a young woman who mischievously plays up her sex appeal

**sex on legs** a person who is regarded as extremely attractive or desirable (if the person is tall, the variant **sex on a stick** may be used)

**sexpot** a person of very great or obvious physical attraction

**shaft** to have sexual intercourse with

**shag** to have sexual intercourse with

**shagger** a person who engages in sexual intercourse

**shag-me shoes** same as **fuck-me shoes**

**shemale** a person, born a male, who has acquired female physical characteristics as a result of hormone treatment but has not had surgery to remove the male genitals

**shoot blanks** same as **fire blanks**

**shtup** to have sexual intercourse with

**sixty-nine** a sexual position in which both partners simultaneously orally stimulate each other's genitals (from the similarity of the position to the shape of the figure 69)

**skeet** to ejaculate

**slack** sexually promiscuous

**slap and tickle** amorous frolicking

**sleep with** to have sexual intercourse with

**sloppy seconds** sexual intercourse with a woman who has just had sex with someone else

**smacker** an enthusiastic or exaggerated kiss

**smack the pony** if a woman 'smacks the pony', she masturbates

**snog** to embrace, cuddle, kiss or indulge in lovemaking

**soap** girls or women considered collectively as sex objects

**soapland** a red-light district

**soixante-neuf** the French equivalent of **sixty-nine**

**something for the weekend** a packet of condoms

**spank the monkey** if a man 'spanks the monkey', he masturbates

**spooge** a US term for semen

**spunk** semen

**stiffy** or **stiffie** an erect penis

**straight** heterosexual

**stud** a sexually potent or active man

**studly** sexually potent

**stud muffin** a US term for a sexually attractive young man

**stuff** to have sexual intercourse with

**suck face** to kiss

**suck off** to perform fellatio or cunnilingus on

**swap spit** to take part in French kissing

**swing** to take part in sexual activity on an uncommitted basis

**swing both ways** to be bisexual

**switch hitter** a US term for a bisexual person

**tit-man** a man for whom a woman's breasts are her principal features of sexual attraction

**titty-bar** a bar where the female staff are topless

**tonsil hockey** French kissing

**toss** to 'toss' or 'toss off' is to masturbate

**touch up** to caress, touch or molest sexually

**wank** to masturbate

**water sports** same as **golden showers**

**well-hung** a man who is 'well-hung' has sizeable genitals

**whack off** to masturbate

**wham bam thank you ma'am** quick impersonal sexual intercourse that brings speedy gratification to the male

**whoopee** to 'make whoopee' is to make love

**yodel in the canyon** engage in cunnilingus

## *Relationships*

Society is built on relationships between individuals, and the slang of any society will reflect this. Some relationships we are born into, as someone's 'sprog' (maybe even 'a chip off the old block'), and some we will create through having a family of our own (turning into 'rents' or someone's 'pappy'). Other relationships are largely elective – they say you can choose your friends but you can't choose your relations – and these include your girlfriend or boyfriend ('bird' or 'boyf'), who might become a marriage partner ('the missis' or the 'old man'), and, of course, your 'buddies'.

Some of the more traditional terms for relationships seem rather old-fashioned in this age of political correctness, and it would be more PC, for example, to refer to your 'significant other' rather than your 'tart'. Relationships between the sexes are perhaps more fluid in the 21st century than ever before. The traditional long-term marriage, with 'two point four children', is increasingly rare and new slang terms may have to be coined to cover modern developments. After all, what *do* you call the person who is your partner without being married? And what about that person's children from a previous relationship who now live with you?

## Glossary

**a bit on the side** extramarital sexual relations, or someone's partner in these

**air kiss** a greeting in which a person performs a simulated kiss but does not touch the other person's face

**arm candy** someone who is invited as a partner to a social event more to add to the glamour of the occasion than for their sparkling conversational skills

**babe** a girl or girlfriend

**bachelor pad** a flat or other residence for an unmarried person

**bag off** same as **cop off**

**beard** a woman who escorts a homosexual man in public to give the impression that he is heterosexual

**better half** a person's 'better half' is their spouse

**bidie-in** a Scottish term for a person's resident lover

**bird** a girlfriend

**boomerang** a young person who, having left the parental home, returns to live there

**boyf** a boyfriend

**bro** and **bruv** both of these terms mean 'brother', but they are often used as affectionate terms of address between males

**buddy** a friend

**cheat on** someone who 'cheats on' their partner is unfaithful to them

**chip off the old block** someone with the characteristics of (usually one of) their parents

**chuck** if you 'chuck' someone, you end your relationship with them

**cohab** someone with whom a person lives together as husband and wife without actually being married (short for 'cohabitee')

**cop off** to have a romantic or sexual encounter

**cradle-snatcher** a person who chooses someone much younger than themselves as a lover or marriage partner

**crush** to 'have a crush on' someone is to be infatuated with them

**dinky** a member of a young, childless couple both earning a high salary and enjoying an affluent lifestyle (from the initial letters of 'double income no kids yet')

**dude** a person; also used as an informal form of address

**dump** if you 'dump' someone, you end your relationship with them

**dumpsville** the hypothetical abode of those who have been 'dumped'

**empty-nester** a parent whose children have left the parental home

**ex** a former partner

**fancy bit** same as **fancy woman**

**fancy man** a woman's lover

**fancy woman** a man's mistress

**fella** a boyfriend

**fling** a brief sexual relationship

**folks** a person's family

**give someone the heave** to end a relationship with someone (alternative items that such an unfortunate may be given include **the old heave-ho**, **the boot** and **the elbow**)

**gone on** infatuated with

**go steady** if you are 'going steady' with someone, you go out regularly together as a couple

**go with** if you are 'going with' someone, you are having a relationship with them

**heart-throb** a person who is the object of great romantic affection from afar

**homeboy** or **homegirl** a friend, especially from your own neighbourhood (often shortened to **homie**)

**hook up** to meet, especially by arrangement

**hubby** a person's husband

**in-laws** relatives by marriage

**intended** someone's 'intended' is their fiancé(e)

**item** two people who are described as 'an item' are in a relationship

**misfortune** an old term for an illegitimate child

**missis** or **missus** a person's wife (often referred to as **the missis**)

**mom** a North American term for 'mother'

**mucker** a best friend or sidekick

**old man** someone's 'old man' is their father or husband (**old boy** is also commonly used)

**old woman** someone's 'old woman' is their mother or wife (**old girl** is also commonly used)

**pappy**, **pop** and **poppa** US terms for father

**rellies** an Australian and New Zealand term for a person's relatives

**rents** 'the rents' are a person's parents

**shack up** to live together as sexual partners

**sidekick** a partner or special friend

**significant other** someone's 'significant other' is their sexual partner

**singleton** a person who is not in a relationship

**sis** a sister

**soccer mom** a US term for a mother who dedicates many hours to driving her children to, and supporting them at, organized recreational activities

**soft spot** if you 'have a soft spot' for someone, you feel affectionate towards them

**spit** someone who is 'the spit', 'the dead spit', 'the very spit' or 'the spitting image' of someone else, especially a relation, is very like the other person

**spoken for** a person who is 'spoken for' is not free or single

**sprog** a child

**squeeze** a person's girlfriend or boyfriend

**stand up** if you 'stand someone up', you fail to appear for an arranged date

**steady** a regular boyfriend or girlfriend

**stuck on** enamoured of

**sweetie** or **sweety**

someone's 'sweetie' is their
beloved
**sweet on** enamoured of
**tart** a girlfriend
**trouble and strife** a wife
(rhyming slang)
**two point four children**
the archetypal size of the
conventional nuclear family

**unc** an uncle
**walker** a US term for a man
of good social standing who
accompanies a woman VIP on
official engagements in the
absence of her husband
**yummy mummy** a young
mother who is regarded as
sexually attractive

## *Illness*

Unless we are particularly healthy or fortunate, we all get ill from
time to time. Those of us not in the medical profession need layman's
terms for the various conditions that might bedevil us, and this is
often where slang comes in to fill the gap. There is no reason to
struggle with the spelling or pronunciation of diarrhoea when 'the
runs' is at your fingertips. No need to worry about what particular
infection may have laid you low when you know that there is a 'bug'
going round. Even if you are rather unsure about your own symptoms,
you can always describe your trouble as 'the dreaded lurgi', or even
'dog's disease'. Such vagueness, however, would be inadvisable when
informing your place of work that you are taking a 'sickie'. And
how else would relative strangers drive a conversation (once the
weather had been exhausted as a topic) if they could not discuss their
respective ailments or the terrible afflictions that had befallen their
acquaintances?

One danger in such exchanges is that of exaggeration. Many of us
will have had 'a bit of a throat' or felt 'all-overish', a little 'ropey' or
'under the weather', but what if your interlocutor claims to be 'in a
bad way'? In your determination not to come out of the exchange
looking like a wimp, you would have no choice but to raise the stakes
to having 'caught your death'.

## Glossary

**all-overish** someone who feels 'all-overish' has an indefinite sense of indisposition

**Aztec two-step** diarrhoea (a variation on **Montezuma's revenge**)

**basket case** a person with all four limbs amputated

**big C** 'the big C' is a euphemism for cancer

**bug** a viral disease

**catch your death (of cold)** to contract a severe cold

**chemo** chemotherapy

**chesty** someone who is 'chesty' is susceptible to disease of the chest

**clap** 'the clap' is gonorrhoea

**clotbuster** any drug used to dissolve blood clots

**collywobbles** abdominal pain or disorder, or simply a nervous stomach

**crabs** someone who has 'crabs' is infested with crab-lice

**crook** an Australian and New Zealand term meaning 'ill'

**death** someone who feels or looks 'like death' or 'like death warmed up' feels or looks very ill indeed

**Delhi belly** diarrhoea, especially as suffered by people visiting India and other developing countries

**dog's disease** an Australian term for any minor ailment, especially influenza

**dose** a 'dose' is an instance of infection with a sexually transmitted disease, especially gonorrhoea

**DTs** someone who has 'the DTs' is suffering from delirium tremens

**flu** influenza

**fluey** someone who feels 'fluey' is experiencing the symptoms of influenza

**gathering** a suppurating swelling, boil or abscess

**ghastly** someone who feels or looks 'ghastly' feels or looks very ill

**gippy** or **gyppy tummy** diarrhoea, a severely upset stomach, thought of as a hazard of holidaying in hot countries

**go down with** to 'go down with' an illness means to contract it

**green about the gills** looking or feeling sick

**gutrot** a stomach upset

**head** someone who says

they have 'a head' or 'one of my heads' is complaining of headache

**heaves** if you have 'the heaves' you are suffering from stomach cramps and nausea

**in a bad way** seriously ill

**jimjams** someone who has 'the jimjams' is suffering from delirium tremens

**kill** if a part of someone's body is 'killing' them, it is causing them great pain

**kissing disease** glandular fever

**lurgy** or **lurgi** any non-specific disease, often in the phrase 'the dreaded lurgy'

**mono** glandular fever (a short form of the technical term 'infectious mononucleosis')

**Montezuma's revenge** diarrhoea, especially caused by travelling in Mexico or eating Mexican food (after Montezuma, the last Aztec emperor of Mexico, who was deposed by the Spanish conquistadors)

**play up** if an impaired part of the body 'plays up', it gives trouble or pain

**pox** syphilis

**rainbow** a highly discoloured bruise

**ropey** if you feel 'ropey', you feel slightly unwell

**runs** 'the runs' is another name for diarrhoea

**shits** 'the shits' is another name for diarrhoea

**shock** a stroke of paralysis

**sickie** a day's sick leave

**skitters** 'the skitters' is another name for diarrhoea

**splitter** someone who has a 'splitter' is suffering from a splitting headache

**squits** or **squitters** 'the squits' and 'the squitters' are names for diarrhoea

**strep** or **strep throat** an acute streptococcal infection of the throat

**throat** someone who says they have 'a throat' or 'a bit of a throat' means that they have a sore throat

**trots** 'the trots' is another name for diarrhoea

**under the weather** indisposed

**virus** when people say they have 'a virus', they really mean a disease caused by a virus

**wog** an Australian term for any germ, bug, infection or illness

**yellow jack** an old name for yellow fever

**zit** a spot or pimple

## Death

Death, which some call the last taboo, is very much the province of euphemism. Those who prefer not to confront head-on the ultimate reality that awaits us all may soften the blow by thinking of death in terms of 'cashing in your chips', 'dropping off the perch' or 'passing away'. Many religious believers take comfort in the conviction that this life is not the only one and prefer to speak of the end of your mortal existence as 'going to meet your maker', leaving for the 'happy hunting-ground' or 'joining the choir invisible'. Others are more blunt and are unafraid to talk of 'snuffing it' or 'kicking the bucket'. In many of the slang expressions concerning death there is an obvious element of treating the whole thing lightly as a means of diminishing its power to terrify us. This is particularly marked among the armed forces (whose acquaintance with death is necessarily more intimate and regular than that of most people) and it is to military sources that we owe such expressions as 'gone for a Burton' and 'buy it'.

### Glossary

**bite the dust** to fall down dead

**brown bread** dead (rhyming slang)

**Burton** in the RAF, if a flier or aircraft has 'gone for a Burton', this means they are dead or destroyed

**burn** to 'burn' someone is to cremate them

**buy it** or **buy the farm** to be killed

**chips** if you 'cash in your chips', you die; if you have 'had your chips' (albeit chips of a different variety), you are either dead or dying

**croak** to die

**curtains** if it's 'curtains for' someone, this means they are about to die

**dead as a dodo** unequivocally dead

**dead duck** a person who cannot survive long

**dead meat** if someone is 'dead meat', they are doomed to die

**deep-six** a US term meaning to kill or bury someone

**departed** 'the departed' or

'the dearly departed' are the dead

**die with your boots on** to die while still working (**die in harness** means the same thing)

**done for** dead or doomed

**drop off the perch** or **twig** to die

**exchange this life for a better one** to die

**fall off the perch** or **twig** to die

**go belly-up** to die

**goner** someone who is dying or seems certain to die

**go to meet your maker** to die

**go west** to die

**had it** someone who has 'had it' is either dead or soon to be so

**happy hunting-ground** the imagined destination for the souls of the dead in Native American culture

**heading for the last roundup** a US term used to mean 'dying' (obviously associated with cowboys in particular)

**in the sky** heaven, or the afterlife, is often described in terms of a particular place 'in the sky', with the precise description tailored to suit the individual involved (for example, a dead rock musician may be said to have 'gone to join the big jam session in the sky' or an American football player may be said to be 'playing on the big gridiron in the sky')

**join the choir invisible** to die

**join the majority** to die

**kick the bucket** or **kick it** to die

**knocking on heaven's door** dying

**meet a sticky end** to die in unpleasant circumstances

**not long for this world** dying

**number** if your 'number is up', you have not long to live

**one foot in the grave** if you have 'one foot in the grave', you are on the brink of death

**on your last legs** about to die

**pass away** or **on** to die

**peg out** or **peg it** to die

**plant** to 'plant' someone is to bury them

**pop your clogs** to die

**pushing up daisies** dead and buried

**quit the scene** to die

**shuffle off this mortal coil** to die (originally from a line in Shakespeare's *Hamlet*)

**six feet under** dead and buried (from the traditional depth of a grave)

**snuff it** to die

**stiff** a dead body

**toast** if a person is told 'you are toast', this means that they are about to die (although the speaker may not have quite such a severe punishment in mind)

**turn up your toes** to die

**wooden overcoat** a coffin

**worm food** someone who, if not already dead, soon will be

## *Insanity*

Why is it such an insult to bring a person's sanity into question? No-one likes to be called a 'loony' or 'dingbat', let alone to be stigmatized with the more extreme 'nutcase' or 'psycho'. We must really prize the condition of being compos mentis to be so touchy about having it doubted. Perhaps it is something to do with our mental state being intimately connected with our personal identity, and the idea that to lose your sanity is to lose your sense of yourself. While insanity is obviously to be feared, and is to a great extent shunned in others, much of the slang connected with this state has humorous overtones. It is easy to make fun of those afflicted; indeed, as late as the 18th century, a trip to the Bethlehem Royal Hospital in London (a 'madhouse' from whose name 'bedlam' is derived) was considered a form of entertainment. People often joke about the things they fear, as if to diminish them, to make them appear more laughable than frightening. No doubt it is to this tendency that we owe psychiatric hospitals being labelled as the 'bughouse', the 'funny farm' or the 'laughing academy'. As with many fields of slang, the more extreme terms are often bandied about in fun and not intended to be taken literally. Even slightly eccentric behaviour will result in someone's being told 'you're mad, you are' or being called a 'looney tune' or, in more recent slang, a 'mentalist'.

## Glossary

**a brick short of a load** slightly mad

**away with the fairies** in a state of abstraction

**bananas** to 'be bananas' or 'go bananas' is to be or become crazy

**barking** or **barking mad** quite mad

**barmy** mentally unsound

**basket case** a nervous wreck

**bats** someone who has 'bats in the belfry' is slightly mad (this is often shortened to describing the person as **bats** or **batty**)

**bonkers** crazy

**booby hatch** a psychiatric hospital

**buggy** slightly mad

**bughouse** a hospital or asylum for the mentally ill

**crackbrain** or **crackpot** a crazy person

**cracked** crazy

**crackers** crazy, unbalanced

**crack up** to suffer a mental breakdown

**cuckoo** slightly mad

**daft as a brush** slightly crazy or eccentric

**dingbat** a foolish or eccentric person

**dippy** insane

**ditz** an eccentric or scatterbrained person

**ditsy** or **ditzy** amiably eccentric or scatterbrained

**doolally** mentally unbalanced (originally services' slang, referring to the town of Deolali, near Mumbai)

**flake** a North American term for an eccentric or crazy person (perhaps shortened from 'cornflake', meaning the same thing)

**fruitcake** a slightly mad person

**funny farm** a hospital or asylum for the mentally ill

**geek** a strange or eccentric person

**go ape** or **apeshit** to go crazy

**go mental** to become mentally unbalanced

**go nuts** to go crazy

**harpic** crazy (Harpic is a proprietary brand of lavatory cleaning fluid, in whose advertising the phrase 'clean round the bend' was used)

**have a screw loose** to be slightly mentally deranged (a variation of this is **have**

a slate loose)

**headcase** a crazy person

**headshrinker** a psychiatrist

**kinky** eccentric or crazy

**kook** a mad or eccentric person

**kooky** eccentric

**laughing academy** a hospital or asylum for the mentally ill

**loco** crazy or mad (originally in US usage, from a Spanish word)

**looney tune** an insane person (from the name of a series of madcap cartoon films made by Warner Brothers)

**loony** a lunatic or mad person (often shortened to **loon**)

**loony bin** a hospital or asylum for the mentally ill

**loopy** slightly crazy

**lose your marbles** to go insane (other things you might similarly lose include **the plot** and, in Scotland, **the place**)

**men in white coats** employees of a psychiatric hospital, often said to be 'coming to take you away'

**mental** mentally unbalanced

**mentalist** someone who is insane

**not all there** not having all of your mental faculties intact

**not playing with a full deck** not having all of your mental faculties intact

**not the full shilling** not having all of your mental faculties intact

**nut** a crazy person (**nutter**, **nutcase** and **nutjob** are variations of this)

**nuthatch** or **nuthouse** a hospital or asylum for the mentally ill

**nutty** mentally unhinged, sometimes in the phrase 'as nutty as a fruitcake'

**oddball** an eccentric person

**off your head** mentally unhinged (you might also be **off your chump**, **off your nut**, **off your onion**, **off your rocker** or **off your trolley**)

**one sandwich short of a picnic** not having all of your mental faculties intact

**out of your skull** insane

**out of your tree** insane

**psycho** a psychopath

**round the bend** or **twist** insane

**schizo** a schizophrenic

**screwball** an eccentric or crazy person

**screwy** eccentric or slightly mad

**shrink** a psychiatrist (shortened from 'headshrinker')
**sicko** a mentally ill person
**spot the loony** an exclamation casting aspersions on someone's sanity, based on something they have just done
**squirrel ranch** or **tank** a US term for the psychiatric ward of a prison
**the lift** (or **elevator**) **doesn't go all the way to the top floor** this person is not of normal intelligence
**the lights are on but nobody's home** this person is not of normal intelligence
**trick cyclist** a psychiatrist
**wacky** crazy

# *Television*

There can be no doubt that one of the most influential innovations of the 20th century was television. By the end of the century, watching TV had become the number one pastime throughout the developed world. In the 21st century it increasingly dominates our lives, with more channels and more ways of receiving them becoming available than ever before (even if it is still possible for the fussy to complain that there is 'nothing on'). You can even watch programmes on your mobile phone. No wonder its slang is so pervasive.

Critics of the 'couch potato' point out that generations are growing up who identify more with characters in 'soaps' than with the real human beings who are living next door, taking cues for their behaviour from the denizens of Walford or Weatherfield rather than from real life. Public opinion is more readily swayed by 'talking heads' or participants in a chat show than by the leader columns of the national press.

Television not only has its own slang, it is also the most wide-reaching medium by which general slang is spread around a country. Terms like 'gobsmacked' and 'minging' would probably have remained (at least for longer) in the areas where they were first used had it not been for their extensive use on the 'goggle-box'. When television broadcasts were first made, a Reithian formality was the order of the day, with presenters speaking in the kind of clipped tones that few outside the older members of the Royal Family would now naturally use. For better or worse, 'BBC English' has been replaced by regional accents and glottal stops – even, heaven forfend, in the national news.

## Glossary

**Auntie** a facetious name for the BBC

**Beeb** 'the Beeb' is a nickname for the BBC

**boob tube** a television set

**box** a television set

**car-crash television** televised material that is disturbing or shocking but at the same time so compelling that the viewer cannot help but watch it

**channel-surf** to switch rapidly between different television channels in a forlorn attempt to find anything of interest

**couch potato** a person whose leisure time is spent sitting shiftlessly in front of the television

**council telly** the main terrestrial television channels only, as opposed to digital or satellite channels

**gag show** a comedy programme

**give it up for** an adjuration much used by TV show hosts, inviting the studio audience to show their appreciation of a performer by cheering or applause

**God slot** a regular spot during the broadcasting schedules for religious programmes

**goggle-box** a television set

**goggler** an avid television viewer

**idiot box** or **idiot's lantern** a television set

**noddy** a sequence in a filmed interview in which the interviewer is photographed nodding in acknowledgement of what the interviewee is saying

**side** a television channel, as in the question 'what's on the other side?'

**sitcom** a situation comedy

**small screen** 'the small

screen' refers to television as opposed to the cinema (which is 'the big screen')

**soap** a soap opera, a sentimental, melodramatic serial concerned with the day-to-day lives of a familly or other small group

**square eyes** an imaginary condition affecting those who watch too much television

**sudser** a soap opera

**talking head** a person talking on television, viewed in close-up

**teaser** a short sequence from a programme shown before the opening titles, to whet the viewer's appetite

**telly** television

**trail** a trailer, a short sequence advertising a forthcoming programme

**tube** a television set

**vee-jay** or **veejay** a broadcaster who introduces and plays music videos (a phonetic spelling of the initials 'VJ', for 'video jockey')

**water-cooler moment** a particularly memorable moment during a television programme (so called because it is likely to be a source of conversation on the following day for workers getting a drink at the office water cooler)

**zap** to change TV channels using a remote control device ('a zapper')

**Part Three**

# Slang of Particular Places and Times

# SLANG IN ENGLISH-SPEAKING COUNTRIES AROUND THE WORLD

## United States slang

US slang is probably the most widely known slang in the world, such has been the dominance throughout the 20th century and into the 21st of American culture – largely through cinema and TV, but also in books, comics and popular music. Once exposed to a wider audience, many American terms quickly become adopted into the slang of other English-speaking countries. Terms like 'buff', 'cool' or 'dude' will be heard from Belfast to Brisbane. However, it is interesting to note that many US terms do not seem to travel. For example 'badass' is perfectly familiar to fans of US films or TV shows in Britain, but no UK teenager would use it seriously. Perhaps the 'ass' element makes it too obviously an American import, and to anglify it into 'badarse' would just be ridiculous. Many other US slang terms are too closely identified with things that are too idiosyncratically American to make any sense elsewhere. Examples of this include 'bobbysoxer', 'cookiepusher' and 'John Hancock'.

The influences on American slang are too numerous and various to go into here, but it has to be noted that the waves of immigration to the United States in the 19th and 20th centuries have left, and continue to leave, their mark (eg 'baloney', 'buttinski' and 'la Migra'), with the Yiddish input remaining particularly strong (as seen in 'mamzer', 'mavin', 'putz' and 'schnorrer'). Many US terms will be found in the lists throughout this book, and the list below does not attempt to include all of these; rather, it serves a useful home for terms not covered elsewhere.

## Glossary

**about east** an old term meaning correctly

**and how!** yes, certainly; very much indeed

**and then some** and even more

**asswipe** a despicable person

**badass** an aggressive or difficult person

**ball-breaker** or **ball-buster** a person or task that is excessively demanding, or a woman who is ruthless, demanding or demoralizing in her treatment of men

**ballsy** gutsy, tough and courageous

**baloney** Bologna sausage, or nonsense

**bazoo** the mouth

**beanery** a cheap restaurant

**belly up to** to go directly or purposefully towards, as in the phrase 'belly up to the bar, boys'

**bent out of shape** angry or upset

**Big Board** the New York Stock Exchange

**big house** 'the big house' is a prison

**big-ticket** expensive

**bindle** a small paper packet

containing an illegal drug

**bite me!** an expression conveying derision, contemptuous dismissal, etc

**bloviate** to speak arrogantly or pompously

**bo** a familiar term of address for a man

**bobbysoxer** an adolescent girl or teenager (from 'bobby socks', ankle-length socks worn, especially formerly, by such girls)

**bodacious** extremely good or marvellous

**bomb** to flop or fail

**booger** a piece of nasal mucus

**boost** to steal (especially to shoplift)

**booster** a shoplifter

**bozo** a fellow or man, especially a dim-witted one

**brewski** a beer

**bs** abbreviation for bullshit, ie nonsense

**buck** a dollar

**bull** a policeman

**bull fiddle** a double bass

**bummed** disappointed or dejected

**burb** a suburb

**burg** a town

**burned up** angry

**butterball** a chubby person

**buttinski** a person who 'butts in' to someone else's business

**buttoned-down** conservative, especially in dress or behaviour

**butt out** to refrain from interfering

**call down** to 'call down' a person is to reprove them angrily

**can** 'the can' is the lavatory

**candy-ass** a weak or feeble person

**car-hop** a waiter or waitress at a drive-in restaurant

**cheaters** an old term for a pair of spectacles

**chewed up** destroyed, defeated or reprimanded

**chickenshit** cowardly

**chorine** a chorus girl

**chump change** an insignificant or insultingly small amount of money

**clam** a dollar

**cockamamie** ridiculous or incredible

**coldcock** to hit someone hard over the head, often knocking them unconscious

**cookiepusher** an effeminate man or sycophant

**cooze** the female genitals, or a woman considered as a sexual object, especially with the suggestion of promiscuity

**copacetic** sound, satisfactory or excellent

**cornflake** an eccentric or crazy person

**cotton-picking** a mildly pejorative intensifying adjective

**cow college** a college in a remote rural area

**coyote** a person who imports or exploits illegal immigrants, especially from Mexico

**critter** a creature, animal

**crock of shit** something considered worthless or nonsense (often now shortened to **crock**)

**crunk** or **crunked** in a state of excitement or intoxication

**cupcake** an attractive woman

**cussword** a swearword

**diddly-squat** nothing at all

**dirtball** a person with few or no scruples

**douche-bag** a despicable person

**down-and-dirty** basic or brutal

**down-home** homely, rustic or rural

**druthers** your 'druthers' are what you would prefer

(shortened and changed from 'I'd rather')

**duck soup** something very easy to do or handle

**dumb-ass** a stupid person

**dweeb** a fool or nerd

**eighty-six** to 'eighty-six' someone or something is to destroy, dismiss or eject them (originally a code term used in bars and restaurants, signifying that a menu item was no longer available or that a troublesome customer should be thrown out)

**fall guy** a dupe or scapegoat

**fanny** the buttocks

**fanny pack** a small bag worn on a belt round the waist

**fat city** easy circumstances or prosperous conditions

**fender bender** a collision between motor vehicles in which little damage is done

**fess up** to confess

**flake** an eccentric or crazy person

**flaky** eccentric or crazy

**fraidy cat** a coward

**full-court press** maximum effort (a basketball metaphor)

**gabfest** an occasion of much talking or gossip

**get bent!** an expression conveying derision, contemptuous dismissal, etc

**gimmies** someone who is excessively concerned with acquiring money may be said to have 'the gimmies' (from the phrase 'give me')

**gimp** a lame person; also used to mean a person who takes a submissive role in sadomasochistic sexual activities

**glom** to snatch or steal

**go figure!** make an effort to understand or explain something puzzling

**goldbrick** someone who shirks work

**gone goose** or **gosling** a hopeless case

**goop** a fool or a rude person; also used to mean an unpleasantly sticky or gooey substance

**GOP** Grand Old Party, the Republican Party

**go to bat for** to defend or take the side of someone (a baseball metaphor)

**gravel** to irritate

**greenback** a banknote, especially a dollar bill

**grifter** a swindler

**grody** dirty, disgusting or inferior

**guck** gooey muck or anything unpleasant

**gyp** to swindle or cheat

**gyrene** an old name for a US Marine

**hang** to spend time with your friends

**have it going on** someone who 'has got it going on' is fashionable or attractive

**have rocks in your head** to lack brains

**heat** 'the heat' is the police

**heinie** the buttocks (from 'hind end')

**hellacious** this can mean both very bad and excellent

**hincty** snobbish, conceited or vain

**hinky** anxious or arousing suspicion

**hog heaven** a condition of supreme happiness, contentment or pleasure

**hog-wild** so angry, excited, etc that you are out of control

**honcho** a boss (from a Japanese word)

**hoop-la** pointless activity or nonsense

**hooters** female breasts

**horn** 'the horn' is the telephone

**hubba hubba** an interjection expressing approval, enthusiasm, pleasure, etc

**hurting** someone who is 'hurting' is in pain or in difficulties

**in a pig's eye!** an exclamation conveying disbelief or refusal (some people substitute 'ass' or another part of the porcine anatomy)

**in spades** extremely, emphatically or to a great extent

**jack** or **jack shit** nothing at all

**jane** a woman

**jarhead** a US Marine

**jawboning** governmental urging of industry to restrict wage increases, accept restraints, etc

**jay** stupid or unsophisticated

**jerk-off** a worthless, contemptible person

**jim-dandy** fine or excellent

**jitney** an old name for a five-cent piece

**jock** a male athlete

**john** the toilet

**John Hancock** your 'John Hancock' is your signature (from one of the prominent signatories of the US Declaration of Independence)

**joint** the penis

**jughead** a stupid person

**juice** alcoholic drink

**juiced** drunk

**juvie** a detention centre for juvenile offenders

**kale** money

**keister** the buttocks

**kicker** an unexpected, especially disadvantageous, turn of events

**kike** a Jew

**like gangbusters** with great speed, impact or effectiveness

**live high on the hog** to live in comfort or luxury

**luck out** to have a piece of good luck

**lunk** or **lunkhead** a fool

**make like** to behave like

**make out like a bandit** to be extremely successful

**make time with** to court or flirt with

**make with** to produce or supply

**mall rat** a young person who spends too much of their time in shopping malls

**mamzer** a detestable or untrustworthy person (from Yiddish)

**mavin** or **maven** an expert (from Yiddish)

**meatball** or **meathead** a stupid person

**megillah** a long or tedious account

**Migra** among Spanish-speaking Americans, 'la Migra' refers to the US immigration authorities

**mondo** extremely or absolutely

**money grab** an opportunity to gain a lot of money in return for little effort

**mook** a foolish or incompetent person

**moon-eyed** drunk

**more bang for your buck** better value for money

**mouse-milking** the pursuit of any project requiring considerable time and money but yielding little profit

**mushmouth** a person who slurs or mumbles in speaking

**my bad** an expression used to admit that you have made a mistake or somehow transgressed

**narc** a narcotics agent

**no-brainer** something entailing no great mental effort

**nooner** any activity undertaken during the lunch break, especially an illicit sexual encounter

**numbnuts** a stupid person

**on the fritz** out of order, not working properly

**on the lam** escaping or running away

**on the money** spot-on or just right

**on the outs** people who are 'on the outs' have fallen out with each other

**palooka** a stupid or clumsy man

**patsy** an easy victim or scapegoat

**pecker** the penis

**peckerwood** a white person from the rural south

**pen** a prison (a shortened form of 'penitentiary')

**picayune** petty

**pissed** annoyed

**pooped** exhausted or out of breath

**preemie** a premature baby

**putz** a penis; also used to mean a stupid person

**R & R** rest and relaxation (or recreation)

**res** or **rez** a Native American reservation

**roomie** a roommate

**sad sack** a person who seems to attract mishap or disaster

**sauce** alcoholic drink

**schlimazel** a persistently unlucky person (like the following words beginning with 'sch-', this comes from Yiddish)

**schlock** something of inferior quality

**schlong** the penis

**schmeck** a taste or sniff

**schmo** a stupid person

**schmuck** a penis; also used to mean a stupid person

**schnook** a pathetic, timid or unfortunate person

**schnorrer** a scrounger or beggar

**scuzzbag** or **scuzzball** an unpleasant or despicable person

**scuzzy** dirty, seedy or unpleasant

**shoot the breeze** to chat informally

**simoleon** an old term for a dollar

**skank** a woman who is unattractive but sexually available

**skivvies** men's underwear

**slanger** a dealer in illegal drugs

**snit** a fit of bad temper or sulking

**snow** to mislead someone or persuade them by flattery

**snowjob** an act of 'snowing' someone

**s.o.b.** an abbreviation of **sonofabitch**

**sonofabitch** an abusive term of address or description

**sorry-assed** pathetic or unfortunate

**stand-up guy** a person who is moral, honest and dependable

**straight arrow** a person who is honest and dependable

**stumblebum** an awkward or inept person

**suck face** to kiss

**sweat** to 'sweat' something is to worry over it

**take a hike!** go away

**tank** to fail, especially at great cost

**that ain't hay** that is no insignificant matter or amount

**the whole nine yards** everything

**ticked off** annoyed

**total** to kill or destroy completely

**tush** or **tushie** the buttocks (from a Yiddish word)

**wack** bad or extreme

**way to go** an interjection expressing approval or agreement

**wazoo** the anus

**wetback** a Mexican illegal immigrant (imagined as having swum or waded across the Rio Grande)

**whizz** to urinate

**wig out** to go crazy

**wingding** a wild party

**wiseass** an irritatingly clever person

**worrywart** someone who worries too much

**yada, yada, yada** tiresome, persistent or meaningless chatter; often used to mean 'and so on'

**ying-yang** the anus

**zing** to criticize or scorn

**zinger** something excellent, clever or surprising

**zip** nothing

## *Canadian slang*

It should be borne in mind that many of the expressions listed under US slang are equally familiar north of that very long and porous border. Everyday slang in Canada is peppered with terms borrowed directly from its larger and culturally dominant neighbour and

Canadians use them unthinkingly as part of their own natural speech. This process became increasingly marked as the 20th century unfolded and Canada's political ties with the 'mother country' of Great Britain were loosened, to be replaced by economic and cultural links with the USA.

This list accordingly concentrates on items that can be identified as peculiarly Canadian. This includes slang terms for things that are Canadian only (such as 'bluenose', 'Gouge and Screw Tax' or 'toonie') as well as specifically Canadian terms for things familiar elsewhere (such as 'flat', 'jam buster' or 'moccasin telegraph'). One specific element of Canadian life that is reflected in the slang is the fact that, owing to its varied imperial history, a large part of the country and population speaks French as its first language. This has come to mean that slang terms of French origin are used in Canadian English, for example 'dep' and 'hab'. Also, as slang often comes into its own as a way of labelling people who are 'different', there are many terms used to designate a French-Canadian person, from 'Frog' to 'pea-souper'. No doubt the variety of French spoken in Quebec contains many words for anglophones, but these are not the province of this book

## Glossary

**baby bonus** family allowance

**bluenose** a native of Nova Scotia

**Canajan** Canadian English

**Canuck** a French-Canadian person

**chippy** touchy, quarrelsome or aggressive

**dep** in Quebec, a 'dep' is a corner shop (from the French word *depanneur*)

**dig** a hard-working student

**double-double** a coffee containing two portions or cream and two sugars

**flat** a case of twenty-four bottles of beer

**forty-pounder** a bottle of spirits with a capacity of forty ounces

**Frog** a French-Canadian person

**garburator** a waste-disposal unit below a kitchen sink

**gorbie** a credulous or ignorant tourist

**Gouge and Screw Tax** Goods and Services Tax, a widely unpopular value-added tax (also called **Grab and Steal Tax**)

**Grit** a member of the Liberal Party

**hab** a tenant farmer or sharecropper (from the French word *habitant*, meaning 'inhabitant')

**Habs** 'The Habs' is the nickname for the Montreal Canadiens ice-hockey team

**Here Before Christ** the Hudson's Bay Company (a nickname based on the company's initials and playing on its longevity)

**hitch** a term of service in the armed forces

**homo** homogenized milk, from which no fat has been extracted

**Hongcouver** Vancouver (playing on the perceived large numbers of immigrants from Hong Kong)

**hydro** electric power, whether actually hydroelectric or not

**jam buster** a doughnut filled with jam

**Jean-Baptiste** a French-Canadian person (from the common Christian name)

**keb** a French-Canadian person (from 'Quebec')

**loonie** a one-dollar coin stamped with a picture of the loon bird on one of its faces

**mick** or **mickey** a small bottle or flask containing alcohol

**moccasin telegraph** the grapevine or gossip

**Mountie** a member of the Royal Canadian Mounted Police

**Newfie** a person from Newfoundland

**pea-souper** a French-Canadian person (also called **Johnny pea-soup**; pea soup being considered typical of their diet)

**pepper** or **Pepsi** a French-Canadian person (from their alleged preference for Pepsi over Coca-Cola)

**pogey** unemployment benefit

**puck bunny** a girl who follows ice hockey, especially one hoping to have sexual relations with players

**redcoat** a member of the

Royal Canadian Mounted Police (from their traditional red uniforms)

**red-eye** a drink of beer and tomato juice

**Rock** 'the Rock' is a nickname for Newfoundland

**rubby** an alcoholic down-and-out reduced to drinking rubbing alcohol

**screech** a strong rum popular in Newfoundland

**Soo** 'the Soo' is a nickname for Sault Sainte Marie in Ontario

**spinny** eccentric or crazy

**Spud Island** a nickname for Prince Edward Island (famous for its potatoes)

**stubble jumper** a prairie farmer, especially a poor one

**T Dot** a nickname for Toronto (from the proliferation of dotcom businesses there)

**Texas Mickey** a very large bottle of alcohol

**timbit** the centre part that is cut out of a doughnut, eaten as a sweet snack (originally coined by the Tim Horton chain of doughnut houses)

**toonie** a two-dollar coin (modelled on **loonie**)

**wawa** on the west coast of Canada, to 'wawa' means to talk (probably imitative of speech sounds)

## Australian slang

Australian English is largely the product of the English spoken by its immigrants from England itself, and also from Scotland, Ireland and Wales. Much of its slang would be perfectly recognizable in these countries, and some terms that may be thought of today as particularly Australian can in fact be traced back to roots in the British Isles. The list given below is intended to cover only slang that is identifiably Australian (although terms such as 'blowie', 'bludge' and 'scroggin' will also be recognized in New Zealand). It includes both urban and rural slang, so not all the terms will be used throughout the vast continent. Among the items listed here are expressions for things that are specifically Australian, such as 'Aussie rules', 'do a Melba' or 'jackaroo', as well as Australianisms for things that are part of the common human experience, such as 'bogan', 'daggy' or 'norks'.

One element that is peculiar to Australian slang is the strain of terms that owe their origin to Aboriginal languages, including 'bingy', 'budgeree' and 'galah'. Another characteristic feature is the Australian tendency to shorten existing words and add the suffix '-o', creating slang usages that are more familiar, everyday and comfortably down-to-earth than the more stilted originals. There are many examples of this: perhaps 'Abo' was the very first, on the model of which followed the likes of 'derro' and 'convo'. Sometimes the source word is not shortened, but the suffix is added to label a person by the kind of work they do, as in 'milko' or 'rabbito'. Although all Australians except those of Aboriginal origin are necessarily descended from immigrants, they have been quick to label incomers with such terms as 'Balt', 'chow' or 'spag'. The British, especially the English, seem to have come off worst, being stigmatized at various times as 'chooms', 'poms', 'pongos' and 'woodbines'.

## Glossary

**Abo** an Aboriginal or Aborigine

**arse** impudence or cheek

**arvo** afternoon

**Aussie rules** Australian rules football

**babbler** a cook (from the rhyming slang 'babbling brook')

**baggy green** any of the caps won by a cricketer playing for Australia

**bag swinger** a bookie or bookie's clerk

**Balt** an immigrant from the Baltic region; also used loosely to mean any European immigrant

**banana-bender** a native of Queensland

**Bananaland** Queensland

**barbie** a barbecue

**beer-up** a drinking bout or rowdy, drunken party

**big-note** to boast about yourself

**Binghi** an Aboriginal or Aborigine (from an Aboriginal word meaning 'brother')

**bingy** the stomach

**bitser** a mongrel dog (because it is made up of 'bits of this and bits of that')

**black stump** a mythical

distance-marker on the edge of civilization, especially in the phrase 'beyond the black stump'

**Blind Freddie** an imaginary epitome of imperceptiveness, especially in the phrase 'even Blind Freddie could see ...'

**blowie** a blowfly

**blow-in** a recent arrival or newcomer

**bludge** to live off the state rather than work

**bludger** a scrounger

**blue** an argument or fight

**bluey** someone with ginger hair

**bogan** a low-class unrefined person

**boilover** a surprising result

**bombo** cheap wine

**bombora** a surfer's term for a large wave that breaks outside the normal surf line

**bonzer** very good

**boofhead** a stupid person

**boshta** an old term meaning 'good'

**boss cocky** a boss

**bot** to cadge or borrow

**break it down!** stop it!

**Bris**, **Brissie** or **Brizzie** Brisbane

**Buckley's** or **Buckley's chance** no chance at all

**bucks' party** a stag party

**budgeree** good (from an Aboriginal term)

**bumper** a cigarette butt

**bung** broken, dead, bankrupt or useless (from an Aboriginal term)

**bunny** a simpleton or scapegoat

**bush tucker** the varieties of food available in the wild to be found by travellers off the beaten track

**buster** a strong south wind

**canary** an old term for a convict

**cark** same as **kark**

**castor** an old term meaning good or excellent

**cat** any timid animal

**chocko** or **choco** a conscripted member of the Australian armed forces in World War II, especially one who never left the country (shortened from 'chocolate soldier')

**choof off** to go away

**chook** a chicken

**choom** an old term for an English person (perhaps reflecting a pronunciation of 'chum')

**chow** an old term for a Chinese person

**chunder** to vomit

**clucky** broody or obsessed with babies

**cobber** a mate or chum

**cockatoo** a lookout

**cockeyed bob** a sudden thunderstorm or a cyclone

**cocky** a small farmer

**cocky's joy** golden syrup

**coit** the buttocks or backside

**coldie** a cold beer

**combi** a camper van

**come the raw prawn** to make an attempt to deceive

**commo** a communist

**compo** redundancy pay

**convo** conversation

**cop it sweet** to accept punishment without complaint

**cornstalk** a tall thin person

**cossie** a swimming costume

**cow** something or someone that is objectionable or despicable, or a trying situation or occurrence, as in the phrase 'a fair cow'

**cronk** ill, of poor quality or fraudulent

**crook** ill

**currency** native-born Australians collectively, as opposed to immigrants

**dag** a person who is eccentric or comic, or a scruffy or socially awkward person

**daggy** unfashionable, scruffy or dishevelled

**daks** trousers (originally a trade name)

**derro** a derelict person

**dice** to reject or abandon

**dingbats** someone who has 'the dingbats' is suffering from delirium tremens

**dingo** a cheat or coward

**dinkum** or **dinky-di** real, genuine or honest

**do a Melba** to make many farewell appearances or return from retirement (like Dame Nellie Melba, the Australian opera singer)

**do a perish** to be close to death due to lack of food or water

**dob** to 'dob a person in' is to inform on them

**dog's disease** any minor ailment, especially influenza

**dole-bludger** someone who would rather live off state benefits than work

**donkey-lick** to 'donkey-lick' an opponent is to defeat them convincingly

**drack** an unattractive woman (from 'Dracula's daughter')

**drink with the flies** to drink on your own

**drongo** a stupid or worthless person

**droob** a stupid or worthless person

**drop your bundle** to lose your nerve or give up

**dry** 'the dry' is the dry season in central and northern Australia

**dunny** a lavatory

**earbash** to talk incessantly, or to nag or scold

**egg** a bookmaker who refuses to take a particular bet

**fizgig** or **fizzgig** an old term for a police informer

**galah** a fool (from an Aboriginal name for a bird)

**garbo** a garbage collector

**g'day** an archetypal Australian greeting (a shortened form of 'good day')

**get off your bike** to lose control of yourself

**go bush** to abandon civilization to live in the bush

**go crook** to lose your temper

**go for the doctor** to make an all-out effort

**good oil** 'the good oil' is reliable information

**go off** to get married, or to be raided by the police

**go off at** to 'go off at' someone is to scold or reprimand them

**go on the shout** to go on a drinking bout

**go to market** to become angry or violent

**greasies** fish and chips

**greasy** a camp-cook in the outback

**grip** a job or occupation

**grog** alcoholic drink, especially beer

**grog-on** or **grog-up** a drinking party or drinking session

**gub** a white person, as opposed to an Aboriginal

**gum digger** an old term for a dentist

**gummies** gumboots

**gussie** an effeminate man

**hoon** a hooligan, or a reckless driver

**hophead** a drunkard

**hornbag** a sexually attractive woman

**illywhacker** a conman

**inky** drunk

**jackaroo** a newcomer, or other person gaining experience, on a sheep or cattle station

**jack up** to refuse or resist

**Jacky** or **Jacky-Jacky** an old term for an Aboriginal or Aborigine

**jillaroo** a female **jackaroo**

**Jimmy Woodser** a solitary drinker or a drink taken on your own

**job** to punch

**Joe Blakes** if you have 'the Joe Blakes', you have the shakes, ie delirium tremens

**John Hop** a police officer (rhyming slang for 'cop')

**josser** an old term for a clergyman

**jumbuck** a sheep

**kark** or **cark** to die

**kidstakes** nonsense or humbug

**king-hit** a knockout blow

**kipper** an old term for a British person

**lair** a flashily dressed man

**long drop** an outdoor toilet

**Lucky Country** 'the Lucky Country' is a term used by Australians for Australia

**map of Tassie** a woman's pubic hair or pubic area (from the perceived resemblance in shape to a map of Tasmania)

**Mary** a woman, especially an Aboriginal one

**middy** a glass of beer, varying in capacity from place to place

**milko** a milkman

**moke** a worn-out or inferior horse

**mong** a mongrel

**mopoke** a dull-witted or boring person

**motser** a large amount of money, especially the proceeds of a gambling win

**moz** a curse or jinx

**naughty** an act of sexual intercourse

**neddy** a racehorse

**new chum** a newly arrived and inexperienced immigrant

**Noah's ark** a shark (rhyming slang)

**norks** a woman's breasts (perhaps from Norco Co-operative Ltd, a butter manufacturer)

**ocker** an oafish, uncultured Australian (after a comic character in the television series *The Mavis Bramston Show*)

**offsider** a subordinate or sidekick

**Old Dart** 'the Old Dart' is a nickname for Britain

**onkus** disordered or bad

**on the knocker** on the nail

**on the nose** unsavoury or offensive

**Oscar** an old term for cash (from the rhyming slang 'Oscar Asche', after an Australian actor)

**Oz** Australia

**perform** to lose your temper

**perv** to stare lustfully at someone

**pick the eyes out of** to choose and take the best parts of

**pike out** to give up

**plonko** an alcoholic

**poddy** a young animal, especially a calf or lamb

**pom** or **pommy** a British person

**pongo** a British person

**poultice** an old term for a large sum of money

**punce** an effeminate man

**put your bib in** to interfere

**rabbito** an itinerant seller of rabbits for eating

**rack off** to go away

**red ned** an old term for cheap red wine

**reffo** a refugee

**reggo** the registration number of a motor vehicle

**rellies** your relatives

**ripper** an admirable person or thing

**rock chopper** a Roman Catholic (playing on the initials RC)

**root** to have sex with

**rort** a racket, or a lively or riotous party

**rorter** a conman

**rorty** lively and enjoyable

**roughie** an outsider in a race, or an unfair trick

**runners** running shoes

**Salvo** a member of the Salvation Army

**sambo** a sandwich

**sanger** a sandwich

**schoolie** a school pupil, a recent graduate from high school, or a schoolteacher

**scroggin** a hiker's snack of mixed fruit and nuts

**serve** verbal abuse or mockery

**sheila** a woman or girl

**shelf** to inform on

**sherbet** beer

**she's apples** everything is fine

**shicker** either strong drink or a drunkard

**shickered** drunk

**shonky** underhand, illicit or unreliable

**shout** to 'shout' someone a drink is to buy one for them

**silvertail** a wealthy socialite or social climber

**skite** to boast

**skivvy** a knitted cotton polo-necked sweater

**slag** to spit

**smoko** a rest or tea-break (originally a break for smoking during the working day)

**snag** a sausage

**souvenir** to 'souvenir' something is to steal it

**spag** an Italian person

**spine-bashing** loafing, lying down or sleeping

**spunk** an attractive person

**starve the bardies** an exclamation of surprise ('bardies' are a kind of insect grub)

**steamer** kangaroo flavoured with pork

**stonker** to kill

**strides** trousers

**Strine** Australian English

**stubby** a small bottle of beer

**sunnies** sunglasses

**swy** a two-year prison sentence

**Tassie** Tasmania

**Tatts** a sweepstake or lottery agency with its headquarters in Melbourne

**tinny** a can of beer

**toady** a toadfish

**toey** nervous or on edge, often with anticipation

**tonk** the penis

**toot** toilet

**trap** an old term for a police officer

**tripehound** a newspaper reporter

**troppo** driven insane

(originally by exposure to tropical heat)

**tube** a can or bottle of beer

**tucker** food

**two-pot screamer** someone who gets drunk on a comparatively small amount of alcohol

**tyke** a Roman Catholic

**wage plug** someone who works for low wages

**walloper** a policeman

**warby** worn-out, decrepit, unwell or unsteady

**wash-up** an outcome or result

**wet** 'the wet' is the rainy season

**whaler** a tramp

**wharfie** a wharf labourer

**white lady** a drink of methylated spirits

**wog** any germ, bug, infection or illness

**woodbine** an old term for an English person (from a popular brand of cigarette)

**Woop Woop** a humorous name for a remote town or district

**wowser** a puritan, teetotaller or spoilsport

**yakka** work, especially in the phrase 'hard yakka'

**yike** a fight

**ziff** a beard

# New Zealand slang

New Zealand slang suffers from the same effect that the United States has on Canada, namely linguistic domination by a more populous neighbour. New Zealanders are exposed to Australian influence in the media as well as through personal contact, and many expressions listed under Australian slang in this book are equally current in New Zealand.

This list is intended to concentrate on bona-fide New Zealand expressions. As with Australia, the local brand of English is very much influenced by the language of the indigenous inhabitants, in this case the Maori, and this is as true of the slang as of more formal expressions. Maori-derived slang terms include 'booai', 'kuri', 'hui' and 'pakeha', but there are also expressions that are hybrids between the two tongues, such as 'half-pie' or 'electric puha'. On the other hand, the abbreviation of 'cousin' to 'cuz', once common in England, is preserved in the English used by young Maoris.

## Glossary

**Anzac Day dinner** a meal involving, or mostly comprising, much drinking of alcohol

**bach** or **batch** a holiday cottage, or a farm worker's cottage (from 'bachelor')

**binder** a meal, especially a filling one

**blue duck** a rumour (especially when unsubstantiated), or a failure

**booai**, **booay** or **boohai** a remote rural area (from Maori)

**box of birds** or **budgies** good, easy or happy

**bugalugs** a term of endearment

**cast** drunk

**cheerios** cocktail sausages

**cuz**, **cuzzy** or **cuzzy-bro** a familiar term of address, especially among young Maoris (from 'cousin')

**egg** a foolish person

**electric puha** marijuana (*puha* is a Maori word for sow thistle)

**Enzed** New Zealand

**Enzedder** a New Zealander

**fernleaf** any New Zealander, but especially a soldier (from the silver fern which is the national symbol)

**fizz boat** or **fizzy boat** a small motorboat

**give your ferret a run** to have sex

**half-pie** not very good, or badly done (from the Maori word *pai* meaning 'good')

**hapu** pregnant (from Maori)

**hollywood** a feigned injury on the sports field or any outburst intended to attract attention

**hooray fuck!** an exclamation used to say goodbye to a disliked person

**hoot** money (from the Maori word *utu*)

**hui** any social gathering (originally a Maori gathering)

**iceblock** an ice lolly

**jandals** flip-flops (from 'Japanese sandals')

**judder bars** speed bumps, also facetiously used to mean haemorrhoids

**Kiwi** a New Zealander

**kuri** a term of abuse (a Maori word literally meaning 'dog')

**lollies** sweets

**mad as a meat axe** very angry

**mollymawk** a fulmar

**monkey** an opossum

**OE** overseas experience, ie travel and work abroad as carried out by graduates before settling on a career

**Other Side** 'the Other Side' is a nickname for Australia (because it is on the other side of the Tasman Sea)

**pack a sad** to be depressed or in a bad mood

**pakeha** a white person (from Maori)

**porangi** slightly crazy (from Maori)

**puckeroo** broken or useless (from Maori)

**rark** to 'rark a person up' is to scold or rebuke them

**scarfie** a university student

**shark and taties** fish and chips

**snarler** a sausage

**swept** having no money at all

**tiki tour** a scenic route or roundabout way to go somewhere

**togs** a swimming costume

**whanau** if you are 'hanging with the whanau', you are spending time with your family

**wop-wops** remote back-country

## South African slang

The variety of English spoken in South Africa bears the mark of a
variety of influences, and the same is true of the slang in use there.
Chief among these linguistic inputs to South African English is Dutch,
and its later variant, Afrikaans, providing such slang terms as 'befok',
'bokkie' and 'vrot'. Other terms owe their origin to local African
languages, including 'babalaas', 'indaba' and 'tsotsi', while Indian
immigrants have also contributed expressions such as 'bunny chow'.

Ever since the days of British imperial expansion at the Cape, the
history of South Africa has been one of conflict between different
ethnic and linguistic groups, especially during the Boer War and the
period of apartheid. This background is still reflected in slang terms
used to refer to members of other groups in South African society.
English-speakers often stigmatize those for whom Afrikaans is the
mother tongue as 'crunchies' or 'hairybacks', while themselves being
derided as 'rooineks' or 'soutpiels'. Terms such as 'African time' and
'munt' reflect attitudes towards black people that perhaps belong
more to the past than to the future of the 'Rainbow Nation'.

### Glossary

**African time** unpunctuality

**babalaas** or **babbelas** a
hangover (from Zulu)

**bakkie** a pick-up truck

**befok** unhappy, insane or out
of order

**bergie** a vagrant or tramp

**be tickets** to be the end

**bioscope** the cinema

**bokkie** a young girl or a
lover (a diminutive of the
Afrikaans word *bok* meaning
'deer')

**bundu** a remote uncultivated
region

**bundu-bashing** travelling in
remote areas

**bunny chow** a dish of
vegetable curry served
inside a hollowed-out half-
loaf of bread (from Hindi
*bania* meaning 'merchant',
vegetarian Hindus being the
primary consumers of this dish)

**Cape smoke** locally made
South African brandy

**chommie** friend (from 'chum')

**crunchie** a derogatory term for an Afrikaner

**dinges** an indefinite name for any person or thing whose name you cannot or will not remember

**donder** to beat up or thrash

**doos** the vagina; also used as an abusive term (an Afrikaans word literally meaning 'box')

**dorp** a town considered as provincial or backward

**gatvol** disgusted or fed up (from Afrikaans, literally meaning 'full anus')

**gesuip** drunk (an Afrikaans word)

**gom** a fool

**hairyback** a derogatory term for an Afrikaner

**howzit** a greeting (probably shortened from 'how is it going?')

**indaba** a problem or concern (from Zulu)

**jol** a party or celebration

**lekker** pleasant or enjoyable

**lightie** a young man, especially a younger brother

**long drop** an outdoor toilet

**moffie** a male homosexual

**monkey's wedding** simultaneous sunshine and light rain

**mooi** fine or good

**munt** or **muntu** a black African

**ou** a man

**poes** the vagina

**pomp** to have sex with (an Afrikaans word literally meaning 'pump')

**rooinek** an Afrikaans nickname for a British or English-speaking person (literally meaning 'red neck')

**sarmie** a sandwich

**scope** short for **bioscope**

**sis** an interjection expressing disgust, contempt, etc

**skeef** askew or crooked

**skollie** a young hooligan or gang member

**soutie** short for **soutpiel**

**soutpiel** an Englishman or English-speaking white South African (from Afrikaans, literally meaning 'salt penis', the implication being that the person has divided loyalties, with one foot in England and the other in South Africa, leaving the genitals dangling in the sea)

**stompie** a cigarette butt

**swak** weak or feeble

**tackies** tennis shoes or

plimsolls (perhaps from their
rubber soles being slightly
sticky)
**tsotsi** a young hooligan or
member of a street gang
**tune** to 'tune' someone is to
tease or be insolent to them
**voetsek** an impolite term of
dismissal (from Dutch, essentially
meaning 'away, I say')
**vrot** rotten; also used to mean
drunk

## *Caribbean slang*

English has been spoken in the Caribbean since the 17th century, but
French, Spanish, Dutch and other languages, not least those of the
black African slaves, have also had wide currency there, and there are
significant variations in slang from island to island. When large
numbers of West Indians emigrated to the United Kingdom in the
latter part of the 20th century, they brought many slang terms with
them which continue in use, not only within the Afro-Caribbean
community, but in wider society too. The growth in popularity of
reggae music in the 1960s and 1970s introduced Britain to
dreadlocked Rastas as well as to such terms, often used in the lyrics of
songs, as 'Babylon', 'natty' and 'skanking'. This process has continued,
with terms such as 'Yardie' becoming notorious in the wider
community, and Caribbean slang terms being adopted for their cool
quotient among black and non-black youth alike (as in the cases of
'massive' and 'punani'). The preservation of West Indian vocabulary
and speech patterns amongst black people in the United Kingdom has
been seen as a badge of identity and this has contributed to the
continued vibrancy of Caribbean slang.

## *Glossary*

**agony** the sensations
experienced during sexual
intercourse
**baby father** a woman's male
sexual partner, to whom she is
not married but who may be
the father of her child
**Babylon** the world of white

people, seen as corrupt; also used to mean the forces of authority, especially the police

**backra** a white person, or white people collectively (from an African language)

**baldhead** or **ballhead** a person (white or black) without dreadlocks

**bans** a lot

**bashment** a party or dance

**batty** a person's bottom

**batty boy** a male homosexual

**boops** a man who supports a female lover

**boopsie** a kept woman

**bumbaclat** or **bumboclot** a sanitary towel; also used as a term of abuse (literally meaning 'bottom cloth')

**chi-chi man** a male homosexual

**cool runnings** an interjection meaning 'everything is fine'

**crucial** excellent or serious

**cut your eye at someone** to look at someone with scorn, or to snub them

**darkers** sunglasses

**day-clean** daybreak

**deaders** meat

**duppy** a ghost

**dutchy** a Dutch cooking pot

**dutty** dirty

**force-ripe** someone who

is 'force-ripe' is precocious, especially in a sexual way (the image being of fruit that is artificially ripened in a greenhouse)

**glamity** the vagina

**hard-ears** stubborn or unwilling to listen

**irie** excellent or wonderful

**jump-up** a social dance

**lime** to loiter or hang about

**marabunta** a bad-tempered woman (literally a kind of wasp)

**massive** a 'massive' is a group of friends or a gang

**natty** a person with dreadlocks

**pickney** a child (shortened from 'piccaninny')

**pum-pum** the vagina

**punani** the female genitals, or women collectively regarded as sexual objects (perhaps from an African word)

**rude boy** a member of a youth movement wearing smart clothes

**skank** to dance to reggae music

**toast** to sing or rap over the rhythm track of a record

**wine** or **wind** to dance in a sexually provocative way

**Yardie** a member of a criminal gang

## Irish slang

Irish people have a reputation for being linguistically inventive and
their long and rich literary tradition supplies ample evidence of this.
The same creativity has been shown in the coining of slang through
the centuries, from 'wigs on the green' to 'plastic Paddies'. The Irish
Gaelic language that puzzled English settlers in the Elizabethan
age continues to influence Irish English, and many slang terms can
be immediately identified as originating in Irish (such as 'amadan',
'gowl', 'flah' and 'scutters'). Many of the racier slang terms reflect
a profound division between town and country in Irish society. The
major cities, particularly Dublin, tend to generate the most slang
vocabulary, and this is apparent in the abundance of disparaging
terms for country dwellers, from 'bogtrotter' to 'culchie' to 'munchie'.
The countryside (or 'the bogs') occasionally throws a counter-punch
with words such as 'jackeen'.

The Irish are often portrayed as being fonder of a drink than many
other people. Whether this is true or is a racial slur is a question
beyond the remit of this book. However, it can certainly be shown
that Irish slang abounds in expressions for drink, drinking and
drunkenness, whether your tipple is a 'ball of malt' or a 'pint of
plain'. It seems safe to say that if you end up 'fluthered', 'jarred' or
'scuttered' in Ireland, you will not be alone.

The island of Ireland does, of course, contain six counties that are part
of the United Kingdom, and a separate discussion of the slang words
of that province can be found under **Ulster slang**. However, many
of the terms listed here will be heard on both sides of the border.

## Glossary

**alko** an alcoholic
**amadan** a fool (an Irish
   word, often transcribed as
**omadhaun**)

**apache** a joyrider
**baby Power** a small bottle,
   or miniature, of Powers Irish
   whiskey

**bags** a mess, as in the phrase 'made a bags of it'

**ball of malt** a glass of whiskey

**banjax** to ruin, destroy or thwart

**baz** pubic hair

**bazzer** a haircut

**black** if a place is 'black', it is crowded with people

**bog ball** a derogatory term for Gaelic football

**bogger** or **bog warrior** someone from rural Ireland

**bogs** 'the bogs' is a derogatory term for rural parts of Ireland

**bogtrotter** an unsophisticated country dweller

**bollocks** or **bollox** a stupid or unpleasant person

**bowsie** a hooligan or street urchin

**buckled** drunk

**bucko** a young lad or chap

**caffler** a fool

**cast** drunk

**cat** something described as 'cat' is very bad or unpleasant (from the Irish phrase *cat marbh* meaning 'mischief')

**catch yourself on** to start thinking sensibly

**chipper** a chip shop

**chiseller** a child

**coodle** excrement

**cop on to yourself** to come to your senses, to start thinking sensibly

**crabbit** cunning or smart

**cratur** 'the cratur' is a term used for whiskey (from 'the creature')

**culchie** a rustic or country labourer

**cute hoor** a clever, devious person (often applied to politicians suspected of corruption)

**cuttie** or **cutty** a young woman or girl

**deadly** very good, excellent

**dirtbird** a term of abuse

**do a legger** to run away

**do a line with** an old-fashioned expression meaning to court or go out with

**eejit** idiot (indicating a characteristic pronunciation)

**feck** 'feck', 'fecking', etc are euphemisms for 'fuck', 'fucking', etc

**Fecky the Ninth** a name used for an idiot

**flah** an attractive girl or woman (from the Irish word *fleadh* meaning 'a party or festival')

**fluthered** very drunk

**foxer** same as **nixer**

**gameball** excellent

**ganky** an unattractive woman

**gee** or **gee-box** the vagina

**gee-eyed** drunk

**gick** excrement

**gicker** the anus or buttocks

**gom** a fool (from an Irish word)

**gooter** the penis

**gouger** a thug or violent criminal

**gowl** the vagina; also used as a term of abuse (from Irish)

**gurrier** a street urchin or lout

**hard chaw** a tough man

**holliers** holidays

**hooley** a party, especially a noisy one

**in flitters** in tatters

**in the nip** naked

**jabs** female breasts

**jackeen** a Dubliner

**jacks** 'the jacks' is a toilet

**jarred** drunk (ie having had a few 'jars' of beer)

**jip** semen

**kip** a brothel; hence, any unattractive or run-down place

**lack** a girlfriend

**langer** the penis

**langered** drunk

**little green man** a small bottle of whiskey

**locked** drunk

**louser** a contemptible person

**lurch** to dance a slow dance close to your partner

**mebs** or **mebbs** testicles

**mickey** the penis

**mortaller** a mortal sin, or anything terrible

**mot** a girl or young woman

**motherless** drunk

**mountainy** a 'mountainy' person is a rough country-dweller, especially if large in size

**munchie** a rustic person

**nixer** a job, especially a spare-time or irregular one, the earnings of which are not declared for tax purposes by the worker (also called a **foxer** in some parts of Ireland)

**omadhaun** see **amadan**

**one and one** a 'one and one' is a portion of fish and chips

**pave** to steal

**pavee** a Gypsy or Traveller (so called because they tramp the pavements)

**pint of plain** a pint of Guinness (seen as the basic Irish beer)

**plastic Paddy** someone of Irish descent (eg the offspring of Irish immigrants to the UK) who makes great play of Irishness

**poppies** potatoes

**praties** potatoes

**puck** a blow

**put on the long finger** someone who 'puts something on the long finger' puts it off or postpones it (as if pushing it away from himself or herself)

**quare** extremely

**quare hawk** an odd person

**rake** a large amount, as in the phrase 'a rake of beers' (from the Irish word *reic* meaning 'generous expenditure')

**rasher** the vagina

**redser** a redhead

**ride and a rasher** a night of sexual intercourse followed by breakfast

**ronnie** a moustache (especially of the thin kind sported by the English actor *Ron*ald Colman)

**rubber dollies** sandshoes, training shoes or running shoes

**runners** running shoes

**sambo** a sandwich

**sanger** a sandwich

**scald** tea (from the Irish word *scal*)

**scaldy** stingy or mean

**scanger** a word that can mean either a stupid woman or a lout

**scoop** a drink of alcohol

**scratch** 'the scratch' is the dole, or unemployment benefit

**scuttered** drunk (from an Irish word meaning 'inconsequential talk')

**scutters** diarrhoea (from the Irish word for the condition, *sciodar*)

**shades** the police

**shift** to engage in lovemaking

**silko** a thief

**skin** a person, especially a friend

**sleeveen** a crafty, smooth-talking person (from the Irish word *slibhin*)

**snapper** a child (shortened from 'bread-snapper', ie a hungry mouth to feed)

**soft** (of weather, or a day) mild and damp

**speedy** a police motorcycle

**stabber** a cigarette butt, or one that is almost finished

**stall the ball** wait a minute

**steever** a kick in the backside

**stick fighting** a derogatory term for the sport of hurley

**strap** a sluttish woman

**swaddler** a Protestant, especially a Methodist

**swiss roll** the anus (rhyming slang for 'hole')

**Tan** an English person (from

the Black and Tans, British auxiliary forces used in Ireland in the 1920s)

**throw shapes** to show off, or to display your physique in boxing moves

**two-bulb** a police squad car (from the two-tone flashing light on its roof)

**tyre biter** a dog; also used to mean an unattractive woman

**Uncle Arthur** Guinness (from the name of the brewery founder Arthur Guinness)

**wagon** a derogatory term for a woman (with the implication that she might offer a 'ride' to many)

**West Brit** someone who is considered excessively anglophile

**wigs on the green** if it is said that 'there'll be wigs on the green', this means that there will be trouble, a fuss or fight (from the removal or dislodgement in earlier times of men's wigs in physical confrontations)

**wojus** very bad or awful (perhaps from a blend of 'woeful' and 'atrocious')

**yockers** testicles

**yoke** a thing

**your man** or **your woman** used to refer to a specific individual without naming names

**your only man** the very thing, or exactly what's required

**yo-yo** a euro

## South Asian slang

English has been in use in South Asia for over two hundred years, having been brought there by British traders and, later, empire-builders. This of course meant that, alongside more formal language, British slang gained currency in such areas as the Indian subcontinent, Hong Kong and what is now Malaysia. Interaction with local languages led to the development of slang terms that were new and peculiar to their environments. For example, British soldiers in the Indian Army began to refer to their rifles as 'bundooks', their sergeants to encourage them with cries of 'jildi!' and officers to console themselves with a 'chota peg' on the veranda. Returning servicemen and other British people who had lived in the East brought many of these words and phrases back to Britain. Among many still in use is 'pukka', whose original meaning of 'cooked or ripe' made it unintentionally appropriate for its association with celebrity chef Jamie Oliver.

Many of the slang terms that evolved in South Asia were essentially the products of hybridization between English and other languages. These crossover terms form part of vocabularies labelled as 'Hinglish' (a hybrid of Hindi and English) and 'Singlish' (Singapore English). The former in particular is increasingly heard in the United Kingdom among communities of Indian descent, and is becoming more widely known with media exposure.

## *Glossary*

**auntie** any older woman, not necessarily a relation

**bangalore** to 'bangalore' a job is to relocate it to India (from the city of Bangalore)

**Bollywood** the Indian commercial film industry (a blend of 'Bombay', now Mumbai, a centre of the industry, and 'Hollywood')

**bundook** a rifle (from Hindi)

**choky** prison (from Hindi)

**chope** to reserve, as in 'this seat is choped' (Singlish)

**chota peg** a small (alcoholic) drink (from Hindi)

**chuddies** underpants (from Hindi)

**cut** in Singapore, to overtake in a motor vehicle

**dadah** in Malaysia, illicit drugs

**deadly** excellent

**eve teasing** the verbal harassment of females by males in public places in India

**filmi** the type of music popularly used in Indian films

**gup** gossip (from Urdu)

**hi-fi** excellent

**isn't it?** a phrase used to seek confirmation at the end of a statement, whether or not it agrees grammatically with the statement itself (as in 'She's looking a lot better, isn't it?')

**jildi** an exhortation to hurry, sometimes heard in the form 'get a jildi on' (from the Hindi word *jaldi* meaning 'speed')

**kiasu** afraid to lose out
(Singlish, from the Hokkien
dialect of Chinese)

**Lollywood** the Pakistani
commercial film industry
(modelled on 'Bollywood',
but taking the initial letter
of Lahore, the centre of the
industry)

**mug** to study (Singlish)

**pukka** thoroughly good or
complete (from Hindustani,
meaning 'cooked or ripe')

**rooty** bread (from the Hindi
word *roti*)

**sian** tired (Singlish)

**solid** excellent (Singlish)

**stepney** a spare wheel or tyre;
also used to mean a married
man's mistress (Hinglish,
perhaps because tyres were
made in Stepney)

**time-pass** a pastime
(Hinglish)

**TK** OK (from the Hindi phrase
*thik hai*)

**toot** stupid (Singlish)

**ulu** remote, backward or
unsophisticated (Singlish, from
Malay)

**uncle** any older man, not
necessarily a relation

**wallah** someone employed in
or concerned with a specific
type of work, eg 'a grocery-
wallah' (from Hindi)

**zap** in Singapore, to photocopy

# REGIONAL SLANG WITHIN THE UNITED KINGDOM

## Scottish slang

People who visit Scotland or who are exposed to the speech of its natives in the media often opine that a language different to English is spoken there. Putting aside the effect of local accents on the pronunciation of common English words, what is left is a mixture of demotic Scots and slang. What constitutes Scots as a distinct language or, as some would have it, a dialect of English, with its influences as varied as Norse, Dutch and French, is beyond the remit of this book. Here we concentrate on slang that is identifiably Scottish in origin.

Slang is essentially an urban phenomenon, and in Scotland it is the major towns, cities and conurbations that are most productive of slang expressions. While centres such as Edinburgh, Aberdeen and Dundee all make their contribution, it has to be said that the slang of greater Glasgow is by far the most pervasive. Perhaps this results from Glaswegian language being most commonly featured in the media, especially in television comedy shows from *Rab C Nesbitt* to *Still Game*. In non-Scottish film and TV portrayals of the typical Scot, it tends to be a 'weegie' who is shown (the issue of why this is usually a violent drunk is a separate matter). The effect is that terms that arose in Glasgow (including 'buroo', 'cludgie', 'ned' and 'Jimmy') became popularized throughout many parts of Scotland. The effect has even spread south of the border where use of words such as 'minger' is now common. One interesting fact about Edinburgh slang is that many of its characteristic terms ('barrie' and 'radge', for example) seem to show a Romany influence that is largely absent from the west of the country.

## Glossary

**away ye go!** a phrase used to express disbelief or dismissal

**bampot** an idiot or fool (**bammer** means the same thing)

**barrie** or **barry** very good or excellent (a term used mainly in the Edinburgh region, derived from a Romany word)

**beezer** something or someone that is 'beezer' is excellent or very good

**bidie-in** a sexual partner with whom someone lives without being married

**blackie** a blackbird

**blootered** drunk (from 'blooter', meaning to beat)

**bucket** a quantity of alcoholic drink

**buftie** or **bufty** a homosexual

**buroo** or **broo** the office at which people receive unemployment benefit (from a pronunciation of 'bureau')

**carfuffle** a commotion or agitation

**carry-out** a meal or alcoholic drink bought and taken away to be consumed elsewhere

**chanty** a chamberpot

**chuddie** chewing gum

**cludgie** a lavatory, especially a communal one

**clype** to tell tales

**crabbit** bad-tempered or irritable

**crivens** or **crivvens** an exclamation expressing amazement or dismay (perhaps euphemistic for 'Christ and heavens')

**diddy** a female breast, a nipple or teat; also used as a disparaging term of abuse

**Doonhamer** a native of Dumfries (from 'doon hame', ie down home, a local way of referring to Dumfries)

**fernytickle** a freckle

**fitba** football

**flit** to move house

**get your hole** to have sexual intercourse

**gub** to 'gub' someone is to strike them on the mouth or defeat them comprehensively ('gub' means the mouth)

**head-bummer** a manager or person in authority

**homer** a job done at home or away from the usual workplace

**jag** an inoculation or injection

**jeely nose** a bleeding nose ('jeely' here means jammy, ie red in colour)

**jessie** an effeminate man or boy

**Jimmy** a term of address for a male stranger

**jings** an exclamation used as a mild oath (probably euphemistic for 'Jesus')

**keeker** a black eye

**kiltie** a wearer of a kilt

**lose the place** to lose your temper

**lumber** a casual sexual partner

**mang** to speak or talk

**midgie** or **midgy** a midge

**minger** an extremely unattractive person

**ned** a young hooligan or disruptive adolescent (possibly from the familiar form of the name Edward)

**numpty** an idiot

**Old Firm** 'the Old Firm' is a name for the two most famous Glasgow football teams, Rangers and Celtic, considered together as the football 'establishment'

**on the broo** someone who is 'on the broo' is receiving unemployment benefit

**outsider** the crusty end-slice of a loaf of bread

**Proddie** or **Proddy** a Protestant

**radge** a bad temper, a rage or an unpleasant person (a variant of 'rage', perhaps influenced by Romany *raj*)

**sannies** sandshoes

**scaffie** a scavenger, ie a street cleaner

**schemie** a person who lives on a council estate (from 'housing scheme')

**scoosh** or **skoosh** something that is easily done

**skelly** or **skellie** having a squint, or cross-eyed

**stotter** a person or thing that is admired

**taddie** a tadpole

**Tally** an Italian

**tammy** a Tam o' Shanter cap

**tube** an extremely stupid person

**very dab** if something is described as 'the very dab', it is exactly what is required

**weegie** a Glaswegian (a term not used by Glaswegians themselves)

**white settler** a wealthy outsider, especially an English person, who moves into a rural area, especially in the Highlands, and makes use of its amenities while making no attempt to blend sympathetically into the local community

**wifie** a woman

# *Ulster slang*

The variety of English spoken in Ulster, or Northern Ireland, has been shaped by two main forces which have often been historically inimical: the Irish-Gaelic-influenced language of the south and that of the largely Protestant community descended from the Scots who settled in the region from the 16th century onwards. This effect is also shown in the slang, and many expressions listed in this book as being Irish and Scottish slang will also be heard in Ulster (especially those concerned with the drinking of alcohol). This list, however, concentrates on language peculiar to Northern Ireland. While 'the Troubles' appear to have been brought to an end by diplomatic means, the sectarian and political tensions involved have left their mark on the region's slang, with terms like 'barrack buster', 'croppie' and 'Taig' continuing to be in common use. However, even during the most violent times of the later 20th century, ordinary people simply had to get on with daily life as best they could, and most of the slang terms here relate to everyday concerns that we all recognize.

## *Glossary*

**are youse gettin?** are you being served?

**away in the head** not in your right mind, or stupid

**away on** a phrase used to indicate disbelief or unwillingness to comply

**barrack buster** a three-litre bottle of cider (originally a name used by paramilitaries for a large home-made bomb used to attack fortified military or police posts)

**blade** a young woman

**blarge** to act in a clumsy or hasty manner

**bowler hat** a rat (rhyming slang)

**bullroot** a derogatory term of address (literally 'bull's penis')

**bull's walt** if someone is 'as thick as a bull's walt' they are very stupid (see **walt**)

**cock relation** someone to whom you are related by marriage

**croppie** or **croppy** a derogatory name for a Roman Catholic (from the 'croppies' or 'croppy boys', Irish rebels of 1798 who cut their hair short like French Revolutionaries)

**delph** crockery, as in the phrase 'she doesn't break much delph', meaning 'she is poor or unimportant'

**dicking** the practice of making observations and passing information to a paramilitary organization

**easy peasy Japanesey** very easy indeed

**empty the bags** to urinate

**ganch** a foolish or boorish person

**hallion** a troublesome or disreputable person

**keep her lit** to keep going without slackening your efforts (perhaps from the idea of continuing to stoke a fire)

**knock your toys in** if you are 'knocking your toys in' you are working very hard

**lig** a fool

**marley** a glass marble

**millie** or **milly** a lower-class girl (from 'mill girl')

**pastie bap** a hamburger in which the burger has been cooked in batter

**pennyboy** someone who performs menial tasks for someone else

**prough** or **pruck** goods obtained for nothing, often stolen

**relax your cacks** don't become tense ('cacks' here means underwear)

**scone** your 'scone' is your head

**some pup** an admirable person

**spide** a young male hooligan who dresses in hip-hop fashions

**Taig** a Roman Catholic (a variant of 'Teague', originally used as a nickname for any Irishman)

**toys** the testicles (from 'toy dolls', rhyming slang for 'balls')

**walt** the penis

**walthead** an idiot

**wee buns** something that is 'wee buns' or 'wee onions' is no bother to do

**wee champion** an attractive young woman

**wee onions** see **wee buns**

**what about ye?** a greeting, equivalent to 'how are you?'

**whipper** an insurance claim for a whiplash injury

**your balls are beef** you are in deep trouble, you are dead meat

# Scouse slang

'Scouse' means Liverpudlian, of course, and a 'Scouser' is a Liverpool native. The word seems to derive from 'lobscouse', a sailors' stew, and Liverpool has a rich history of nautical connections. Like many cities that have been major ports, and thus acted as melting pots for a wide range of linguistic influences, Liverpool has long been well known for its distinctive slang. It was, perhaps, not until the 1960s that the rest of Britain and the English-speaking world became more widely aware of Scouse speech, with the emergence of The Mersey Sound, particularly exemplified by The Beatles, who didn't moderate their accents or use of slang in interviews. Liverpool writers, including poets like Roger McGough, playwrights like Willy Russell and screenwriters like Alan Bleasdale, also helped expose Liverpool language to a wider audience. The process was further boosted by the existence of Liverpool's own TV soap, *Brookside*, which brought the everyday slang of the city into millions of homes around the country between 1982 and 2003.

Language of course does not respect municipal boundaries, and some of the expressions listed below may well be familiar outside Liverpool, even when they originated on Merseyside.

## Glossary

**antwacky** old-fashioned

**arlarse** someone who is 'arlarse' acts in a crafty or underhand manner

**back crack** a back alley

**bezzie mate** a best friend

**bizzy** a police officer

**blind butty** a 'butty' with nothing on it, ie a slice of bread

**bluenose** a supporter of Everton Football Club (who traditionally play in blue)

**brass** a prostitute

**buck** a young tearaway

**buckess** a young female tearaway

**Chrizzy** Christmas

**cob** a bad mood or state of being angry, as in the phrase 'to have a cob on'

**conny-onny** condensed milk

**Corpy** 'the Corpy' is the City Corporation

**docker's doorstep** a particularly thick slice of bread

**do one** to go away or run away

**go Bismarck** to become violently angry (a play on 'berserk')

**jangle** to have a 'jangle' means to gossip

**jigger** a lane between houses

**kaylied** drunk

**kidder** a friendly term of address

**knockoff** stolen goods

**la**, **lah** or **lar** a friend; used as a friendly term of address

**Lanky** a native of Lancashire

**latch lifter** an amount of money sufficient to buy one drink in a pub

**leccy** or **lecky** the electricity supply

**Liverpool kiss** a head-butt

**loop-di-loop** soup

**made up** highly delighted or chuffed

**Mersey Funnel** 'the Mersey funnel' is a nickname for Liverpool's Roman Catholic cathedral (from its shape)

**moby** a mobile shop

**nudger** a sandwich

**our kid** Scousers may call their younger brother 'our kid'

**over the water** if someone goes 'over the water', they cross the River Mersey from Liverpool to the Wirral peninsula

**Paddy's Wigwam** Liverpool's Roman Catholic cathedral (from its shape, and the perception that Catholics are of Irish descent)

**pipe** 'the pipe' is a nickname for the Mersey Tunnel

**queen** an affectionate term of address for a female

**rat catcher** a Roman Catholic (from the initials 'RC')

**rednose** a supporter of Liverpool Football Club (who traditionally play in red)

**scally** a rogue or scoundrel

**scuffer** a policeman

**soash** social security

**soft lad** a disrespectful term of address for a male, implying stupidity

**sound** used to describe anything considered excellent

**wack** or **wacker** a familiar term of address for a companion or friend

**woollyback** an unsophisticated person from out of town (sometimes shortened to **wool**)

# *Geordie slang*

A Geordie is a native of Tyneside, a collective name for the communities centred along the river Tyne, including Newcastle, Gateshead, Jarrow, and North and South Shields. The whole area is often referred to as 'Geordieland', and while outsiders might label the natives of nearby Sunderland as 'Geordies', they would not themselves use this term (neither would true Geordies, who would call them 'Mackems').

The Tyneside conurbation grew up along with coal mining – we still talk about the fatuity of 'taking coals to Newcastle' – and major heavy industries like shipbuilding, and the local slang evolved features typical of these areas, such as preoccupation with hard work and hard play. Many of the words and turns of phrase associated with Tyneside became more widely known in Britain through the hit television series *Auf Wiedersehen, Pet* (originally shown in the 1980s, but many-sequelled and much-revived). Like many formerly industrial areas, Tyneside has been trying to reinvent itself, and the typical Geordie (if one exists) would no longer be a collier, seaman or factory worker. Such a person, however, may still like to sup good beer, whether it be called 'dog' or 'broon', and regularly turn out with the 'Toon Army'.

## *Glossary*

**back end** the latter part of autumn

**badly-liked** disliked

**black and white** a supporter of Newcastle United Football Club

**broon** brown ale

**cackhouse** a lavatory ('cack' here means excrement)

**cacky** excrement

**Canny Toon** Newcastle ('canny' is a general term of approval which is also found in Scots use; 'toon' is a variant of 'town')

**clod** a penny

**Darlo** Darlington

**dog** brown ale

**Geordie** a native of Tyneside (a diminutive form of 'George')

**hacky** filthy

**hadaway** an expression used

to indicate disbelief

**hatstand** someone who is 'hatstand' is insane

**hinny** a term of endearment for a woman (from 'honey')

**howay** an expression used to give encouragement, as in the footballing chant 'Howay the lads!'

**hoy** to throw

**ket** a sweet or other pleasant thing to eat

**kidder** a friendly term of address, especially to a young person

**Mackem** a native of Sunderland or Wearside

**Magpies** a nickname for Newcastle United Football Club (from their black-and-white strip)

**marrow** or **marra** a mate or companion

**nettie** a lavatory

**newky broon** Newcastle Brown Ale, a proprietary brand of beer

**palatic** drunk (perhaps from 'paralytic')

**pet** a friendly term of address

**red and white** a supporter of Sunderland Football Club

**sackless** stupid or useless

**tab** a cigarette

**Toon Army** the supporters of Newcastle United Football Club

## *Northern English slang*

The North of England is an enormously wide and varied region. In geographical terms it includes the industrialized areas centred on Manchester, Liverpool and Tyneside (the last two being dealt with separately in this book under **Scouse slang** and **Geordie slang**), as well as more rural and agricultural areas such as Cumbria and the Yorkshire Dales. Natives of many of these areas (whether 'Lankys', 'Mancs' or 'Tykes') would probably resent being lumped together, not least those on either side of the Pennines, protesting that local slang varies greatly. While this is true, it suits the scope of this book to treat the region as a whole, although this is not necessarily to fall into the southern English habit of dismissing these areas with caricatured phrases such as 'it's grim up north' or 'ee by gum'.

One of the most popular and long-enduring soap operas on British television has been the Manchester-set *Coronation Street* (first broadcast in 1960), and this has probably been most responsible for regularly exposing people outside the North to such vocabulary as 'chuck', 'daft ha'porth' and 'like piffy on a rock' (whatever that actually means). Manchester slang became even more prominent when 'for one shining moment' in the late 1980s and early 1990s, as 'Madchester', it eclipsed both Liverpool and London as the national focus for youth culture, pop music and fashion.

## Glossary

**bab** to defecate

**babby** a baby

**barmcake** a silly or slightly mad person (literally a kind of soft bread roll)

**bin off** to get rid of

**bizzy** a police officer

**bobbins** something that is 'bobbins' is not very good (perhaps from 'bobbins of cotton', rhyming slang for 'rotten')

**butty** a sandwich (probably from 'buttery')

**chuck** a term of endearment

**chuff** a euphemism for 'fuck'; also used to refer to the vagina

**claggy** muddy

**clog toe pie** a kick

**daft ha'porth** a silly or stupid person ('ha'porth' means a halfpenny's worth)

**ecky thump** an exclamation of surprise, etc (a phrase that is something of a caricature and is often used by natives in the full knowledge of this)

**effing and jeffing** swearing

**gadgy** a man (probably from Romany)

**give over** to cease or desist

**gobby** excessively talkative or cheeky

**gobshite** a stupid person

**gobsmacked** shocked, taken aback or astounded (now widely used outside the North as well)

**grand** excellent or highly enjoyable

**happen** perhaps

**heck as like** a phrase used to express disbelief or unlikelihood, as in 'Will she heck as like', meaning

'I don't believe she will'

**kaylied** drunk

**Lanky** a native of Lancashire

**lanky streak of piss** a tall thin person

**leccy** or **lecky** the electricity supply

**like piffy** someone who is left standing 'like piffy' is ignored, left on their own or forgotten about (variations of the phrase include **like piffy on a rock** and **like piffy on a rock bun**)

**live tally** to cohabit without marriage

**Madchester** a nickname for Manchester (coined in the late 1980s when the city was a Mecca for pop music and fashion; perhaps from the extensive use of the drug MDMA, or else from the local expression of keenness, 'mad for it')

**made up** highly delighted

**mam** mother

**Manc** a Mancunian

**natter** to be peevish

**nobbut** nothing but

**nowt** nothing

**our kid** the speaker's younger brother

**owt** anything

**parky** chilly

**scally** a rogue or scoundrel

**scran** food

**sithee?** do you see?

**soft** silly or stupid

**summat** something

**ta-ra** goodbye

**Tyke** a native of Yorkshire

**wag off** to play truant from school

**wazz** to urinate

# Midlands slang

The Midlands are the central parts of England, including such areas as Staffordshire and Leicestershire. Much of the region is rural and was traditionally associated with fox-hunting, but the Midlands also includes such heavily-industrialized areas as the Black Country and the Potteries. The city of Birmingham (known as 'Brum') dominates the region and its slang is the most prominent strain in the list below, although some terms from the East Midlands (for example 'beeroff' and 'croggy') are also included.

Some elements of what has been documented as Midlands slang are really only pronunciations of standard English words in the distinctive (often stigmatized as 'flat and unlovely') accents of 'Brummies' and other Midlands natives; other terms much used locally are common to the slang of other parts of the country. The list below, however, represents an attempt to isolate slang that is peculiar to the region.

## Glossary

**any road up** anyway

**bab** a friendly term of address for a woman

**bag** someone who 'has a bag on' is in a bad mood

**Balti Triangle** an area of Birmingham's city centre famous for its Asian restaurants

**beeroff** an off-licence

**beeza** a BSA motorcycle

**blart** to weep

**bost** broken (probably from 'bust')

**bostin** very good, excellent

**Brum** Birmingham (from 'Brummagem', an old form of the city's name)

**Brummie** a person from Birmingham

**croggy** a ride on the crossbar of a bicycle

**donnies** the hands

**glarnies** marbles

**half-soaked** not very clever or quick on the uptake

**jitty** a narrow alley between a row of houses

**kaylied** drunk

**mardy** petulant or grumpy

**miskin** a dustbin

**morkins** a stupid person

**on a line** someone who is 'on a line' is annoyed

**outdoor** an 'outdoor' is an off-licence

**tittybabby** a suckling infant; also used as a derogatory name for someone considered immature

**tussock** a cough

**tutty pegs** a child's term for the teeth

**twitchel** a narrow alley between a row of houses

**wag it** to play truant from school

**yamp** a person who is considered stupid or mentally subnormal

**yampy** stupid or mentally subnormal

## West Country slang

The West Country is the name given to south-western England, including primarily Cornwall, Devon, Dorset, Somerset and Gloucestershire. Its accent is perhaps one of the most caricatured in Britain, with everyone thinking they can do it by throwing in 'ooh arr' every now and again. Much of the region is rural, but the cities of Bristol and Plymouth have histories not only of industry but also of nautical connections, not least with the Royal Navy. Bristol was once one of the major ports in England and grew rich on, among other things, the slave trade, and it is the slang of Bristol that dominates the list below. Labelled 'Bristle', the regional argot consists of many local pronunciations of standard English words, but there are also genuine indigenous slang terms, such as 'dog up' and 'macky'. The highly popular television sketch show *Little Britain* (first aired in 2003) features a character called Vicky Pollard who speaks in rapid-fire Bristolian and is responsible for popularizing regional phrases such as 'give someone evils'.

### Glossary

**ank** to move quickly

**babber** a baby; also used as an affectionate term of address

**cacks** underwear

**daps** plimsolls or running shoes

**dog up** to 'dog someone up' is to stare at them aggressively

**emmet** in Cornwall, an 'emmet' is a tourist (from an old dialect word for an ant)

**fire up** to 'fire a person up' is to physically assault them

**gashead** a supporter of Bristol Rovers Football Club

**give evils** to 'give someone evils' is to stare at them censoriously or aggressively

**grockle** a tourist or incomer in south-west England

**gurt** very large

**jammer** someone who is lucky (from 'jammy')

**jan** a tramp

**Janner** a person from Devon

**jasper** a wasp

**kiddies** a group of people who are described (or describe themselves) as 'the kiddies' are the best at the activity concerned

**macky** very large
**pisser** an awkward or painful fall (perhaps referring to the contribution made by drunkenness)

**raggy** a roll-up cigarette
**scutler** a woman of dubious morals
**topper** the crusty end-slice of a loaf of bread

## Southern English slang

In England, the South is tricky to define. There are those who say that everything below Watford is in the South; others would separate off the South-West and South-East. If London is excluded (as it is in this book), the area is constricted further, but still includes a wide-ranging area from rural Hampshire to Kent and Essex, where 'Estuary English' (a form of the language heavily influenced by the Cockney of nearby London) is spoken. In the ports of the south coast the influence on local slang of the seafaring life is palpable, but this brand of language has already been treated in this book under the heading of Nautical slang. Of course, slang terms found in London and the surrounding area will also be current in the South, but the list below attempts to identify slang that is specific to the South.

### Glossary

**ackle** to work or function
**ballyrag** to bully or scold
**bit an' drap** something to eat and drink, a meal
**bosh** to 'bosh' a job is to do it quickly and carelessly
**bruv** a friendly term of address between males (shortened from 'bruvver', a pronunciation of 'brother')
**cheeselog** a woodlouse

**crousty** ill-tempered
**dewbit** breakfast
**doobry** a thing whose name is unknown or temporarily forgotten
**Essex Girl** an archetypal working-class female from south-east England, with low-brow tastes and supposedly limited intelligence
**Essex Man** an archetypal

working-class male from south-east England, without cultural interests or good taste but with a large disposable income which he spends freely, mainly on consumer goods and entertainment

**joppety-joppety** a state of nervous agitation

**luzz** to 'luzz' something is to throw or pass it

**noggerhead** a foolish person

**Pompey** a nickname for Portsmouth

**tinklebobs** icicles

## *London slang*

Some writers prefer to label the slang peculiar to London as 'Cockney slang'. A Cockney is defined as a person born in London, strictly within hearing of Bow Bells, which, of course, would make him or her an East Ender. The Cockneys, especially the market traders among them, are credited with creating **rhyming slang**, and this type of language is mainly covered in a separate section of this book. Sometimes, when only the first part of a piece of rhyming slang is used, it may be difficult to identify it as such, and, for those not in the know, some examples are given here, such as 'boat', 'hampton' and 'hampsteads'. While much of the slang in the following list may indeed be Cockney, and Cockneys continue to be widely seen as the archetypal Londoners, 21st-century London is very much larger than the East End. The London of pearly kings and queens and *Knees-up Muvver Brown* is largely perpetuated for the benefit of tourists.

As well as being the capital and seat of government of the United Kingdom, London is one of the major cities of the world and continues to be a melting pot of widely disparate influences and cultures. Like any capital it is a centre of the arts, the media and fashion. What is new and trendy there soon becomes fashionable elsewhere, and this is as true of slang as anything else. Slang terms that originate in London are picked up quickly around the country (never more so than in this age of instant communications), and what is said in highly popular television programmes like *Minder, Only Fools and Horses* and *EastEnders* is soon assimilated and bandied about by mere provincials. Some London slang resists being uprooted, however. Sometimes this is because there is a particularly local reference involved, as in 'Brixton briefcase' or 'Croydon facelift'; in other cases, local equivalents seem more appropriate (for example 'John' would be out of place in Glasgow and would be replaced by 'Jimmy', likely to be a more common name there). Occasionally, London pronunciation is the barrier: 'tin bath' would not rhyme exactly with 'laugh' elsewhere, nor would 'round the houses' with 'trousers'.

The list below contains only a smattering of the slang used in the capital; expressions covered in many of the other subject lists in this book are just as likely to be heard on the streets of London, not only those which originated there.

## Glossary

**afters** a period of drinking in a pub after it has officially closed for the night

**barnet** your 'barnet' is your hair (shortened from the rhyming slang 'Barnet Fair')

**boat** the face (shortened from the rhyming slang 'boat race', referring to the annual university rowing race on the River Thames)

**Brixton briefcase** a large portable hi-fi with built-in speakers (from their popularity among black youths in the Brixton area)

**browns** 'a browns' is a cigarette

**charlie** a fool, often heard in the phrases 'a proper charlie' or 'a right charlie' (perhaps from 'Charlie Hunt', rhyming slang for 'cunt')

**ching** five pounds sterling

**chip** to depart

**Croydon facelift** the effect on a young woman's face of pulling the hair back very tightly into a pony-tail

**cushty** very good or excellent

**diamond** used to describe anything that the speaker approves of highly, as in the phrase 'a diamond geezer' meaning a splendid fellow

**do the off** to depart (a variant is the rhyming slang **do the Frank**, after the broadcaster Frank Bough)

**dutch** your 'dutch' is your wife (perhaps short for 'Duchess of Fife', rhyming slang for 'wife')

**gack** or **gak** cocaine

**gaff** a person's private accommodation

**gertcha** a phrase of dismissal, disbelief, etc (from 'get away with you')

**go into one** to lose your temper

**gooner** a supporter of Arsenal Football Club (from 'gunner')

**guv** a respectful form of address to a boss or older man (from 'governor')

**gypsy's** an act of urination (shortened from 'gypsy's kiss', rhyming slang for 'piss')

**hampsteads** the teeth (from rhyming slang 'Hampstead Heath')

**hampton** the penis (shortened from 'Hampton Wick', rhyming slang for 'prick')

**hanging** something that is 'hanging' is of inferior quality

**have it away on your toes** to run away

**herbert** a despicable or insignificant person, as in the phrase 'a spotty little herbert'

**her indoors** the speaker's wife (popularized by the television series *Minder*)

**John** a term of address for a man

**knees-up** a riotous dance or party (the image being of dancers lifting up their legs)

**leave it out!** stop it!

**love a duck!** a mild exclamation

**lovely jubbly** excellent or wonderful (apparently coined in the 1980s by John Sullivan, writer of the BBC sitcom *Only Fools and Horses*)

**minces** the eyes (from rhyming slang 'mince pies')

**moody** not genuine, but fake or counterfeit

**muller** or **mullah** to beat severely, defeat heavily or murder

**mullered** or **mullahed** intoxicated

**nang** excellent

**nosh** to perform oral sex

**Oxo cube** 'the Oxo cube' is the London Underground (rhyming slang for **Tube**)

**pictures of the Queen** banknotes

**porky** a lie (from rhyming slang 'pork pie')

**porridge wog** a Scottish person

**round the houses** trousers (rhyming slang)

**seeing-to** to 'give someone a seeing-to' means to have sex with them; it can also mean to give someone a beating

**shoeing** a 'shoeing' is the same as a 'kicking', in the sense of a physical beating, but can also mean a vigorous effort at something

**Smoke** 'the Smoke' is a nickname for London

**sort** a woman, especially an attractive one

**stroll on!** an exclamation of surprise, disbelief, etc, often used ironically

**tin bath** laugh (rhyming slang, owing to pronunciation of 'bath' as 'baff')

**Tube** 'the Tube' is the London Underground

**up west** in or to the West End of London

**well hard** someone who is 'well hard' is considered tough

**wolly** a pickled olive or cucumber

# SLANG THROUGH THE AGES

The following section deals with slang expressions in terms of when they are first recorded as being in use. Dating the first appearance of words and phrases is always difficult, but with slang the problems are exacerbated by the fact that slang was often seen as an inferior, even deplorable, brand of language, and as such not worthy of being written down. In the light of this, the ascribing of dates to slang terms is always approximate; to say that an expression belongs to the 16th century or the 20th century often just means that it was first recorded then, not that no-one in the preceding or subsequent few years ever said it.

The lists in this section are not intended to be a complete record of the slang of the period concerned – for one thing, this would involve tedious repetition of material covered in other lists in the book. Rather they aim to give a flavour of the slang of each period, concentrating on items whose specificity, longevity or relative novelty is particularly interesting, as well as vocabulary not included in other specific lists.

## *The 16th century*

The slang that begins to be recorded in the 16th century is very much the language of the underworld, which most readers would regard with fear and hostility. In this period glossaries of 'thieves' cant' were published. The purpose of these collections was ostensibly to put readers on their guard against the wiles of confidence tricksters and other criminals, but they also offered readers vicarious thrills, much in the way that today's audiences continue to enjoy crime stories. The plays of Shakespeare and his contemporaries included some of this vocabulary as well as the more fashionable slang terms of the day.

It is remarkable how modern some of the terms sound. If he were around today and inclined to put himself about a bit, a person from the 16th century would have no trouble in recognizing a 'bruiser' or someone who 'chuntered on', and might well find himself in such a 'pickle' as to contract a dose of 'the clap'. Some terms, on the other hand, are quite strange to us, such as the use of 'niggle' to mean sexual intercourse or a 'cheat' as being a thing in general.

## Glossary

**Abraham-man** an unruly beggar, especially one feigning insanity (said to be named after the Abraham ward in the Bethlehem Royal Hospital, a psychiatric hospital in London)

**barnacles** spectacles

**bawcock** a fine fellow (from the French phrase *beau coq*)

**bawdy basket** a female beggar or thief, often selling obscene literature

**bing** to go

**bousingken** a low drinking-shop (obviously related to the later word 'booze')

**brass** money

**bruiser** a prize-fighter or violent person

**bung** a purse, or someone who steals one

**candle-waster** someone who studies late into the night

**cheat** a thing in general

**chunter** to mutter or grumble

**clack** the tongue

**clap** 'the clap' meant (and still does mean) gonorrhoea

**clink** prison

**cly** to seize or steal

**commodity** a whore

**coney-catcher** a confidence trickster ('coney' here means a rabbit)

**costard** the head

**cove** a chap

**crush a cup** to drink a glass of wine

**darkmans** night

**dell** a young girl or prostitute

**doxy** a loose woman

**duck** a term of address for a darling or sweetheart

**duds** clothes

**fap** drunk

**frig** to masturbate

**geck** a fool

**gob** the mouth

**grease** to bribe

**greedy guts** a greedy person

**have** to have sex with

**higgledy-piggledy** in confusion

**horn** an erection of the penis

**hunks** a miserly curmudgeon

**in hot water** in trouble

**jark** a seal on a (usually counterfeit) document

**jay** a flashy, immoral woman

**jobernowl** a stupid person

**lazybones** an idle person

**lick** to defeat

**lift** to steal

**lug** the ear

**martin** the victim of a robbery or confidence trick

**maund** to beg

**mill** to beat or thrash

**mutton** a prostitute

**nab** the head

**niggle** to have sexual intercourse

**nip** a robber or cutpurse

**noddle** the head or brain

**not know a B from a bull's foot** to know nothing

**pickle** a predicament

**pins** legs

**pocky** confounded or damned (essentially the same as 'poxy')

**prat** the buttocks

**prick** the penis

**prig** a thief

**rotgut** cheap, poor-quality alcoholic drink

**ruddock** a gold coin

**saucebox** an impudent person

**shaver** a chap

**sheep-biter** a contemptible person

**shift** to go away or move quickly

**skipper** to sleep rough in barns

**streetwalker** a prostitute

**strummel** straw or hair

**traffic** a whore

**upright-man** a sturdy beggar or leader of a gang

**whittle** to confess at the gallows

**win** or **wing** a penny

## The 17th century

The slang of this period is still firmly tied to the world of thieves, jailbirds and whores, with vocabulary like 'bracelets', 'collegiate' and 'nubbing-cove', but it also expands into everyday life, with terms like 'broke', 'hubby' and 'knock off' becoming current. It was a period that saw great upheaval, in which civil war ravaged Britain, ending with the execution of a king. The Restoration which followed saw an upsurge in drama, and contemporary slang was very much in evidence in the works of popular playwrights such as Etherege, Wycherley and Vanbrugh. The wider English-speaking world begins to make its mark on slang in this period, with the appearance in the American colonies of terms like 'juice', meaning alcoholic drink, and in southern Africa of 'Kaffir'.

## *Glossary*

**bang** an act of sexual intercourse

**betty** a burglar's jemmy

**bogtrotter** an Irishman

**bone** to seize or arrest

**box** the vagina

**bracelets** handcuffs

**broke** bankrupt or having no money

**Brum** Birmingham

**bub** strong drink

**bust a gut** to work very hard

**butter-print** a child

**canary** a guinea or sovereign

**canary-bird** a jailbird or convict

**chat** a louse

**chicken** afraid; also used to mean a coward

**chiv** a knife

**cit** a town-dweller, not a gentleman (from 'citizen')

**claret** blood

**cock** the penis

**collar** to arrest

**collegiate** a prison inmate

**come** or **come off** to achieve sexual orgasm

**cook the books** to falsify accounts

**cracked** crazy

**cully** a pal, or a man in general

**darbies** handcuffs

**dead men** emptied bottles

**diver** a pickpocket

**do** to cheat or swindle

**elevated** drunk

**fence** a receiver of stolen goods

**flush** having money

**gripe** a usurer

**grub** food

**hog** a shilling

**hoof it** to walk

**hopping mad** very angry

**hubby** a husband

**in with** friendly with

**invite** an invitation

**juice** alcoholic drink (originally American)

**Kaffir** a black person in southern Africa

**kick** the fashion

**knob** the penis

**knock off** to stop work

**lay** a sexual partner

**leg it** to run away

**mill** to rob

**mobility** the common people (a play on 'mob' and 'nobility')

**mouse** to hit someone in the face

**muff** a woman's genitals

**mulligrubs** colic or sulkiness

**mumper** a beggar

**nab** a hat

**nim** to steal

**nub** the gallows (also **nubbing-cheat**)

**nubbing-cove** a hangman

**overshot** drunk

**pal** a friend

**paw** a hand

**phiz** the face (from 'physiognomy')

**pickled** drunk

**pike** to go quickly

**pinch** to steal

**plant** a thief's hoard

**plover** a dupe, or a prostitute

**puke** to vomit

**quid** a pound sterling

**rhino** money

**rhinocerical** rich

**sawney** a fool

**slimy** obsequiously servile

**smelt** a half-guinea

**sock** to hit or punch

**son of a bitch** a term of abuse

**spanker** a gold coin

**sponger** someone who lives at other people's expense

**squitters** diarrhoea

**stingo** strong malt liquor

**stretcher** a lie

**Taffy** a Welshman

**Taig** a Catholic in Northern Ireland

**tail** the female genitals or the penis

**tarpaulin** a sailor

**tit** a female breast or nipple

**tribulation** if goods were said to be 'in tribulation', they had been pawned

**tony** a simpleton

**turn in** to go to bed

**turn off** to 'turn someone off' meant to execute them by hanging

**what's-its-name** something whose name cannot be recalled at the moment

**when pigs fly** never

## The 18th century

In this era, slang still includes underworld terms, such as 'beak', 'cop' and 'hoister', but the emphasis appears to shift even more markedly towards the common experiences of society at large. Fashion is important, with the new-fangled trousers coming to replace breeches and being labelled as 'indescribables'. Heavy drinking was plainly prevalent, with numerous terms for being drunk coming into use, such as 'bosky', 'cockeyed' or 'half-seas-over'. Another social indicator is the large amount of sexual slang. Much of this we would still recognize today (such as 'hump', 'quim' and 'screw'); other terms, for whatever reason, have faded out of memory (as in the case of 'smoke').

The novel was becoming important in literary circles, and slang often features in the works of, for example, Henry Fielding and Tobias Smollett. It is to the satirist Jonathan Swift that we owe the creation of the term 'yahoo', which is still familiar to the modern ear. The American colonies were lost to Britain in this period, but the Atlantic came to be referred to as 'the pond', and terms like 'pappy' and 'toot' were among the imports from that part of the world. India too makes its contribution, with 'bundook' and 'pukka'.

## Glossary

**all my eye** nonsense
**all the go** in fashion
**all there** sane, not stupid
**bam** to hoax or deceive (shortened from 'bamboozle')
**beak** a magistrate
**bite** a playful imposition or act of swindling
**blasted** used as a mild expletive
**blunt** cash
**bob** a shilling

**bog** a toilet
**bogus** fake or spurious (of American origin)
**bollocks** the testicles
**bosky** somewhat tipsy
**botheration** petty trouble
**bounce** to reprimand
**breadbasket** the stomach
**breeze** a quarrel
**broadbrush** not worked out in detail
**bundook** a rifle (from Hindi)

**bunk** to flee or play truant

**cabbage** to steal or purloin

**cake** a madcap or fool

**caning** a severe beating or defeat

**cat** a malicious or spiteful woman

**catch your death of cold** to catch a very bad cold

**chap** a man, boy or fellow (originally from an Old English term meaning 'trader')

**character** an odd or eccentric person

**chatterbox** someone who chatters or talks incessantly

**clout** a blow

**cockeyed** drunk

**cod** a lie (originally Irish)

**college** a prison

**confab** to talk (shortened from 'confabulate')

**cool** all of, not less than (as in 'a cool thousand pounds')

**coot** a foolish, silly person

**cop** to capture or arrest; hence to acquire or obtain

**corporation** a pot-belly

**cram** a lie

**crazy** extravagantly enthusiastic or passionate

**crocus** a quack doctor

**cut** to run away

**daisy-cutter** a fast horse

**dandy** fine

**dish** to outwit

**doctor** brown sherry

**drill** to pierce with a bullet or bullets

**flabbergasted** confounded

**frisk** to search

**gams** the legs

**glim** an eye

**glorious** tipsy

**gosh** a mild exclamation

**half-seas-over** slightly drunk

**hoister** a shoplifter

**hop** a dance party

**hump** to have sexual intercourse with

**hush money** money paid for silence

**indescribables** trousers

**infernal** unpleasant or annoying

**jarvey** a hackney-coach driver

**jiff** or **jiffy** an instant

**jump** to attack

**kick the bucket** to die

**knowledge box** the brain

**leathering** a beating

**let on** to disclose or divulge

**livestock** domestic or body vermin

**madly** extremely

**mag** a halfpenny

**mark** a gullible person, especially a conman's victim

**mighty** very (originally American)

**misery** a doleful person

**mizzle** to leave or decamp

**mot** a young girl or woman (in Irish usage)

**nail** to catch

**napper** the head

**nix my dolly** never mind

**nose** an informer

**number one** oneself

**oaken towel** a cudgel

**oiled** drunk

**Paddy** an Irishman

**pappy** a father (in American usage)

**peepers** the eyes

**pesky** annoying or troublesome

**piddle** to urinate

**pile** a fortune

**pond** 'the pond' is the Atlantic Ocean

**pony** a sum of twenty-five pounds

**pop off** to die

**prad** a horse

**pukka** genuine (from Hindustani)

**quim** the female genitals

**rum** odd or strange

**Sandy** or **Sawney** a Scot

**saphead** a fool

**savvy** to know or understand

**scab** a strikebreaker (in American usage)

**screw** to have sexual intercourse with

**shaft** the penis

**shit** to defecate

**shithouse** a toilet

**shooting iron** a firearm

**skew-whiff** crooked or awry

**sky parlour** an attic

**smasher** a person who passes bad money

**smoke** to have sexual intercourse with

**snaffling lay** the profession of highway robbery

**snob** a shoemaker or cobbler, or an apprentice to one of these

**spiflicate** to destroy

**spit** an exact replica

**sprog** a child

**stash** to stop or desist

**suck the monkey** to insert a tube into a cask and drink the contents

**swab** a naval officer's epaulette

**swag** plunder

**sweat** to extract a confession or evidence from someone (originally American)

**swell** a fashionable or finely dressed person

**swipes** inferior or weak beer

**swizzle** a strong, mixed alcoholic drink

**syebuck** a sixpence

**ta** thank you

**tail** the buttocks

**thingumabob** something whose name cannot be recalled at the moment

**throw up** to vomit

**tilbury** a sixpence (this being the ferry fare across the Thames from Gravesend to Tilbury)

**toot** a drinking binge (in American usage)

**top** to kill, especially by hanging

**towel** to cudgel

**understandings** the legs, feet or footwear

**upper storey** the brain

**weeny** very small

**whack** to strike hard; also used to mean a share

**wipe** a handkerchief

**yahoo** an unrefined loutish person (coined by Jonathan Swift in *Gulliver's Travels* (1726) for a class of animals which are human in form but which have the understanding and passions of brutes)

## *The 19th century*

The 19th century was very much the age of empire, and saw the rise of English to the status of a world language. Slang terms from all over the English-speaking world show the extent of Britain's interaction with its far-flung possessions, with, for example, 'Abo', 'Buckley's' and 'cobber' entering the language from Australia. However, the independent United States of America also became a world power, and its particular slang was increasingly recorded there and exported to Britain. Many of these US terms are still familiar to us, whether or not they have been adopted into British use, including 'bushed', 'dough', 'creep', 'greenback' and 'heist'.

This was also an age of greater literacy: printed sources such as newspapers and magazines proliferated, and great novelists, from Thackeray to Trollope and George Eliot, were widely read. Chief among them, of course, was Charles Dickens, and his enjoyment and vivid use of slang immortalized many usages in print.

## Glossary

**Abo** an Aboriginal (in Australian usage)

**ack emma** before midday (in military slang)

**all mouth and no trousers** given to making boasts that are not backed up by your actions

**all over the shop** disordered, everywhere

**and no mistake** assuredly

**axe** dismissal from a job

**bad** excellent, tough or attractive (in American usage)

**bag** to catch or obtain

**bags** trousers

**bags I** I lay claim to

**bait** a rage

**bald-headed** without restraint or regard for consequences

**balls** guts or courage; also used to mean nonsense

**bang-up** excellent

**barmy** mad

**barnet** the hair (shortened from the rhyming slang 'Barnet Fair')

**barney** an argument

**battle-axe** an intimidating woman

**bazoo** the mouth (in American usage)

**beanpole** a tall thin person

**bellyache** to complain

**bender** a spree

**benny** an overcoat (probably, from 'Benjamin', a tailor's name)

**bevvy** alcoholic drink

**biccy** a biscuit

**biff** to hit

**big fish** an important person

**bigmouth** a talkative and often boastful or indiscreet person

**bint** a young woman

**bird** a woman or girlfriend

**blag** a robbery

**bleeder** a person

**bleeding** a euphemism for 'bloody'

**bobbery** a noisy disturbance

**bobby** a policeman (familiar form of 'Robert', after Sir Robert Peel, Home Secretary at the passing of the Metropolitan Police Act in 1828)

**bobby-dazzler** anything excellent

**bod** a person

**bodacious** extremely good (an American usage rediscovered in the 1960s)

**boko** the nose

**bonce** the head

**bone up on** to study (in American usage)

**bookie** a bookmaker

**boomer** anything large or successful

**boozer** a public house

**bosh** nonsense, foolish talk

**boss** excellent (in American usage)

**boss cocky** a boss (in Australian usage)

**bounder** a person whose moral conduct is objectionable

**box** a coffin

**boys in blue** the police force

**brainbox** the cranium, or a very clever person

**brass** effrontery or cheek

**brass monkeys** very cold

**brolly** an umbrella

**bs** bullshit (in American usage)

**buck** a US dollar

**bucket shop** the premises of an unregistered stockbroker (in American usage)

**Buckley's** or **Buckley's chance** no chance (in Australian usage)

**buddy** a friend (in American usage)

**bug** a fault (in American usage)

**bumf** lavatory paper; also used as a derogatory term for official documents

**bunce** profit or gain

**bunch of fives** a fist

**bun fight** a tea party

**bushed** exhausted

**butterfingers** someone who lets something they ought to catch slip through their fingers

**buzz** an immediate sensation of pleasure from alcohol or drugs (in American usage)

**cagey** wary or secretive

**Canuck** a Canadian (in American usage)

**catch it** to be scolded or reprimanded

**caution** an alarming or amusing thing or person

**celestial** a Chinese person

**cert** a certainty

**chancer** an opportunist

**chat up** to talk informally and flirtatiously to

**cheapskate** a miserly person

**cheese it** to desist or run away

**chin-chin** cheers, or farewell

**chipper** cheerful, fit and well

**chizz** a cheat

**chronic** deplorable

**cinch** something easy

**circs** circumstances

**civvy** civilian

**clinch** an embrace

**clobber** clothes

**clock** to record a certain speed or time

**clout** influence

**cobber** a mate or chum (in Australian usage)

**cocksucker** a sycophant

**come a cropper** to have a fall

**come off it!** don't be ridiculous!

**comeuppance** a deserved rebuke or punishment

**comfy** comfortable

**cool** satisfactory, agreeable or good

**cop** or **copper** a policeman

**corker** anything excellent

**crackerjack** an excellent thing (in American usage)

**creep** an unpleasant person (in American usage)

**crib** a person's home (in American usage)

**cuckoo** slightly mad

**dead duck** a failure

**dekko** a look

**digs** lodgings

**dippy** eccentric

**dip your wick** to have sex

**do in** to kill

**do over** to beat up

**doss** to sleep

**dotty** eccentric

**dough** money (in American usage)

**doughboy** an American infantryman (a US military use dating back to the Mexican War of 1847)

**draw it mild** to refrain from exaggeration

**dude** a man (in American usage)

**earthly** the slightest chance

**elevenses** an eleven o'clock snack

**faff about** to waste time

**fanny** a woman's genitals

**fat chance** little or no opportunity or prospect (originally American)

**firebug** an arsonist

**fit up** to incriminate someone falsely

**fix** a dilemma

**flash** to expose yourself

**fling** a brief sexual relationship

**foxy** sexually attractive

**fuck all** nothing

**fuck up** to damage or mar

**funny business** deceptive behaviour

**geek** a misfit

**geezer** a man

**get outside of** to eat or drink

**glad rags** your best clothes

**goody** a character on the side of justice

**grapevine** a source of rumour

**greenback** a US dollar

**guy** a man

**half-cut** drunk

**ham** a bad actor

**handle** a name

**hang out** to lodge or reside

**hard-on** an erection of the penis

**harp** a harmonica

**heist** to steal money (in American usage)

**his nibs** or **her nibs** a mock title for an important person

**hock** to pawn

**homeboy** someone from the same neighbourhood as yourself (in American usage)

**honky-tonk** a disreputable drinking haunt (in American usage)

**how come?** how does that come about?

**hunky-dory** in a good position or condition

**in a pig's whisper** immediately

**jacksie** the buttocks or anus

**jerry** someone who builds cheap flimsy houses

**jolly** very

**kibosh** to put an end to

**kinky** eccentric (in American usage)

**knee-trembler** sexual intercourse in a standing position

**knock into the middle of next week** to hit very hard

**lashings** an abundance

**lead towel** a bullet

**lickety-split** very quickly

**loaded** intoxicated

**London particular** a London fog

**lulu** an outstandingly bad or impressive thing or person

**meal ticket** a guarantee of success

**miss the boat** to be too late, to miss your chance

**monkey** the sum of five hundred pounds

**mug** to attack with the intention of robbing

**narky** irritable

**neck** to kiss and cuddle

**needle** to irritate

**nifty** stylish

**nope** no

**not half bad** quite good

**off your rocker** insane

**OK** satisfactory

**out of sight** excellent

**parky** cold

**peeler** a policeman (after Sir Robert Peel; see **bobby**)

**peg leg** a wooden leg

**perk** an incidental benefit

**phoney** counterfeit, fake

**pic** a picture

**pig** a police officer

**poke** to have sex with
**pub** a public house
**pull** to arrest
**rattler** a cab
**ring** the anus
**ripping** excellent
**rozzer** a policeman
**sap** a fool
**sawbones** a doctor
**scarper** to run away
**scorcher** a day of scorching heat
**screwy** eccentric or slightly mad
**scrubber** an unattractive woman
**shag** to have sexual intercourse with
**sheila** a girl or woman (an Australian usage)
**shenanigans** mischief or antics
**shooter** a gun
**skint** without money
**sky pilot** a military chaplain
**smartypants** an irritatingly clever person
**snatch** the female genitals
**snotrag** a handkerchief
**sov** a pound sterling (shortened from 'sovereign')
**squiffy** tipsy
**stiff** a corpse
**stunner** a very attractive person, especially a woman
**swiz** a fraud or great disappointment
**tenner** a ten-pound note
**the real McCoy** the genuine article
**tidy** fairly good or big
**todger** the penis
**tummy** the stomach
**Uncle Sam** the United States
**-ville** a suffix denoting a supposed world, milieu, etc frequented by a specified type of person or characterized by a specified quality, as in 'squaresville' or 'dullsville'
**wank** to masturbate
**yellow** cowardly

# World War I

The most important event of the earlier 20th century was undoubtedly the Great War of 1914–18. Many thousands of young men from around the English-speaking world were uprooted from home, in most cases for the first time, and exposed to forms of language that they would never have normally encountered. As well as the established military slang that spread from the regulars to the conscripts (which has been discussed in the earlier section on **Military slang**), terms were coined that were specific to the new and horrifying mode of war that took place in the trenches of the Western Front (for example, 'blighty', 'over the top' and 'whizzbang'). British soldiers not only came into contact with comrades from other parts of the British Isles, helping the spread of hitherto localized slang such as Cockney rhyming slang, but also with Canadians, Australians, New Zealanders, South Africans and Americans, and became familiar with much of their slang too. Soldiers' experience of trying to converse with French speakers also contributed to British slang, with 'boche', 'napoo', 'plonk' and 'san fairy ann' entering the language.

## *Glossary*

**ace** an airman of the highest quality, especially one who has downed several enemy aircraft

**Archibald** an anti-aircraft gun or its fire (also called **Archie**)

**AWOL** absent without official leave

**Big Bertha** a big German gun, such as those used to shell Paris in 1918 (an uncomplimentary reference to the girth of Frau Berta Krupp, whose husband owned the Krupp steelworks where these were made)

**blighty** a wound necessitating a return home (ie back to 'Blighty')

**boche** a German, especially a German soldier (originally a French term)

**bolshie** awkward or intractable (from 'Bolshevik', a Russian revolutionary)

**conchy** or **conchie** a conscientious objector

**dog tag** a soldier's metal identity disc

**Dora** The Defence of the Realm Act (1914), which imposed wartime restrictions

**Eyetie** an Italian

**Fred Karno's Army** the conscript British army that replaced the largely regular force at the beginning of the war (from the name of a popular music-hall comedian)

**gasper** a cigarette

**Hun** a German

**imshi!** go away! (from Arabic)

**Jerry** a German, or Germans collectively

**Kaiser Bill** the German emperor Wilhelm I

**kaput** ruined, broken or not working (from German)

**napoo** no more, good for nothing or dead (from the French phrase *il n'y en a plus* meaning 'there is no more of it')

**Old Contemptibles** the British Expeditionary Force to France in 1914 (from the Kaiser's probably apocryphal reference to them as 'a contemptible little army')

**over the top** to go 'over the top' meant to go out of one's trench and attack the enemy

**pineapple** a hand grenade or a bomb

**pipsqueak** a type of German shell

**plonk** wine, especially of poor quality (perhaps from the French *vin blanc* meaning 'white wine')

**Russki** a Russian

**san fairy** (or **ferry**) **ann** it doesn't matter (a phonetic reproduction of the French phrase *ça ne fait rien*)

**souvenir** to 'souvenir' something is to steal it (in Australian usage)

**strafe** to bombard or assail (from the German *strafen* meaning 'to punish')

**when the balloon goes up** when the trouble starts or when the proceedings begin (from the observation balloons that would be sent up before a battle)

**whizzbang** a light shell of high velocity which is heard arriving shortly before it explodes

## The 1920s

The slang of the decade that followed the Great War seems to be marked by the desire of the young to enjoy themselves, no doubt as a contrast to what had gone before. Writers such as PG Wodehouse and F Scott Fitzgerald chronicled 'flappers', 'bimbos' and their partners, determined to 'party', no matter what the 'dismal Jimmies' had to say. Recreational drugs had always been available, but their use seems to have become wider at this time, with terms like 'coked up', 'H', 'junkie' and 'nose candy' becoming current. Similarly, sexuality seems to have become more open. While the Victorians may have been reluctant to believe that there was such a thing as lesbianism, and Oscar Wilde labelled homosexuality as 'the love that dare not speak its name', in the 1920s many more people understood what was meant by 'fag', 'homo' or 'lesbo'. Fitzgerald called the period 'The Jazz Age', and it was this imported music that brought many American slang terms to Britain through its associated terminology and song lyrics. The burgeoning cinema also played its part in this process, with words like 'heart-throb' and 'weepy' being first recorded.

## Glossary

**and how!** yes, very much (in American usage)

**attaboy** an interjection expressing encouragement or approval (possibly a corruption of 'that's the boy')

**beaver** a woman's genitals

**Big Apple** 'the Big Apple' is a nickname for New York City

**bimbo** a person, especially one who is young and physically very attractive but dim, naïve or superficial

**booty** the vagina, or the buttocks (in American usage)

**bop** to strike

**bubbly** champagne

**buy** to accept or believe (in American usage)

**buzz** to make a phone call (in American usage)

**carry the can** to take the blame

**chute** a parachute

**cock up** to do or perform very badly

**coked up** under the influence of cocaine

**cop a plea** to plead guilty to a lesser charge

**cowboy** someone who behaves recklessly or irresponsibly

**crackers** crazy or unbalanced

**cruise** to go round public places looking for a sexual partner

**dismal Jimmy** a pessimist

**fag** a male homosexual (in American usage)

**fat cat** a prosperous person (in American usage)

**fave** favourite

**flab** excess body fat

**flapper** a flighty young woman, especially one ostentatiously unconventional in dress or behaviour

**for the high jump** in trouble (originally this meant 'sentenced to be hanged')

**fry** to execute by electrocution (in American usage)

**fuzz** the police

**gaga** deranged or senile

**geek** a carnival freak (in American usage)

**gig** a concert

**H** heroin

**haywire** all awry

**heart-throb** a person who is the object of great romantic affection from afar

**hokum** nonsense or sentimentality

**homo** a homosexual

**hot pants** sexual desire

**icky** sentimental

**junkie** a drug addict

**lesbo** or **lez** a lesbian

**level with** to be frank with

**loopy** insane

**malarkey** fuss

**Mickey Finn** a spiked drink

**minder** a bodyguard

**motherfucker** an objectionable person or thing

**nite** night

**nooky** sexual intercourse

**nose candy** cocaine

**party** to participate in parties, or to have a good time

**peachy** very good or excellent

**pissed** drunk

**potty** insane

**poxy** unpleasant or contemptible

**samey** alike or monotonous

**scram** to go away

**speed cop** a policeman who watches out for speeding motorists

**stud** a sexually potent or active man

**tickety-boo** fine or satisfactory

**up the pole** pregnant

**weepie** a highly emotional film, play or book

## The 1930s

The 1930s was a more politicized decade than the 1920s. Against a background of worldwide economic depression, politics of left and right vied for the allegiance of the public, and terms like 'commie' and 'leftie' first entered the slang lexicon. Exposure of British audiences to American slang continued to widen through the proliferation of wireless radio sets and the cinema, where 'talkies' now came in, full of American 'patter' and wisecracks, and a new kind of hero in the form of the 'private eye'. Film stars were increasingly the greatest celebrities of the day, and were described variously as 'bombshells', 'cheesecake' and 'sex goddesses'. It is perhaps surprising to see, among young black Americans, especially jazz musicians, the emergence of slang terms that are most often associated with the 1960s, such as 'dig', 'groove', 'groovy' and 'lick'. On the other hand, many would have thought that 'mother's ruin' was of much older vintage than the 1930s.

## Glossary

**anchors** brakes, especially of a motor vehicle

**baddy** a villain in a film or radio show

**bags** plenty

**bash** an attempt

**bent** stolen

**berk** a fool

**bollock** to reprimand

**bombshell** an attractive young woman (in American usage)

**bonk** to hit or thump

**boob** a female breast

**bread** money (in American usage)

**browned off** fed up

**bull dyke** a masculine lesbian

**butch** a masculine lesbian

**buzz** a thrill (in American usage)

**cane** to defeat thoroughly

**Charlie** cocaine

**cheesecake** women with sex appeal (in American usage)

**commie** a communist

**corny** sentimental, old-fashioned or dull through overuse

**crunch** the critical moment

**dig** to understand

**dog** an unattractive woman

**drip** a weak person

**dum-dum** a stupid person

**dyke** a lesbian

**fart about** to waste time

**fatso** an overweight person

**five-o'clock shadow** the

new growth of hair that becomes noticeable on a man's shaven face in the late afternoon

**fix** a shot of heroin or another drug

**funny money** counterfeit money

**gaff** a person's home

**get down** to 'get someone down' means to depress them

**get up someone's nose** to annoy them

**go overboard** to go to extremes of enthusiasm

**grass** a police informer

**groove** to experience pleasure

**groovy** good

**gunk** any unpleasant substance

**hepcat** or **hepster** a fashionable, well-informed person

**hoo-ha** a fuss

**it** Italian vermouth, as in 'gin and it'

**juke** to dance

**knockers** a woman's breasts

**leftie** a socialist

**lick** a short instrumental passage or flourish

**mainline** to take a narcotic drug intravenously

**mother's ruin** gin

**odds and sods** miscellaneous things

**oppo** a mate or pal

**pad** a person's home

**pinko** a communist

**pix** pictures

**pizzazz** flair

**platter** a gramophone record

**pot** marijuana

**pressie** a present

**private eye** a private investigator

**readies** cash

**sausage dog** a dachshund

**scanties** women's underpants

**sex goddess** a female film star with sex appeal

**shag** an act of sexual intercourse

**snatch** a robbery or kidnapping

**snazzy** attractive, smart or fashionable

**souped-up** if an engine is 'souped-up', it has been modified to increase its power

**spliff** a marijuana cigarette

**swish** a male homosexual

**swiz** to defraud or cheat

**talkies** films with a soundtrack as opposed to silent films

**tizzy** a state of confusion

**toots** an affectionate term of address

**tops** the best

**walk it** to win easily

**wide boy** an astute or wily person

**write-off** an aircraft that has crashed and been destroyed

**yob** or **yobbo** a teenage lout

**you can say that again** you are absolutely right

## *World War II and the 1940s*

Another World War (1939–45) again meant the exposure of a generation of young men to the slang both of the armed forces and of other areas and parts of the English-speaking world. However, unlike World War I, this was 'total war' in which the bombing of cities meant that civilians were for the first time on the front line. Because of this, slang terms directly relating to the war became widely known throughout the general population, instead of purely amongst combatants. These included 'Brylcreem Boys', 'doodlebug', 'flak' and 'moaning minnie'. American usages continued to be spread by the cinema and also by the presence in Britain of the US Air Force and of thousands of GIs in the build-up to D-Day. With so many British men in the services, the absence of manpower on the home front led to many women doing jobs previously held by men, bringing, among other things, the 'clippie' onto the scene. By the time hostilities ended, for many 'demob happy' conscripts, a return to 'civvy street' couldn't come quickly enough.

## *Glossary*

**admin** administration

**badmouth** to criticize

**bad news** someone or something that is troublesome or irritating

**bandit** an enemy aircraft

**bang on** absolutely or correctly

**belt up** to be quiet

**benny** an amphetamine tablet (from 'benzedrine')

**boffin** an intellectual or expert

**boffo** successful

**Brylcreem Boys** a disparaging term used by other forces for members of the RAF, whether or not they actually used the proprietary brand of hair cream in question

**bull** tediously excessive discipline, such as unnecessary drill or polishing of kit

**Burton** in the RAF, if a flier or aircraft had 'gone for a Burton', this meant they were dead or destroyed

**busty** having a large bust

**cake hole** the mouth

**chairborne** working at a desk

**chocko** or **choco** an Australian term for a conscripted member of the Australian armed forces in World War II, especially one who never left the country (shortened from 'chocolate soldier')

**choppers** teeth

**civvy street** civilian life after a period of service in the armed forces

**clippie** a female bus or tram conductor

**clobber** to hit or defeat

**clueless** ignorant, stupid or helpless

**come out (of the closet)** to reveal your homosexuality (originally American)

**crash** or **crash out** to fall asleep or become unconscious

**Dear John letter** a letter from a woman to her husband, fiancé, etc (especially one serving in the armed forces) ending their relationship

**demob happy** excited by the prospect of release from the armed forces

**ditch** to 'ditch' an aircraft is to bring it down in the sea

**doodlebug** the V-1, a German flying bomb

**do the business** to have sexual intercourse

**dreamboat** a wonderful, desirable person

**dreamy** lovely

**drop a clanger** to make a mistake

**eager beaver** an enthusiastic person

**flak** anti-aircraft fire

**flannel** flattery

**foul-up** a mistake

**freeload** to sponge off others

**fubar** an American term used to describe a chaotic or hopeless position (from the initial letters of the phrase '*f*ucked *u*p *b*eyond *a*ll *r*ecognition')

**gauleiter** an overbearing wielder of petty authority (from the Nazi title for a chief official of a district)

**gen** information

**get the chop** to be dismissed

**get weaving** to start moving quickly

**get your rocks off** to achieve sexual orgasm

**gizmo** a gadget

**glamourpuss** a glamorous person

**glossy** a glossy magazine

**gobbledygook** jargon

**grass** marijuana

**gubbins** an indeterminate thing

**hairy** frightening

**hash** hashish

**hassle** trouble or inconvenience

**hiya** a greeting

**horn** the telephone (an American usage)

**jelly** gelignite

**jungle juice** alcoholic liquor

**loo** a lavatory

**Mickey-Mouse** inferior

**milk run** a routine military flight

**moaning minnie** a World War II German mortar that produced a shrieking noise when fired; also used to mean an air-raid siren

**mousetrap** unexceptional cheese

**mucker** a friend

**natter** to gossip

**Nip** a Japanese person

**nit** an idiot

**no-no** an impossibility

**pissed off** annoyed

**preggers** pregnant

**psycho** a psychopath

**pussy** a weak, cowardly man

**rat race** a hectic and unproductive situation

**ropey** bad

**Scouse** Liverpudlian

**shufti** a look or glance

**smack** heroin

**snafu** an chaotic situation (an American acronym for *situation normal all fouled (or fucked) up*)

**sprog** a raw recruit

**square** a person of boringly traditional outlook

**stacked** having a large bust

**tail-end Charlie** the aircraft bringing up the rear in an air-force formation; hence any person who comes at the end

**tash** a moustache

**TTFN** goodbye (from the initial letters of the phrase '*ta-ta for now*')

**up the duff** pregnant

**up yourself** smugly pleased with yourself

**zilch** nothing

## The 1950s

One of the most far-reaching social developments of the 1950s was the coming of television to an increasing number of homes. This soon made an impact on slang, with its detractors labelling it as the 'boob tube' or 'idiot box', while devotees were only interested in what was 'on the box'. The fact that many of the programmes shown were made in the United States only increased the prevalence of American slang in Britain. The emergence, also in the United States, of rock'n'roll (as epitomized by Elvis 'the Pelvis' Presley) created what was perhaps the first real youth culture, not only there but in Britain too. 'Teddy Boys' sporting 'DA' haircuts, sideboards, 'drainpipes' and 'brothel creepers' were soon a feature of the streets of British towns. Technological developments were also reflected in the slang of the period with the likes of 'chopper' and 'nuke'.

### Glossary

**and all that jazz** and all that kind of thing, and so on

**A-OK** fine or well

**axe** a guitar or other musical instrument

**bag** to denigrate or criticize

**bang on** to talk at length

**basket case** a nervous wreck

**bent** homosexual

**bog off** to go away

**bollock-naked** completely naked

**bomb** a lot of money

**bomber** a capsule of an illicit drug

**bonkers** crazy

**boob tube** a television set

**bop** to dance

**box** a television set

**brothel creepers** men's soft shoes with thick rubber soles

**cancer stick** a cigarette

**champers** champagne

**chopper** a helicopter

**chunder** to vomit (in Australian usage)

**cool it** to calm down

**cop out** to avoid responsibility

**DA** an abbreviation for **duck's arse**

**DJ** or **deejay** a disc jockey

**drainpipes** very narrow trousers

**duck's arse** or (US) **ass** a man's hairstyle in which the hair is swept back to a point on the neck resembling a duck's tail, especially worn by **Teddy boys**

**fantabulous** wonderful

**flip** to become angry or excited, or go mad

**funky** of or like blues music (in American usage)

**funny farm** a psychiatric hospital

**get the message** to understand

**give someone five** to shake hands or slap hands above your head

**go spare** to become furious

**hang-up** an obsession

**head** someone who takes hallucinogenic drugs

**headshrinker** a psychiatrist

**ho** a woman, especially a prostitute (in black American usage)

**hooter** the nose

**horse** heroin

**hunky** sexually attractive

**idiot box** or **idiot's lantern** a television

**jugs** a woman's breasts

**knackered** exhausted

**kooky** eccentric

**lippy** lipstick

**mouth off** to talk impudently or indiscreetly

**nuke** a nuclear weapon

**OD** a drug overdose

**piss-up** a drinking session

**raver** an uninhibited, lively person

**Roller** a Rolls-Royce car

**rush** the euphoria experienced after taking a drug

**sci-fi** science fiction

**sex kitten** a young woman with overt sex appeal

**shindig** a noisy quarrel

**shooting gallery** a place where addicts gather to inject drugs

**sickie** a day's sick leave

**stroppy** awkward, obstreperous or quarrelsome

**swinger** someone who is up to date and in the social swim

**swinging** trendy or lively

**Ted** a **Teddy boy** or **Teddy girl**

**Teddy boy** an unruly adolescent affecting a dandyish style of dress (so called because their clothes were reminiscent of those worn during the reign of Edward VII)

**Teddy girl** the female equivalent of a **Teddy boy**

**ticked off** annoyed or angry

**veggies** vegetables

**widdle** an act of urination

**Yorkie** a Yorkshire terrier

# *The 1960s*

The 1960s was a time of great social change, and this is reflected in
the slang of the era. In terms of youth culture, at the beginning of
the decade rock'n'roll was still at its height; by its end, there existed
a full-blown counterculture as exemplified by the lifestyle of the
hippies. The slang of drug use, especially of hallucinogens like 'acid',
was prevalent, especially in the lyrics of psychedelic rock, which spoke
of 'bad trips' and 'blowing your mind'. In Britain, Merseyside, home
of the Beatles, vied with 'swinging London' for dominance of fashion
and music, and use of terms like 'into', 'grotty' and 'heavy' came to
define how trendy an individual appeared to be. However, alongside
the 'trippy' world of 'freaks' and their music, more conventional
lifestyles continued to unwind, in which people contracted 'square
eyes' from watching too much television or got 'bevvied' and
sometimes into a spot of 'bovver'.

Perhaps surprisingly, major events in the world seemed to leave little
or no mark on the slang of the decade, which ignored the space race
and the Cold War, and took only a cursory glance at the war in 'Nam'.

## *Glossary*

**acid** the drug LSD

**arse bandit** a male
homosexual

**bag** a person's interest or
speciality

**banger** a decrepit old car

**barking** mad

**bee stings** small female breasts

**bevvied** drunk

**blow your** or **someone's
mind** to go or cause someone
to go into a state of ecstasy
under the influence of a
drug or of an exhilarating
experience

**bovver** rowdy behaviour and
violence of street gangs

**bovver boots** heavy lace-up
boots, as worn by **bovver
boys**

**bovver boy** a youth involved
in rowdy behaviour

**breadhead** someone
considered to have an
unhealthy or excessive interest
in money

**bummer** a bad trip on drugs, or any nasty experience

**buns** the buttocks

**Charlie** a name given by US forces in Vietnam for the Vietcong or a member of the Vietcong (from 'Victor Charlie', the communications code letters for VC)

**chase the dragon** to inhale the fumes of melting powdered heroin

**closet queen** someone who is keeping their homosexuality secret

**codswallop** nonsense

**crash** to suffer the unpleasant after-effects of a drug high

**crashpad** a place providing temporary sleeping accommodation

**dickhead** a term of abuse

**dipstick** a fool

**disco** a discotheque

**dishy** attractive

**doobie** a marijuana cigarette

**dork** a foolish or awkward person

**downer** a depressant drug or a depressing experience

**filth** the police

**flasher** someone who exposes himself in public

**folkie** a performer or devotee of folk music

**freak** a hippie

**freak out** to have a hallucinatory experience on drugs, or to have a strong fit of anger or anxiety

**get your act**, **yourself** or **your shit together** to organize yourself

**get your knickers in a twist** to become harassed

**give someone stick** to subject someone to censure or abuse

**glitch** a minor problem

**go bananas** to lose your temper

**grok** to understand

**grotty** ugly or dirty

**grunge** a messy or sticky substance

**heavy** profound or affecting

**how does that grab you?** what do you think of that?

**humongous** huge, enormous

**into** keen on or interested in

**Jesus freak** a devout Christian

**left-field** out of the ordinary (originally a baseball term)

**let it all hang out** to be relaxed

**liquid lunch** an instance of drinking alcohol at lunch-time instead of eating food

**looney tune** an insane person (from the name of a

series of madcap cartoon films made by Warner Brothers)

**magic mushrooms** mushrooms with naturally hallucinogenic qualities

**mind-blowing** amazing

**moon** to present your bare buttocks to public view

**muso** a musician

**Nam** Vietnam

**no way** or **no way José** an emphatic denial or refusal to believe

**number** a marijuana cigarette

**on your bike!** a contemptuous expression of dismissal

**pillock** a stupid person

**PJs** pyjamas

**poppers** amyl nitrate or butyl nitrate inhaled from a crushed capsule

**porn** pornography

**pseud** a pretentious person

**queer-bashing** verbal or physical attacks on homosexuals

**raunchy** coarsely or openly sexual

**rent boy** a young male prostitute

**rip-off** a fraud or theft, or something that exploits the success of something else

**sarnie** a sandwich

**sex bomb** a person with a lot of sex appeal

**sexpert** an expert in sexual behaviour

**shrink** a psychiatrist (shortened from 'headshrinker')

**skinflick** a pornographic film

**skin up** to make up a marijuana cigarette

**spaced out** in a dazed or stupefied state, such as that caused by the taking of drugs

**speed** amphetamine

**square eyes** an imaginary condition affecting those who watch too much television

**technicolour yawn** an act of vomiting

**teeny-bopper** a young teenager, especially a girl, who enthusiastically follows the latest trends in pop music, clothes, etc

**tranny** a transistor radio

**trendy** a fashionable person

**trippy** hallucinatory, or reminiscent of a drug experience

**Trot** a Trotskyist

**wheeler-dealer** someone who engages in shrewd bargaining

**yonks** a long time

**za** a pizza (in American usage)

## The 1970s

The 1970s were perhaps more characterized by social conflict than the 1960s. Industrial unrest led to national strikes, power cuts and a three-day working week; in youth culture, hippies gave way to the more confrontational punks. Perhaps because of these trends, the list below contains more insults (such as 'airhead', 'div', 'nutjob' and 'scrote') than terms of endearment or encouragement. Society seemed to be deeply divided, with the 'Sloane Rangers' and the affluent flashing their 'plastic' living in stark contrast to the millions of unemployed people struggling to get by 'on the Social'.

### Glossary

**airhead** an idiot

**awesome** great or wonderful

**bean counter** an accountant

**Bolivian marching powder** cocaine

**bonk** to have sexual intercourse with

**boob tube** a woman's garment of stretch fabric covering the torso from midriff to armpit

**breaker** someone broadcasting on Citizens' Band radio

**bunk off** to play truant

**chippy** having a chip on your shoulder

**chopsocky** a genre of films featuring martial arts

**clean up your act** to regulate your behaviour or put your affairs in order

**clone** a copy or replica, or a person who imitates another

**cred** the quality of being fashionable or acceptable to your peers (from 'credibility')

**ditz** an eccentric person

**ditzy** eccentric

**div** or **divvy** a fool

**do a runner** to abscond

**drink** a bribe

**earner** a profitable job

**Friday afternoon car** a new car with many faults in it (supposedly built on a Friday afternoon when workers' concentration is poor)

**fuck-me shoes** (or **pumps**) shoes considered as being sexually alluring

**gas-guzzler** a car that consumes large amounts of petrol

**gazump** the buyer of a house is 'gazumped' when the seller raises the price of the property just before contracts are due to be signed

**get your kit off** to take off your clothes

**give it some wellie** to apply great force

**go commando** to forgo the use of underpants

**guilt trip** a prolonged feeling of guilt

**happening** fashionable or up-to-the-minute

**headbanger** a fan of heavy metal music

**lib** liberation, as in 'women's lib'

**nutjob** an insane person

**one of them** a homosexual

**on the Social** living on Social Security benefits

**out of order** unacceptable

**Paki-bashing** the act of making racially motivated attacks on Asian people

**palimony** alimony paid to a cohabitee to whom a person was not married

**plastic** or **plastic money** credit cards

**plod** a policeman

**scrote** a despicable person

**scuzzy** dirty or seedy

**shit-for-brains** a stupid person

**shunt** a motor accident

**sick as a parrot** extremely disappointed

**Sloane Ranger** a young person, typically upper-class or upper-middle-class and female, who favours expensive casual clothing suggestive of rural pursuits, speaks in distinctively clipped tones, evinces certain predictable enthusiasms and prejudices, and is resident (during the week) in the Sloane Square area of London or a comparable part

**space cadet** someone who regularly takes drugs, and is often 'spaced out'

**splatter film** or **movie** a film in which graphic scenes of gory mutilation, amputation, etc are depicted, employing various special effects

**streaker** a person who runs naked in public

**street cred** approval among working-class youths

**touchy-feely** involving emotion and personal contact

**wanky** stupid or contemptible

**weeny-bopper** a very young fan of pop music (modelled on the earlier 'teeny-bopper')

**wuss** a weak or timid person (in American usage)

## The 1980s

This was the decade in which compact discs appeared and AIDS was identified, and it seems to have been a time when society was splintering into a multitude of different 'tribes'. New Age travellers and 'crusties' flocked to music festivals, often in the teeth of opposition from 'Nimbys', while 'Essex Man' and 'Essex Girl' were more concerned with conspicuous consumption and 'dinkies' went to 'power breakfasts'. In musical terms, rap became important, and with it the slang of 'gangstas' and 'posses' came to prominence. Recreational drugs introduced new slang: the term 'crack' became familiar, and even 'acid' was revived from the faraway sixties for use at 'acid house' parties and raves; but there were still plenty of 'lager louts' regularly getting 'slaughtered'. Patterns of spending and consumption were changing, with more people heading for shopping malls than to the corner shop, and picking up cash from an ATM (the infamous 'hole in the wall') rather than visiting their local bank.

### Glossary

**acid house** a youth movement which involved large gatherings of people to dance to loud repetitive music, often accompanied by the taking of drugs such as Ecstasy

**air kiss** a greeting in which a person performs a simulated kiss but does not touch the other person's face

**beer goggles** a supposed source of impaired vision due to drinking alcohol, causing potential sexual partners to appear more attractive than they really are

**boombox** a large portable radio and cassette player

**brainiac** a highly intelligent person

**brat pack** a group of young and popular film actors who came to prominence in Hollywood in the 1980s

**brill** brilliant

**buff** having attractively well-developed muscles

**bunny-boiler** a woman who is likely to behave in a deranged manner when spurned (from the behaviour of a character in the film *Fatal*

*Attraction*, made in 1987)

**butthead** a stupid person

**casual** a member of a gang of hooligans who frequent football matches and deliberately start fights, etc

**couch potato** a person whose leisure time is spent sitting shiftlessly in front of the television

**crack** a form of cocaine mixed with other substances

**crackhead** a user or addict of crack

**crusty** a person who appears fashionably unkempt, often with matted hair or dreadlocks, as part of an alternative lifestyle

**dinky** a member of a young, childless couple both earning a high salary and enjoying an affluent lifestyle (from the initial letters of '*d*ouble *i*ncome *n*o *k*ids *y*et')

**dis** or **diss** to disrespect

**dope** excellent

**Essex Girl** an archetypal working-class female from south-east England with low-brow tastes and supposedly limited intelligence

**Essex Man** an archetypal working-class male from south-east England without cultural interests or good taste but with a large disposable income which he spends freely, mainly on consumer goods and entertainment

**foodie** or **foody** a person who is greatly (even excessively) interested in the preparation and consumption of good food

**gangsta** a US term for a member of a criminal gang

**gaydar** the supposed ability of a person, especially a homosexual, to sense whether or not someone else is homosexual

**gazunder** the seller of a house is 'gazundered' when the buyer lowers the sum offered just before contracts are due to be signed

**get a life** to start to live life to the full

**get real** to wake up to reality

**ghetto-blaster** a large portable device for playing recorded music

**go ballistic** to become violently angry

**handbag** to wreck or undermine

**himbo** a man who is attractive but unintelligent

**hole in the wall** a cash dispenser

**in your dreams!** that's not likely

**jelly** a capsule of the drug Temazepam®

**knob** to have sexual intercourse with

**lager lout** an alcohol-fuelled aggressive young man

**loved up** in a state of euphoria, especially after taking drugs

**mall rat** a young person who spends too much of their time in shopping malls

**massive** a 'massive' is a group of friends or a gang

**minder** a bodyguard or personal advisor

**mosh** to dance energetically to loud rock music

**Nimby** someone who is willing for something to happen so long as it does not affect them or take place in their locality (from the initial letters of 'not in my back yard')

**nuke** to 'nuke' food is to cook or heat it in a microwave oven

**posse** a gang, or a group of friends

**power breakfast** or **lunch** a high-level business discussion held over breakfast or lunch respectively

**power dressing** the wearing, by businesswomen, of smart suits tailored on austerely masculine lines so as to give an impression of confident efficiency and have a daunting effect on colleagues and contacts

**sesh** a drinking session

**slaughtered** very drunk

**techie** a devotee of or expert in computer technology

**touch base** someone who 'touches base' with another makes contact with them, often without any specific reason

**toyboy** the young male lover of an older woman

**trainspotter** a person who takes an obsessive interest in something

**trannie** a transvestite

**VPL** visible panty line

**woofter** a male homosexual

**Yardie** a member of a West Indian gang or Mafia-like syndicate involved in drug-dealing and related crime

**yoof** an adjective applied to magazines, programmes, etc pandering to contemporary youth culture

**zapper** a television remote control

# The 1990s

This decade saw the amazing exponential growth of the Internet and
the World Wide Web, accompanied by a whole new vocabulary of
technical and slang terms (many of which are discussed in the section
on **Computer and Internet users' slang**). The development
of e-mail allowed 'cybernauts' to correspond instantly with like-
minded individuals across the world, even indulging in 'flame wars'.
No innovation comes without its downside, however, and the Internet
was soon the haunt of fraudsters and sexual predators seeking to
'groom' new victims. Back in 'meatspace', people were, unsurprisingly,
still interested in getting 'off their tits', whether using alcohol (albeit
sometimes in new forms like 'alcopops') or new, 'designer' drugs like
ecstasy (known, among other names, as 'E' or 'disco biscuits'). Despite
pessimists' predictions about a millennium bug that would cause
computer chaos at the dawn of the year 2000, 'Y2K' arrived without
noticeable mishap.

## Glossary

**air rage** uncontrolled anger
or aggression on an aeroplane

**alcopop** a commercially sold
drink containing alcohol but
packaged and tasting like a
soft drink

**anorak** someone who has
an obsessive interest in the
statistics and trivia associated
with a particular subject

**bad hair day** a day that
starts badly, characterized by
difficulty with your hair

**bi-curious** a term used to
describe someone whose
sexual orientation is not so
firmly fixed as to preclude
thoughts about bisexual
experimentation

**big up** to express approval and
respect for

**chick lit** fiction written to
appeal to young women

**chuddies** underpants (from
Hindi)

**crunked** excited

**cybernaut** an Internet user

**disco biscuit** a tablet of the
drug ecstasy

**E** the drug ecstasy or a tablet
of this

**flame war** an acrimonious

exchange of e-mail messages

**Frankenstein food** or **Frankenfood** food made or derived from genetically modified plants or animals

**gaylord** a male homosexual

**groom** to cultivate an apparently harmless friendship, especially on the Internet, with a child whom the individual intends to subject to sexual abuse

**happy-clappy** enthusiastic in religious practices

**heroin chic** a trend in the fashion industry in which models are used who portray a pale emaciated appearance thought to resemble that of heroin addicts

**hottie** a sexually attractive person

**jazz mag** a pornographic magazine

**large it** to enjoy yourself unrestrainedly

**meatspace** the physical world, as opposed to cyberspace

**munter** an unattractive person, especially a woman

**off your tits** drunk or under the influence of drugs

**out** to 'out' someone is to make their homosexuality public without their permission

**scissor sister** either of two lesbians who, during sex, open their legs like scissor blades in order to bring their genitals into contact

**shedload** a large amount

**trailer trash** in the USA, poor and uneducated people, typically living in trailer parks

**tree-hugger** an environmentalist

**twenty-four-seven** all the time (ie 24 hours a day and 7 days a week)

**wake up and smell the coffee** to become realistic

**Y2K** the year 2000

## The 21st century

At the time of writing, the 21st century has yet to complete its first decade, yet the English language has already generated a great variety of slang terms that were unknown in the 20th century. New terms are coined continually, many achieving wide currency almost instantly. Others may only enjoy a brief vogue and fall into disuse almost as quickly as they appeared. Such is the nature of all neologizing, but especially in the protean world of slang. The following is a list of slang expressions that have been recorded for the first time in the last few years.

## Glossary

**aluminium cookie** a compact disc

**back, sack and crack** cosmetic depilation of the male back, scrotum and buttocks-cleft

**bingo wings** flaps of skin that hang down from the upper arms, (so called because they are often displayed by people raising a hand to claim victory in bingo)

**bleeding edge** a part or area of an organization, branch of study, etc that generates extremely innovative ideas

**bling** or **bling bling** jewellery, especially of a large and conspicuous style

**blinging** ostentatious, especially in showing off your personal wealth

**booze cruise** a ferry trip across the Channel for the purpose of buying cheap alcohol

**Britney Spears** beers (rhyming slang, from the name of the American singer)

**chatterati** the chattering classes

**chav** a boorish, uneducated person who appears to have access to money but not to taste

**chavette** a female **chav**

**council telly** the main terrestrial television channels only, as opposed to digital or satellite channels

**daisy-cutter** a powerful bomb designed to explode close to the ground

**digerati** expert computer users

**dogging** the activity of visiting isolated public places, usually at night, to engage in, or observe other people engaging in, sexual activity, especially in parked cars

**flag up** to draw to someone's attention

**gay** unfashionable, worthless

or inferior (this is just the latest meaning adopted by this extraordinarily mutable little word)

**happy slapping** the practice of physically attacking an unsuspecting victim while an accomplice records the incident on a camera-equipped mobile phone

**milf** a sexually attractive older woman (from the initial letters of '*m*om *I*'d *l*ike to *f*uck')

**monstering** an instance of harsh criticism or treatment

**muffin top** a roll of fatty flesh that spills out over the top of a pair of low-cut trousers

**retrosexual** a man with attitudes that hark back to the days before the New Man

**roasting** a form of group sexual activity in which a person is penetrated in more than one orifice at the same time

**sex up** to make more interesting or attractive

**silver surfer** an older person who enjoys using the Internet

**stooze** to borrow money at a low rate of interest and invest it to make a profit

**tangoed** someone who has been 'tangoed' has an orange-coloured complexion due to inexpert application of an artificial tanning product (after a slogan for an orange-flavoured fizzy drink)

**trout pout** a facial disfigurement resulting from excessive collagen being implanted into the lips

**whale tail** if a woman is revealing the top of her thong above her low-cut trousers, the shape of this leads her to being described as sporting a 'whale tail'

**yummy mummy** a sexually attractive woman who has children

# Index

## A

abandonware 64
Abby Singer 23
ABH 10
abigail 71
a bit of all right 190
a bit of muslin 190
a bit of rough 190
a bit of skirt 190
a bit on the side 199
ablutions 2
Abo 171, 225, 272
aboard 94
about east 215
Abraham-man 264
a brick short of a load 208
abs 181
accounted for 104
AC/DC 190
ace 2, 60, 74, 86, 277
ace queen 71
acid 52, 288
acid freak 52
acid-head 52
acid house 293
ack emma 2, 272
ackle 258
actioner 23
Adam and Eve 142
admin 147, 283
adrift 7
advance 18
aerial 102
aerial ping-pong 76
a fate worse than death 131
afraid of the dark 86
African time 234
afters 76, 116, 260
agate 71
agatha 71
A-gay 71
aggie 71

aggro 123
agony 236
agony aunt 18
agony column 18
agricultural 81
air 96, 100, 102
air ball 96
air express 71
airhead 291
air kiss 199, 293
air rage 123, 296
air shot 74, 86
alamo 71
alcopop 296
A-list 153
A-list gay 71
alkie 110
alko 238
alky 110
all day and night 49
alley oop 96
all-in 106
all mouth and no trousers 272
all my eye 268
all-natural 28
all-overish 203
all over the shop 272
all that 57
all the go 159, 268
all the rage 159
all there 268
all the threes 108
Aloha State 178
alphasort 64
also-ran 89
aluminium cookie 298
amadan 238
amber fluid 110
amber gambler 163
amber nectar 110
ambidextrous 71
ambulance-chaser 10

am-dram 23
ammo 2
amy 71
anchors 163, 281
and all that jazz 286
and how! 215, 279
and no mistake 272
andrew 7
and then some 215
angel 11, 23, 71
angel dust 52
angel food 71
angelina 71
angel with a dirty face 71
Anglo 171
ank 257
Anna Kournikova 106
anorak 296
another place 156
ante 106
ante up 106
anti 104
antimony 18
antwacky 250
any road up 256
Anzac Day dinner 232
A-OK 286
apache 238
APB 14
apple polisher 60
apples and pears 142
appro 33
Archibald 2, 277
Archie 2, 277
are youse gettin? 248
Argie 168
arlarse 250
arm candy 199
arse 225
arse bandit 136, 288
arseholed 110
Arthur Scargill 86

artic 163
arvo 225
as I live and breathe 127
a slate loose 209
as nature intended 131
aspro 71
ass pro 71
asswipe 215
assy 71
Athenian 71
attaboy 279
Auld Reekie 176
Auntie 211
auntie 71, 243
Aunt Nellie fakes 26
Aunt Nells 26
Aussie 168
Aussie rules 225
away in the head 248
away on 248
away with the fairies 208
away ye go! 246
awesome 291
AWOL 277
axe 21, 151, 272, 286
axeman 21, 147
Ayrton Senna 120, 142
Aztec two-step 187, 203

**B**
bab 254, 256
babalaas 234
babbelas 234
babber 257
babble 104
babbler 225
babbling brook 142
babby 254
babe 190, 199
baby bonus 222
baby catcher 11
baby dyke 71

baby father 236
Babylon 236
baby Power 238
baby spanner 7
bach 232
bachelor pad 199
back bench 18
back crack 250
back door 86, 167
back end 252
back in the day 57
backra 237
back, sack and crack 298
back scuttle 28
back-up 14
bad 272
bada-bing, bada-boom 47
badass 215
bad beat 106
baddy 23, 281
badge 49
Badger State 178
bad hair day 296
badly-liked 252
badmouth 283
bad news 283
badonkadonk 69, 181
bafflegab 156
bag 52, 94, 256, 272, 286, 288
baggie 52
baggies 100
baggy green 81, 225
bagman 47
bag off 57, 190, 199
bagpiping 71, 190
bags 159, 239, 272, 281
bags I 60, 272
bag swinger 36, 225
bail out 86, 100
bait 57, 272
Bajan 168
bajan 62

bakkie 234
Balaam 18
baldhead 237
bald-headed 272
ball 190
ball-breaker 215
ball-buster 215
baller 69, 96
ballhead 237
ball of malt 239
balls 272
ballsy 215
bally 131
ballyrag 258
baloney 215
Balt 171, 225
baltic 145
Balti Triangle 256
bam 268
bammer 69, 246
bampot 246
banana 39
banana-bender 176, 225
Bananaland 176, 225
banana republic 156
bananas 208
bandbox 94
bandit 2, 86, 283
bang 18, 52, 57, 190, 266
bangalore 243
banger 90, 116, 163, 288
bang for your buck 33
bangin' 57
bang on 283, 286
bang on the drum 108
bang to rights 14, 39
bang up 39, 49
bang-up 272
banjax 239
banker 36
bank shot 96
bans 237

baphead 57
baps 181
barbie 116, 225
bare 57
bareback 190
barely legal 28
barf 187
barfly 110
bark 187
barking 208, 288
barking iron 123
barking mad 208
Barlinnie drumstick 49
barmcake 254
barmy 208, 272
barnacles 264
barn door 98
barnet 260, 272
Barnet Fair 142
barney 272
barrack buster 248
barrelhouse 190
barrie 246
Barry White 142
bash 190, 281
basher 159
bashment 237
basket 71, 181
basket case 11, 203, 208, 286
bat 110
batch 232
bathroom 131
bats 208
battle-axe 272
batty 182, 208, 237
batty boy 136, 237
bawcock 264
bawdy basket 264
Bay State 178
baz 239
bazoo 182, 215, 272
bazzer 239

b-ball 97
beach bunny 100
beak 10, 39, 60, 268
beamer 81, 164
bean counter 33, 147, 291
beanery 116, 215
beanie 159
beano 116
beanpole 182, 272
Beantown 26
bear 30, 71, 167
beard 36, 199
bearded clam 182
bear in the air 167
bear market 30
beast 39, 49, 57
beastie 179
beat 190
beat-'em-up 64
beautiful game 76
beautiful people 159
beaver 182, 279
Beaver State 178
beaver tail 100
bed 18
bed-and-breakfast deal 30
bed-leg 49
Beeb 211
beef bayonet 182
beefcake 190
Beehive State 178
beer goggles 293
beeroff 256
beer tokens 120
Beertown 26
beer-up 225
beer vounchers 120
bee stings 288
beetle-crusher 3
beetle-crushers 159, 182
beetle off 3
beeza 256

beezer 182, 246
befok 234
be helping the police with their
    inquiries 131
behind 131, 182
be intimate with 131
bejant 62
belle 71
bells and whistles 64
bellyache 272
belly up to 215
belt 123
belt up 283
Beltway 156
bench-warmer 74
bender 110, 136, 272
bend the elbow 110, 131
benny 52, 272, 283
bent 39, 281, 286
bent out of shape 215
bergie 234
berk 136, 281
Berkeley Hunt 142
best bib and tucker 159
beta 98
be tickets 234
better half 199
betty 40, 266
bevvied 110, 288
bevvy 110, 272
bezzie mate 250
b.f. 26
bi 190
Bible-basher 173
Bible-pounder 173
Bible-thumper 173
biccy 116, 272
bi-curious 296
bidie-in 199, 246
biff 123, 272
Big Apple 176, 279
Big Bang 30

Big Bertha 277
Big Board 215
big brown eyes 182
big bucks 120
big C 131, 203
Big Easy 176
big fish 272
big girl's blouse 136
big house 49, 215
big league 153
bigmouth 272
big noise 153
big note 120
big-note 225
big slick 106
Big Smoke 176
big-ticket 215
big up 296
big wall 98
bigwig 153
bike 190
biker 164
bikie 164
bilge 7
Bill 40
billy goat 179
Bim 168
bimbo 136, 279
bin 40
binder 232
binders 90
bindle 52, 215
bing 264
Binghi 171, 225
bingo wings 182, 298
bingy 182, 225
bin off 254
bint 272
bioscope 234
bird 23, 40, 49, 199, 272
birdcage 89, 92
bird lime 142

biscuit 3
bishop 190
Bismarck 36
bit 49
bit an' drap 258
bitch slap 123
bite 268
bite me! 215
biter 69
bite the dust 205
bit on the side 131
bitser 179, 225
bivvy 98
bivvy bag 98
bizzy 40, 250, 254
BJ 190
black 40, 239
black and white 252
blackie 246
black knight 30
black Monday 30
black ops 3
blackout 108
black stump 176, 225
bladdered 110
blade 248
blag 40, 272
blank 104, 106
blarge 248
blart 256
blast 94
blasted 110, 268
blatt 18
bleeder 11, 84, 272
bleeding 131, 272
bleeding edge 298
Blighty 176
blighty 3, 277
blimey 127
blind butty 250
blind-drunk 110
blinder 74

Blind Freddie 226
blind interview 18
bling 58, 69, 159, 298
blinging 298
B-list 153
blitzed 110
bloatware 64
blob 81
blog 64
blogger 64
blogosphere 64
bloke 7
blood 104
blood work 11
blootered 110, 246
blotto 110
bloviate 215
blow 40, 52
blow away 123
blow chunks 187
blowie 179, 226
blow-in 226
blowjob 190
blow me 127
blow me down 127
blow off 187
blow off the stage 21
blow-out 116, 164
blow someone's mind 52, 288
blow your mind 288
bludge 151, 226
bludger 226
blue 123, 226
Blue Beret 3
blue bet 36
blue-chip shares 30
blue duck 232
blue juice 100
blue nose 176, 222, 250
blue on blue 3
blue rinse brigade 153
blue ruin 111

blue-sky thinking 33
bluey 226
blunt 268
bo 215
board 97
boat 260
boatie 62
boat race 142, 182
bob 120, 268
bobbery 272
bobbins 254
bobby 272
bobby-dazzler 272
bobbysoxer 215
bobpoint 98
boche 168, 277
bod 272
bodacious 215, 272
body fascism 159
body packer 52
boff 123, 190
boffin 3, 283
boffo 26, 283
bog 268
bogan 153, 226
bog ball 239
bogey 187
bogger 239
bog off 286
bogs 239
bogtrotter 136, 168, 239, 266
bogus 268
bog warrior 239
bogy 187
boho 153
bohunk 136, 168
boilermaker 111
boilover 74, 226
bokkie 234
boko 182, 272
Bolivian marching powder 291
bollock 281

bollock-naked 286
bollocks 182, 239, 268
bollox 239
Bollywood 23, 243
bolshie 277
bolt 104
bomb 23, 79, 92, 120, 215, 286
bombed 53
bomber 53, 98, 286
bombo 111, 226
bombora 100, 226
bombshell 281
bona 26
bonce 273
bone 14, 190, 266
boner 190
bones 11, 47
boneshaker 164
bone up on 273
bong 18
bonk 123, 190, 281, 291
bonkers 208, 286
bonzer 226
booai 232
boob 281
boobies 131, 182
boobs 131, 182
boob tube 159, 211, 286, 291
booby hatch 208
boof 50
boofhead 226
booger 215
boogie board 100
boohai 232
bookie 36, 273
boombox 293
boomer 273
boomerang 199
boondocks 176
boops 237
boopsie 237
boost 40, 215

booster 215
boot 3, 151
boot camp 3
bootie 3
booty 69, 182, 279
booty call 69, 190
bootylicious 69, 191
booze 111
booze cruise 111, 298
boozer 111, 273
booze-up 111
bop 123, 279, 286
boracic 120
boracic lint 142
borgata 47
borsch belt 23
borsch circuit 23
bosh 258, 273
boshta 226
bosie 81
bosky 268
boss 273
boss cocky 147, 226, 273
bost 256
bostin 256
bot 64, 226
botheration 268
bottle 36, 111, 123
bottle and glass 142, 182
bottom fisher 30
bottoming 90
bottomish 30
bouldering 98
bounce 268
bouncer 120
bounder 273
bousingken 264
bovver 123, 288
bovver boots 288
bovver boy 288
bowled over 104
bowler hat 142, 248

bowler-hat 3
bowsie 239
bow-wow 179
box 182, 211, 266, 273, 286
box of birds 232
box of budgies 232
boyf 58, 199
boy racer 164
boys in blue 40, 273
bozo 215
bracelets 40, 266
Brahms and Liszt 111, 142
brain 123
brainbox 273
brain bucket 98
brainiac 60, 293
brass 40, 250, 264, 273
brass hat 3
brassic 120
brass monkeys 145, 273
brat pack 293
bread 281
breadbasket 182, 268
breadhead 288
breaker 167, 291
break it down! 226
break up 104
breeder 71
breeze 268
brekkie 116
brew 116
brewer's droop 191
brewski 111, 215
brick 97
brickie 147
bricks-and-mortar 33
bridesmaid 74
brief 10, 40
brig 50
brill 293
bring off 191
bring the house down 23

bring to the table  33
briny  7
Bris  176, 226
Brissie  176, 226
Bristol cities  142, 182
Brit  168
Britney Spears  111, 142, 298
Brixton briefcase  260
Brizzie  176, 226
bro  199
broad  191
broad-brim  173
broadbrush  268
broad in the beam  182
broiler  145
broke  120, 266
brolly  273
broo  246
broon  252
brothel creepers  159, 286
brown bread  142, 205
browned off  281
browns  260
brown sugar  53
bruise  104
bruiser  123, 264
Brum  176, 256, 266
Brummie  176, 256
brush  104
bruv  199, 258
Brylcreem Boys  3, 283
bs  215, 273
bub  266
bubbly  111, 279
buck  215, 250, 273
buckess  250
bucket  97, 145, 246
bucket shop  30, 273
buckeye  176
Buckeye State  178
buckled  239
buckle my shoe  108

Buckley's  226, 273
Buckley's chance  226, 273
bucko  7, 239
buckshee  120
bucks' party  226
buddy  199, 273
budgeree  226
buff  58, 293
buftie  246
bug  11, 65, 203, 273
bugalugs  232
buggy  208
bughouse  208
buildering  98
bukkake  28
bulks  18
bull  3, 30, 40, 50, 215, 284
bull dyke  136, 191, 281
bullet  50, 92, 106, 151
bull fiddle  215
bull market  30
bullroot  248
bull's walt  248
bum  151, 191
bumbaclat  237
bumbag  159
bumboclot  237
bumf  273
bumfreezer  159
bummed  215
bummer  53, 289
bump  18
bump and grind  191
bumper  81, 226
bumper belay  98
bump off  123
bump uglies  191
bum rap  40
bumsucker  137
bunce  273
bunch of fives  123, 273
bundle  123

bundook 3, 243, 268
bundu 234
bundu-bashing 234
BUNDY 13
bun fight 273
bung 40, 226, 264
bunghole 28, 182
bunk 269
bunk off 60, 291
bunny 81, 226
bunny-boiler 293
bunny chow 234
buns 182, 289
bunsen 81
bunsen burner 142
buppy 153
burb 176, 215
burg 176, 215
Burlington Bertie 36
burn 40, 205
burned up 216
buroo 246
burp 187
Burton 3, 205, 284
bus 164
bush 182
bushed 273
bush league 94
bush tucker 226
bust 3, 14
bust a cap 123
bust a gut 266
bust a nut 28
busted 120
busted flush 106
buster 145, 226
busty 284
butch 71, 281
butcher's hook 142
bute 89
butt 182
butterball 216

butterfingers 273
butter-print 266
butters 57
butthead 294
buttinski 216
button 47
buttoned-down 216
button man 47
butt out 216
butty 254
buvare 26
buy 279
buy it 3, 205
buy the farm 3, 205
buzz 273, 279, 281
buzzer-beater 97
by-blow 137
by George 127
by gum 127
by heck 127
by jiminy 127
by jingo 127
by Jove 128
by Jupiter 128
by the Great Cham's beard 128
by the Lord Harry 128

## C

cab-rank principle 10
cab-rank rule 10
cabbage 40, 86, 269
cabbie 164
cack 187
cackhouse 252
cacks 257
cacky 252
caesar 11
caff 116
caffler 239
cagey 273
Cain and Abel 142
cake 269

cake hole 182, 284
calaboose 50
calendar 50
call 106
call down 216
can 7, 50, 182, 216
Canajan 222
canary 14, 40, 50, 226, 266
canary-bird 50, 266
cancer stick 286
candle-waster 264
candy-ass 216
candyman 53
cane 281
caning 269
canned 111
Canny Toon 252
can of corn 94
canteen culture 147
Canuck 168, 222, 273
canvas 84
cap 104
caper 40
Cape smoke 111, 234
capo 47
carb 164
car-crash television 211
card 89
cardi 159
careware 65
carfuffle 246
car-hop 147, 216
cark 226
carny 147
carpet 3, 36, 50, 76, 86
carpetbagger 156
carpet muncher 191
carry 40, 53
carry-out 246
carry the can 279
carsey 26
carve up 124

case 40
cash in your chips 131
cast 104, 232, 239
casting couch 23
castor 226
casual 294
cat 21, 179, 226, 239, 269
catch a wave 100
catch it 273
catch your death 203
catch your death of cold 203, 269
catch yourself on 239
cat-fight 124
cathouse 191
cattle market 191
cauliflower ear 84
caulk 7
caution 273
cave 60
celestial 273
cement overshoes 47, 124
cert 273
chain gang 92
chain lightning 111
chairborne 284
Chalfont St Giles 142
chalk 36
chalkface 60
chalk player 36
-challenged 131
champ 74, 84
champers 111, 286
chancer 273
channel-surf 211
chanty 246
chap 269
chapel 173
char 116
character 269
charity stripe 97
charity toss 97
charley horse 74

Charlie 3, 53, 104, 281, 289
charlie 260
charper 26
charpering omi 26
chart-buster 21
charver 27
chaser 3, 111
chase the dragon 53, 289
chassis 182
chat 266
chatterati 298
chatterbox 269
chat up 273
chav 137, 153, 298
chavette 298
cheap shot 92
cheapskate 273
cheat 40, 264
cheaters 216
cheat on 199
check 104
cheerios 232
cheese 58
cheesecake 281
cheese-eater 50
cheese-eating surrender monkeys 137
cheese it 40, 273
cheeselog 258
Chelsea tractor 164
chemo 11, 203
cherry 81, 191
chesty 203
Chevy 164
chewed up 216
chewie 116
chew the scenery 24
chew up the scenery 24
Chiantishire 176
chi-chi man 237
chicken 71, 266
chicken colonel 3

chickenfeed 120
chickenhawk 71
chickenhead 69
chickenshit 216
chicken wings 98
chick flick 24
chickhead 98
chick lit 296
chill 58
chill pill 58
Chinaman 81
China plate 142
chin-chin 273
Chinee 171
Chinese 116
Chinese burn 60
ching 260
Chink 137, 171
Chinky 137, 171
chin music 81, 94
chip 260
chip off the old block 200
chipper 116, 239, 273
chippy 116, 147, 222, 291
chips 147, 205
chirps 58
chiseller 239
Chi-town 176
chiv 40, 124, 266
chizz 60, 273
chocko 3, 226, 284
choky 40, 50, 243
chommie 235
choof off 226
chook 226
choom 168, 226
chop 104, 116, 151
chope 243
chopper 124, 164, 182, 286
choppers 182, 284
chops 21
chopsocky 24, 291

chorine 216
chota peg 243
chow 171, 226
Chrizzy 250
chrome dome 182
chronic 53, 60, 69, 273
chuck 116, 200, 254
chucker-out 147
chuck it down 145
chuck up 187
chuck wagon 116
chuddie 246
chuddies 159, 243, 296
chuff 254
chummy 14
chump change 216
chunder 187, 227, 286
chung 58, 191
chunter 264
church 173
chute 279
cinch 273
circs 273
circus catch 92
cit 266
civilian 47
civvy 273
civvy street 284
clack 264
claggy 254
clam 216
clap 203, 264
claret 84, 182, 266
clean 40
clean air 91
clean sheet 76
clean someone's clock 124
clean up your act 291
cleffer 26
click 4
clickety-click 108
clicks and mortar 33

clickstream 65
climb the ladder 92
clinch 273
clink 40, 50, 264
clip 47
clip joint 40
clippie 284
C-list 153
clobber 124, 159, 273, 284
clock 124, 164, 182, 274
clocker 53
clod 252
clodhopper 159
clogger 76
clog toe pie 254
clone 40, 291
close down 76
closet 72
closet queen 72, 289
clotbuster 12, 203
clothes-horse 159
clout 269, 274
clucky 227
cludgie 246
clueless 284
clunker 164
cly 264
clype 246
c-note 120
CNS-QNS 13
coalbox 4
cob 250
cobber 227, 274
cobblers 182
cobbler's awls 142
cock 182, 266
cockamamie 216
cockatoo 41, 227
cockeyed 111, 269
cockeyed bob 227
cockle 36
cock relation 248

cocksman 191
cocksucker 274
cockteaser 191
cock up 279
cocky 227
cocky's joy 227
cod 269
codswallop 289
co-ed 60, 62
coffin 81
coffin-dodger 137
cohab 200
coin 26
coit 182, 227
cojones 182
coke 53
coked up 53, 279
cokehead 53
coldcock 124, 216
coldie 227
cold snap 145
cold turkey 53
collar 14, 266
collateral damage 131
college 50, 269
collegiate 266
collywobbles 203
Colombian necktie 47
comare 47
combi 164, 227
come 191, 266
come a cropper 274
come down 53
come off 266
come off it! 274
come on stream 33
come on to 191
come out 72, 284
come out of the closet 284
come shot 28
come the raw prawn 227
come-to-bed eyes 191

comeuppance 274
comfortable 120
comfort station 132
comfy 274
commie 156, 281
commo 156, 227
commodity 264
company doctor 33
compare 47
competish 26
compo 151, 227
con 41
con artist 41
concert party 30
conchy 137, 277
coney-catcher 264
confab 269
con game 41
conk 124, 182
con man 41
connect 84
connection 53
conny-onny 250
consigliere 47
contract 47
con trick 41
convo 227
convoy 167
con woman 41
coodle 239
cook 21, 53
cookiepusher 216
cook the books 33, 266
cook up 53
cool 269, 274
cooler 50
coolhunter 159
cool it 286
cool runnings 237
coon 137, 171
coot 269
cootie 179

cooze 183, 216
cop 14, 269, 274
copacetic 216
cop a plea 10, 279
cop it sweet 227
cop off 58, 191, 200
cop on to yourself 239
cop out 286
copper 41, 274
copshop 41
copter 164
cor 128
corked 111
corker 274
corned beef 142
cornflake 216
Cornhusker State 178
cornstalk 183, 227
corny 281
corporate raider 30
corporation 269
corpse 24
Corpy 251
correctional facility 132
corridor of uncertainty 81
corridor work 33
cory 183
Cosa Nostra 47
cosh 124
cossie 159, 227
costard 264
cotch 58
cotched 58
cottaging 72, 191
cotton-picking 216
couch potato 211, 294
council telly 211, 298
course specialist 89
cove 264
cow 137, 227
cowabunga! 101
cowboy 28, 106, 279

cow college 62, 216
cow corner 81
cow shot 82
coyote 216
CPR 12
crabbit 239, 246
crabs 180, 203
crack 53, 183, 294
crack a crib 41
crackbrain 208
cracked 208, 266
cracker 137, 153
crackerjack 274
crackers 208, 279
crackhead 53, 294
crackling 191
crackpot 208
crack up 208
cradle-snatcher 200
cram 269
crank 53
crap 187
crash 53, 284, 289
crash out 284
crashpad 289
crate 164
crater 99
cratur 111, 239
crazy 269
cream 69
cream crackered 142
cream pie 28
cream your jeans 191
creative accountancy 34
cred 291
creep 274
creeping Jesus 137, 173
creepy-crawly 180
crib 58, 69, 191, 274
crikey 128
crim 41
crimp 99

crimper 147
crinkly 137
cripes 128
crippleware 65
critter 180, 216
crivens 128, 246
crix 26
croak 124, 205
croc 180
crock 216
crocked 111
crock of shit 216
crocus 12, 269
croggy 256
cronk 227
crook 203, 227
crooked number 94
croppie 248
crousty 258
crovey 58
crown 124
crown jewels 183
Croydon facelift 260
crucial 237
cruise 191, 279
crumbs 128
crump 58
crumpet 191
crunch 281
cruncher 101
crunchie 235
crunk 69, 216
crunked 69, 216, 296
crush 200
crush a cup 264
crusty 153, 294
cry 104
cub 18
cubbing 104
cuckoo 208, 274
cuffs 14
culchie 239

cully 266
cum 191
cum shot 28
cunny 183
cunt 183
cupcake 216
cuppa 117
currency 227
curse 132, 187
curtains 205
curves 183
cushty 260
cuspy 65
cussword 216
custodian 76
cut 21, 60, 92, 243, 269
cute hoor 239
cut-offs 159
cut the cheese 132, 187
cuttie 239
cut up 164
cut your eye at someone 237
cuz 232
cuzzy 232
cuzzy-bro 232
cybernaut 65, 296
cyberslacking 65
cybersquatting 65

**D**
DA 160, 286
dabs 14, 41
dadah 243
daddy 50
daft as a brush 208
daft ha'porth 254
dag 227
daggy 160, 227
dago 137
daisy chain 31
daisy-cutter 4, 82, 269 298
daisy roots 142, 160

daks 160, 227
dance floor 86
dance the blanket hornpipe 191
dandy 269
Danny La Rue 108
daps 257
darbies 14, 41, 266
darkers 237
darkey 171
dark horse 156
darkie 171
darkmans 41, 264
darky 171
Darlo 252
dauber 108
Davy Jones 7
Davy Jones's locker 7
dawg 69
dawn raid 31
day-clean 237
DBI 13
dead as a dodo 205
deadbeat 151
dead-cat bounce 31
dead cert 36
dead duck 205, 274
deaders 237
deadly 239, 243
dead man's hand 106
dead marines 111
dead meat 205
dead men 111, 117, 266
dead presidents 120
dead tree edition 65
dealer 53
Dear John letter 284
death 203
deathmatch 65
death wobbles 99
decaff 117
decider 74
deck 101, 102, 124

deck ape 7
deck out 99
deebo 58
deejay 21, 286
deep 58
deepie 24
deep-six 124, 205
dee-wee 14
def 69
defrag 65
dekko 274
Delhi belly 187, 203
deli 117
dell 264
delph 249
delts 183
demo 21
demob happy 4, 284
demon drink 111
dep 222
departed 205
derby 76
derro 227
desk jockey 147
Desmond 62
deuce 50, 97
devil-dodger 173
devil's darning-needle 180
dewbit 258
dewdrop 187
dial 183
diamond 260
dice 227
dick 41, 183
dickhead 137, 289
dicking 249
dicky-bird 142
dicky dirt 142, 160
diddle 191
diddly-squat 216
diddy 246
die 24

die in harness 206
die with your boots on 206
DIFFC 13
differently-abled 132
dig 62, 76, 82, 222, 281
digerati 65, 298
digger 50
dig in 117
digs 274
dime 50, 69
dinarly 27
ding 101
dingbat 208
dingbats 111, 227
dinge 137, 171
dinger 94
dinges 235
dingo 227
dinkum 227
dinky 200, 294
dinky-di 227
dip 41
diplomatese 156
dippy 208, 274
dipstick 137, 289
dip your wick 191, 274
dirtball 216
dirtbird 239
dirty air 91
dis 294
disco 289
disco biscuit 53, 58, 296
dish 94, 97, 269
dishy 289
dismal Jimmy 279
diss 294
ditch 4, 284
ditsy 208
ditz 208, 291
ditzy 208, 291
div 291
dive 76, 84, 176

diver 41, 266
divvy 291
DJ 160, 286
D-list 153
DMs 160
do 41, 124, 191, 266
do a legger 239
do a line with 239
do a Melba 227
do a perish 227
do a runner 291
dob 41, 227
docker's doorstep 251
doctor 7, 111, 145, 269
dodger 117
dog 36, 252, 281
doggie 180
dogging 192, 298
doggy fashion 28, 192
dog player 36
dogs 183
dog's-body 7
dog's disease 203, 227
dog-soldier 4
dog tag 4, 277
dog up 257
dog-whistle politics 156
do in 274
dole 151
dole-bludger 151, 227
dole-ite 151
doley 151
dolly 27, 82
dolly-mop 192
dome 183
domestic 14
domme 28
don 47
dona 27
donder 124, 235
done for 206
dong 183

donkey 76
donkey-lick 74, 227
donnies 256
doobie 53, 289
doobry 258
doodlebug 284
doo-doo 187
doofus 137
doolally 208
do one 251
Doonhamer 246
doorstep 117
doos 235
do over 274
dope 53, 69, 294
Dora 277
do-re-mi 120
dork 289
dorp 176, 235
dose 203
dosh 120
doss 187, 274
dosser 151
do the business 192, 284
do the Frank 261
do the horizontal mambo 192
do the off 261
do the wild thing 192
dotty 274
double-bubble 50, 120
double carpet 36
double-double 222
double header 94
double penetration 28
double witching hour 31
douche-bag 216
dough 120, 274
doughboy 4, 274
doughnutting 157
Douglas Hurd 62
dove 53, 157
down 58

down-and-dirty 216
downer 53, 289
down-home 176, 216
downtown 97
doxy 192, 264
DP 28
drack 137, 227
drag 104, 164
drag king 72
drain 97
drainpipes 160, 286
drat 128
drat and double drat 128
draw 106
draw dead 106
draw it mild 274
dreamboat 284
dreamy 284
dribbler 86
drill 124, 269
drink 7, 41, 120, 291
drink with the flies 111, 227
drip 281
drive-by 124
drongo 137, 228
droob 137, 228
droop snoot 164
drop a clanger 284
drop a dime 15
drop off the perch 132, 206
drop off the twig 132, 206
drop the hammer 91
drop your bundle 228
drunk tank 15
druthers 216
dry 24, 58, 157, 228
DTs 111, 203
dub 50
duck 82, 264
duck's arse 160, 286
duck's ass 160, 286
duck soup 217

dude 200, 274
duds 160, 264
duff 183
duff up 124
duke it out 124
dukes 124, 183
dumb-ass 217
dumbbell 137
dum-dum 281
dump 187, 200
dumper 101
dumpsville 200
dun 69
dunk 97
dunny 228
duppy 237
dust 124
dustbin lids 142
dutch 261
Dutch pink 183
dutchy 237
dutty 237
duvet day 147
dweeb 137, 217
dyke 137, 192, 281
dynamo 74
dyno 99

**E**
E 53, 296
each way 36
eager beaver 284
earbash 228
earhole 37
earlies 147
early bath 76
early doors 76
earn a crust 120, 147
earner 147, 291
earthly 274
Easter egg 65
easy over 117

easy peasy Japanesey 249
eatery 117
eating irons 117
eat lead 124
eats 117
ecky thump 254
economy 132
edge 99
eejit 239
eek 27
effing and jeffing 254
egg 4, 24, 37, 86, 228, 232
egg beater 164
egghead 61
Egyptian 99
eighty-six 217
ekker 61
el 164
elderly prim 12
electric puha 232
elevated 111, 266
elevenses 117, 274
E-list 153
Elvis 99
Emerald Isle 176
Emma Freuds 142
emmet 257
Empire State 178
empty-nester 200
empty the bags 249
end run 92
enforcer 47
engine 76
enin 37
ENT 12
Enzed 176, 232
Enzedder 168, 232
equalizer 124
erk 4
Essex Girl 153, 258, 294
Essex Man 153, 258, 294
eventide home 132

eve teasing 243
ex 200
exchange this life for a better one 132, 206
excuse my French 133
exes 34, 120
exhibition football 77
exhibition stuff 77
exotic dancer 132
eye 192
eye-opener 111
Eyetie 137, 168, 277

**F**

face 15, 37, 41, 53
face-ache 137
face-fungus 183
facer 124
facetime 34
facial 28
faff about 274
fag 137, 279
faggot 137
fag hag 72
fairy 137
fall guy 217
fall off the back of a lorry 132
fall off the perch 132, 206
fall off the twig 132, 206
family 47
family jewels 183
fan 94
fancy bit 200
fancy man 200
fancy woman 200
Fannie Mae 31
fanny 183, 217, 274
fanny batter 192
fanny pack 160, 217
fantabulous 287
fantasy 53
fantod 7

fap 264
Farmer Giles 142
fart 187
fart about 281
fashionista 160
fashion victim 160
fast-track 147
fat cat 279
fat chance 274
fat city 217
fatso 137, 281
fave 58, 280
featherbed 34
feck 132, 239
Fecky the Ninth 239
Fed 41
feed 117
feed your face 117
feel 58, 192
feele 27
feeling no pain 132
felch 192
fella 200
fem 192
femme 72, 192
fence 41, 266
fender bender 164, 217
fernleaf 233
fernytickle 246
fess up 217
fetch up 187
fifteen-man game 79
fight 84
filer 34
fill in 124
filmi 243
filth 41, 289
filthy 95
filthy rich 120
fin 120
finance 132
finger 65

finger-fuck 192
fire blanks 192
firebug 41, 274
fire up 257
firewater 111
firm 15
firmware 65
fish 50
fist 192
fist-fuck 192
fisting 28
fit 58
fitba 246
fit up 41, 274
five-finger discount 41
five-o'clock shadow 183, 281
five-oh 69
fiver 120
fix 54, 274, 282
fizgig 41, 228
fizz 111
fizz boat 233
fizzer 4
fizzgig 41, 228
fizzy boat 233
flab 183, 280
flabbergasted 269
flagrante delicto 192
flag up 298
flag waver 157
flah 239
flak 4, 284
flake 54, 208, 217
flaky 217
flame 65
flamed 99
flame war 65, 296
flannel 284
flapper 280
flash 41, 274
flasher 289
flash the leather 95

flat 222
flat spot 91
flatten 124
flick 24
flier 74
flimp 41
fling 200, 274
flip 287
flit 246
flivver 164
FLK 13
floater 15
floorer 61, 124
floozie 192
flop 97
floss 69
flow 69
flu 203
fluey 203
fluffer 28
flunk 62
flunk out 62
flush 120, 266
fluthered 239
flutter 37
fly 69, 160
fogey 137
fogle 160
fogy 137
fold 106
folding green 120
folding money 120
folkie 289
folks 200
foodie 117, 294
fool around 192
footer 77
footie 77
Footsie 31
force-ripe 237
forearm pump 99
foreigner 147

for goodness' sake 128
form 15, 41
for Pete's sake 128
for the high jump 280
for the love of Mike 128
forty-pounder 222
forty winks 187
fo shizzle 69
fo sho 69
foul-up 284
four ball 82
four by two 137, 142, 171
fourpenny one 124
foxer 239
foxy 192, 274
frag 4
fraidy cat 217
frame-up 41
Frankenfood 117, 297
Frankenstein food 117, 297
frat 62
frat house 62
freak 289
freak out 54, 289
Fred Karno's Army 277
freebase 54
freeload 284
free-rider 147
freeware 65
freeze 92
freeze-out 106
French 192
French kiss 192
French letter 192
fresher 62
Freud Squad 12
Friday afternoon car 164, 291
fried egg 87
friendly fire 132
friend of Dorothy 72
friend of mine 48
friend of ours 48

frig 192, 264
frightener 41
frillies 160
Frisco 176
frisk 269
Frog 137, 168, 222
frog and toad 142
Froggie 137, 168
frog-strangler 145
front bottom 132, 183
front door 167
frosting 28
froth-blower 111
frozen rope 95
fruit 137, 192
fruitcake 208
fruit fly 72
fruity 192
fry 41, 280
fry-up 117
fubar 284
fuck 192
fuck all 274
fuck buddy 192
fuck-me pumps 193, 291
fuck-me shoes 193, 291
fuck up 274
fugly 58
full 112
full and frank exchange of views 132
full blues 7
full-court press 217
full-figured 132
fundie 173
funkhole 4
funky 287
funny business 274
funny farm 208, 287
funny money 120, 282
fuzz 41, 280
fuzzy-wuzzy 171

# G

G 120
gabfest 217
gack 261
gadgy 254
gaff 261, 282
gaffer 148
gaga 280
gage 54
gag show 211
gagster 24
gak 261
galah 137, 228
galoot 4
gam 193
game 41
gameball 240
game on! 77
game plan 92
gamer 65
gams 183, 269
ganch 249
gandy dancer 148
gang bang 193
gangbanger 15, 48
gangbuster 15
gangsta 48, 69, 294
gangster's moll 48
ganky 240
gaper 82
gapper 62, 95
garbo 148, 228
garburator 223
gardening 82
gardening leave 132, 151
garryowen 79
gas 79
gas-guzzler 164, 291
gash 7, 183
gashead 257
gasper 277
gasser 12

gat 124
-gate 157
gate fever 50
gathering 203
gator 180
gatvol 235
gauleiter 284
gay 58, 298
gaydar 72, 294
gay deceiver 160
gaylord 297
gazongas 183
gazump 34, 292
gazunder 34, 82, 294
GBH 10, 124
g'day 228
gear 54, 160
geck 264
gee 240
gee-box 240
geechee 171
gee-eyed 240
gee-gee 180
gee-gees 89
geek 65, 137, 208, 274, 280
geekspeak 66
gee whiz 128
geezer 274
geezerbird 58
geezergirl 58
gelt 120
gen 285
gender bender 193
generously proportioned 132
Geoff Hurst 62
Geordie 176, 252
gertcha 261
gesuip 235
get a life 294
get bent! 217
get down 282
get into bed with 34

get into someone's knickers  193
get into someone's pants  193
get it on  193
get it up  193
get jiggy  193
get laid  193
get off  193
get off with  193
get off your bike  228
get outside of  117, 274
get out the vote  157
get real  294
get religion  173
get the chop  285
get the message  287
get up someone's nose  282
get weaving  285
get your act together  289
get your ashes hauled  193
get your ducks in a row  34
get your end away  193
get your hole  246
get your kit off  193, 292
get your knickers in a twist  289
get your leg over  193
get your oats  193
get your rocks off  193, 285
get yourself together  289
get your shit together  289
g.f.  26
ghastly  203
ghetto-blaster  294
ghostbuster  148
Gib  176
gick  240
gicker  240
gig  21, 148, 280
GIGO  66
gill  41
gimme  87
gimme cap  160
gimmies  217

gimp  217
gippo  4, 137, 169, 171
gippy tummy  187, 203
girls  79
giro  151
git  137
give evils  257
give head  193
give it some wellie  292
give it up for  24, 211
given best  104
given law  104
give one  193
give over  254
give someone five  287
give someone stick  289
give someone the boot  200
give someone the elbow  200
give someone the heave  200
give someone the old heave-ho
  200
give your ferret a run  233
gizmo  285
glad eye  193
glad rags  160, 274
glamity  237
glamour  132
glamourpuss  285
glarnies  256
glass  97, 124
glass ceiling  148
glass chin  84
glasshouse  4, 101
glass jaw  84
glim  183, 269
glitch  66, 289
glitterati  160
GLM  13
glom  217
glorious  269
glossies  18
glossy  285

gloveman 82
G-man 41
gnarly 101
gnashers 183
gnat's piss 112
gnome 31
go 187
goalie 77
go all the way 193
go ape 208
go apeshit 208
gob 8, 183, 187, 264
go ballistic 125, 294
go bananas 289
gobble 193
gobbledygook 285
gobby 254
go belly-up 206
go Bismarck 251
gobshite 137, 254
gobsmacked 254
go bush 228
go bust 34, 120
go commando 160, 292
go crook 228
God-botherer 137, 173
godfather 48
God forbids 142
God help us 128
go down 15, 41, 50
go down on 193
go down with 203
God slot 211
God squad 173
Godzone 176
go-faster stripes 164
gofer 148
go figure! 217
go for a song 120
go for the doctor 228
goggle-box 211
goggle-eyed 183

goggler 211
gogglers 183
goggles 183
going-over 125
go in hard 77
go into one 261
GOK 13
goldbrick 148, 217
golden bowler 4
golden duck 82
golden handcuffs 148
golden handshake 151
golden hello 148
golden parachute 151
golden showers 29, 193
golden sombrero 95
Golden State 178
gold star 72
golf widow 87
golly 128
gom 235, 240
go mental 208
GOMER 13
gone goose 217
gone gosling 217
gone on 200
goner 206
gong 4
gonk 58, 193
go nuts 208
good areas 82
good buddy 167
goodfella 48
good heavens 128
good lord 128
goodness 128
goodness gracious 128
goodness me 128
good oil 228
goody 24, 274
goofball 54
go off 193, 228

go off at 228
go off on one 58
goofy foot 101
gook 137, 171
goolies 183
goomare 48
goombah 48
goon 15
gooner 261
go on the shout 228
goop 217
goose 193
goose bumps 187
goosegog 117
gooter 240
go overboard 282
GOP 157, 217
Gopher State 178
gorbie 223
gorblimey 128
gosh 128, 269
go spare 287
goss 18
go steady 200
Gotham 177
go to bat for 217
go to market 228
go to meet your maker 132, 206
gouch out 54
Gouge and Screw Tax 223
gouger 240
go under 34
gov 15
government-inspected meat 72
go west 206
go with 200
gowl 240
goy 173
go yard 95
Grab and Steal Tax 223
grad 62
grad school 62

graf 18
graft 42, 148
grand 120, 254
grand salami 95
grandstand 74
Granite State 178
grapevine 274
grass 42, 54, 282, 285
grass up 42
grauncher 148
Grauniad 18
gravel 217
graveyard shift 148
gravy 42
gravy train 34, 148
grease 264
greaseball 138, 171
grease monkey 148
greaser 8, 138, 165, 171
greasies 117, 228
greasy 117, 148, 228
greasy spoon 117
great unwashed 154
Great Wen 177
Great White Way 24
greedy guts 264
Greek love 193
green 120
green about the gills 203
greenback 121, 217, 274
Green Beret 4
greenhouse 4
greenie 187
green room 101
greens 193
green stuff 120
green-wellie 154
greeny 187
grey funnel line 8
grey knight 31
grey market 31
grey pound 34

gridiron 92
griff 18
grift 42
grifter 42, 217
grind 102, 193
grinding rail 102
grind rail 102
gringo 138, 171
grip 148, 228
gripe 266
grip tape 102
Grit 223
grockle 257
grody 217
grog 112, 228
grog-on 112, 228
grog-up 112, 228
groise 61
grok 289
grommet 101
groom 297
groove 21, 91, 282
groovy 160, 282
grope 193
grotty 289
groundhopper 77
groupie 21
groupware 66
growl and grunt 138, 142
growler 112, 165, 183
grub 117, 266
grubber 79
grundle 183
grunge 289
grunt 4
guardee 4
gub 138, 171, 228, 246
gubbins 285
guck 218
guest of Her Majesty 50, 132
guilt trip 292
guinea 138, 169

guinea pig 34
gully 69
gum digger 12, 228
gummies 228
gumshoe 42
gun 42, 165
gunfire 4
gunk 282
gun moll 42
gunsel 42
gup 243
guppie 72
gurrier 240
gurt 257
gussie 228
gussy up 160
gut 183
gutrot 112, 203
guts 117
guv 15, 261
guy 275
gyp 42, 218
gyppy tummy 187, 203
gypsy's 261
gypsy's kiss 142
gyrene 218

**H**

H 54, 280
hab 223
Habs 223
hack 18, 97, 148
hacker 66, 87
hackette 18, 148
hacking gear 105
hacky 252
hadaway 252
had it 206
hail Mary 92
haircut 50
hairy 285
hairyback 235

half 61
half a century 108
half a ton 121
half-cut 112, 275
half-inch 142
half-pie 233
half-pipe 102
half-seas-over 112, 269
half-soaked 256
hallion 249
ham 24, 84, 275
ham-and-egger 84
hammer 31, 74
hammered 112
Hampstead Heath 142, 183
hampsteads 261
hampton 261
Hampton Wick 142
hand 37
handbag 294
handbags 77
handful 37
handjob 193
handle 167, 275
hand relief 194
hang 218
hang-dogging 99
hang five 101
hanging 261
hang out 275
hang ten 101
hang-up 287
hankie 160
Hank Marvin 142
happen 254
happening 292
happy 112
happy-clappy 173, 297
happy hunting-ground 206
happy slapping 58, 125, 299
hapu 233
hard 194

hard chaw 240
hard-ears 237
hard hat 154
hard man 15, 42
hard-on 275
hard stuff 112
hard up 121
hard yards 79
harman 42
harmans 42
harp 22, 275
harpic 208
Harry Potter 106
hasbian 72
hash 54, 285
hash house 117
hash slinger 117
hassle 285
hatches, matches and dispatches
  18
hatchet man 42, 125
hater 69
hatstand 253
hat-trick 77, 82
have 194, 265
have a bun in the oven 132
have a screw loose 132, 208
have a slate loose 133, 208
have a watermelon on the vine
  132
have cash-flow problems 133
have issues 133
have it away 194
have it away on your toes 261
have it going on 218
have it large 58
have nothing on 42
have rocks in your head 218
have the hots for 194
have your collar felt 42
hawk 157
haymaker 84

hayseed 138, 154
haywire 280
head 8, 54, 203, 287
headbanger 292
head-bummer 246
headcase 209
heading for the last roundup 206
heads 8
headshrinker 209, 287
heart attack on a plate 117
heartsink 12
heart-throb 200, 280
heat 42, 95, 218
heater 42, 125
heave 151
heavens above 128
heaves 204
heavies 18
heavy 42, 289
heavy artillery 87
Hebe 171, 174
heck as like 254
hedgehog 4
heeler 157
heidie 61
Heinie 169
heinie 183, 218
Heinz 180
Heinz varieties 108
heist 42, 275
helicopter view 34
hellacious 218
hell's bells 128
helm 24
helmer 24
helmet 15
hen fruit 117
hentai 29
hepcat 282
hepster 282
herb 54
herbert 261

Here Before Christ 223
her indoors 261
her nibs 154, 275
heroin chic 160, 297
hick 138, 154, 177
hickey 194
hiding 125
hi-fi 243
higgledy-piggledy 265
high 54
high cheese 95
higher-ups 148
high-hat 154
high heat 95
high muck-a-muck 154
hill 4
himbo 294
hincty 218
hinky 218
hinny 253
hip 160
his nibs 154, 275
hit 42, 48, 54, 125
hitch 4, 50, 223
hitman 42, 48, 125
hit on 194
hit the bottle 112
hit the bricks 50
hit the canvas 84
hiya 285
ho 69, 138, 287
hock 275
hodad 101
hog 266
hog heaven 218
hog it 117
hog-wild 218
hoister 42, 269
hokum 280
hole 50, 77
hole card 107
hole in the wall 294

holliers 240
hollywood 233
holy Joe 148, 174
holy moly 129
holy Roller 174
holy shit 129
holy smoke 129
homeboy 48, 69, 200, 275
homegirl 69, 200
homer 95, 148, 246
homie 48, 70, 200
homo 223, 280
honcho 34, 148, 218
Hongcouver 223
honk 187
honker 101
honky 138, 171
honky-tonk 275
hooch 112
hood 42, 70
hoof 79
hoofer 24
hoof it 266
hoo-ha 282
hooker 42
hookey 61
hook up 200
hooky 42
hooley 240
hoon 228
hoop-la 218
hoops 97
hooray fuck! 233
Hooray Henry 154
hoosegow 50
hoosier 177
hoot 233
hooter 183, 287
hooters 183, 218
hop 54, 269
hophead 54, 112, 228
hopping mad 266

hops 97
horn 194, 218, 265, 285
hornbag 194, 228
horny 194
horse 54, 287
horse opera 24, 26
horse's hoof 138, 142
hospital pass 79
hoss 180
hot 15, 42, 160, 194
hot button 157
hot corner 95
hot-desking 34
hot-dog 101
hot-gospeller 174
hot hatch 165
hot pants 194, 280
hot place 174
hot seat 42
hottie 58, 194, 297
hotting 42
hot-wire 43, 165
hound 180
house 108
housey-housey 108
howay 253
how come? 275
how does that grab you? 289
how's your father 133, 194
howzit 235
hoy 253
hubba hubba 218
hubby 201, 266
hug the touchline 77
hui 233
humongous 289
hump 194, 269
humper 148
Hun 169, 278
hungry 77
hunk 194
hunks 265

hunky 287
hunky-dory 275
hurl 187
hurting 218
hush money 269
hustle 43
hustler 43, 194
hutch 82
hydro 223
hype 12, 54

**I**
IC 12
ice 43, 48, 54, 125
iceblock 233
iced 70
iceman 43, 48
icky 280
iddy-umpty 4
I declare 129
idiot box 211, 287
idiot's lantern 211, 287
I'll be a monkey's uncle 129
I'll be hornswoggled 129
I'll go to the foot of our stairs 129
illywhacker 43, 228
impost 89
impot 61
improv 24
imshi! 4, 278
in a bad way 204
in a pig's eye! 218
in a pig's whisper 275
indaba 235
indescribables 269
index 184
Indian 117
Indie 19
indulge 133
Indy 500 91
infernal 269
in flagrante delicto 194

in flitters 240
in full cry 105
in hock 50
in hot water 265
ink-jerker 19
ink-slinger 19, 148
inky 112, 228
in-laws 201
inside 15, 43, 51
inside job 15, 43
in spades 218
inspect the facilities 133
intended 201
interstate 95
in the can 24
in the family way 133, 187
in the groove 22
in the nip 240
in the sky 206
in the zone 74
into 289
invite 266
in with 266
in your birthday suit 133
in your dreams! 295
irie 237
Irish lager 8
iron 125
iron hoof 138, 142
isn't it? 243
it 112, 194, 282
item 201
It Girl 160
ivories 22, 184

**J**
J 54
jab 12
jabs 240
jack 121, 218
jackaroo 149, 228
Jack Dusty 8

jackeen 177, 240
jack in 66
jack off 194
jacks 240
jack shit 218
jacksie 184, 275
Jack tar 8
jack up 54, 228
Jacky 171, 228
Jacky-Jacky 171, 228
jaffa 82
Jag 165
jag 246
jail 87
jam 97, 99
jam buster 223
jam jar 142, 165
jammer 257
jammies 161
jan 257
jandals 233
jane 218
Jane Doe 10
jangle 251
jankers 4
Janner 257
Jap 169
japan 174
jar 112
jarhead 218
jark 265
jarred 112, 240
jarvey 269
jasper 257
java 117
jawboning 149, 218
jay 218, 265
jazz 194
jazz mag 29, 194, 297
Jean-Baptiste 223
jeely nose 246
jeepers creepers 129

jelly 54, 285, 295
jemimas 161
jemmy 117
jerk 138
jerk off 194
jerk-off 218
jerkwater 177
jerk your peter 194
Jerry 169, 278
jerry 275
jessie 138, 247
Jesus freak 174, 289
jiff 269
jiffy 269
jigger 251
jiggy 161
jiggy-jiggy 194
jildi 243
jillaroo 149, 229
Jim Crow 171
jim-dandy 218
jim hat 194
jiminy cricket 129
jimjams 112, 204
Jimmy 247
jimmy hat 194
jimmy riddle 142, 187
Jimmy-the-one 8
Jimmy Woodser 112, 229
jings 129, 247
jip 240
jism 194
jitney 121, 218
jitty 256
jizz 194
joanna 143
job 15, 43, 125, 229
jobbie 187
jobernowl 265
jobs for the boys 157
jobsworth 149
Jock 169

jock 4, 75, 218
joe 117
Joe Baxi 143, 165
Joe Blake 143, 180
Joe Blakes 112, 229
Joe Sixpack 154
joey 180
jogger's nipple 75
John 261
john 43, 218
John Doe 10
John Hancock 218
John Hop 43, 143, 229
johnny 194
Johnny pea-soup 223
John Thomas 184
joint 50, 54, 218
join the choir invisible 133, 206
join the majority 133, 206
jol 235
jolly 4, 37, 89, 275
jonty 8
joppety-joppety 259
josser 149, 229
journo 149
joyrider 165
judder bars 233
jug 50, 99
jughead 219
jugs 184, 287
juice 112, 219, 267
juiced 112, 219
juke 282
jumbuck 180, 229
jump 165, 194, 269
jump bail 10, 43
jumper 97
jumping Jehoshaphat 129
jump ship 8
jump someone's bones 194
jump-up 237
jungle 87

jungle bunny 138, 171
jungle juice 112, 285
junk bond 31
junkie 54, 280
juvie 51, 219

## K

K 95, 121
kack 187
Kaffir 171, 267
kaffirs 31
Kaiser Bill 278
kale 219
kangaroo 165
kangaroo court 10
kangaroos 31
kaput 278
kark 229
Kate 4
Kate Carney 4, 143
kaylied 251, 255, 256
kayo 84
keb 223
kecks 161
keeker 247
keelie 177
keep her lit 249
keepie-uppie 77
keister 184, 219
keks 161
Kelly's eye 108
ket 253
key of the door 108
keypal 66
Keystone State 178
kiasu 244
kibosh 275
kick 267
kicker 19, 102, 107, 219
kicking 58, 125
kick it 133, 206
kick the bucket 133, 206, 269

kick turn 102
kick upstairs 149
kidder 251, 253
kiddies 257
kidstakes 229
kike 138, 171, 219
kiki 72
kill 204
kill fee 19
killing 121
kiltie 247
kinchin 43
king-hit 229
kink 194
kinky 194, 209, 275
kip 240
kipper 169, 184, 229
kipper and plaice 143
kipper tie 161
kisser 184
kissing disease 204
kit 161
kitchen 22
kitchen cabinet 157
kitchen police 4
kite 5, 121
kitty 180
Kiwi 169, 233
kludge 66
klutz 138
knackered 287
knackers 184
knees-up 261
knee-trembler 194, 275
knicks 161
knob 184, 194, 267, 295
knock 82, 125, 195
knock at the door 108
knockback 51
knockers 184, 282
knocking on heaven's door 206
knocking shop 43, 195

knock into the middle of next
   week 275
knock off 43, 149, 251, 267
knock out 34
knock up 195
knock your toys in 249
knowledge box 269
ko 84
kook 101, 209
kooky 209, 287
Kraut 169
krunk 70
kuri 233

**L**
L 165
la 251
lack 240
lad 133
la-di-da 154
ladyboy 195
Lady Godiva 121, 143
Lady Macbeth strategy 31
lady of the night 133
lag 51
lager lout 112, 295
lah 251
lair 229
la-la land 177
lallie 27
lamp 125
lamps 184
lancejack 5
lander 125
langer 240
langered 240
Lanky 251, 255
lanky streak of piss 255
lar 251
large it 58, 297
larrup 125
larry 12

lashed 112
lashings 275
latch lifter 251
lather 125
latty 27
laugher 75
laughing academy 209
laughing gear 184
launder 43
laundry 92
lavender marriage 72
law 43
lawn meet 105
lay 195, 267
lay an egg 24
lazybones 265
lead 19, 125
lead poisoning 133
lead towel 125, 275
leaf 54
leak 187
leather 125
leathering 269
leatherneck 5
leave it out! 261
leccy 251, 255
left-field 289
left-footer 174
leftie 157, 282
leg 37
legal eagle 10, 149
leg-business 24
leggy 82
leg it 267
legless 112
leg-man 195
leg-opener 112
leg-over 195
legs 26, 87
legs eleven 108
lekker 235
lemon 72

lensman 24, 26
lesbo 280
let go 133
let it all hang out 289
let off 133, 187
let on 269
let one go 187
letterman 75
letty 27
level playing field 34
levels you devils 37
level with 280
lez 280
lib 292
lick 22, 265, 282
lickety-split 275
lids 15
lifer 51
lift 15, 43, 265
lig 249
lightie 235
light into 125
like gangbusters 219
like piffy 255
like piffy on a rock 255
like piffy on a rock bun 255
lily law 72
lime 237
limey 169
line 54, 105
linen draper 143
Lionel Blairs 143, 161
lip out 87
lippy 161, 287
lipstick lesbian 72
liquidate 133
liquid lunch 112, 289
liquid sunshine 145
liquored up 112
little green man 240
live high on the hog 219
Liverpool kiss 251

livestock 180, 269
live tally 255
liveware 66
load 112
loaded 112, 121, 275
loaf 184
loaf of bread 143
LOBNH 13
lobster 5
locked 240
lock-in 112
lockout 19
loco 209
loid 43
LOL 13
lollies 233
lollipop 91
lollipop lady 149
lollipop man 149
lollipop woman 149
lolly 121
Lollywood 244
Londonistan 177
London particular 275
Lone Star State 178
long 62
long ball 95
long drop 229, 235
long shot 75
loo 285
loon 209
looney tune 209, 289
loonie 223
loon-pants 161
loons 161
loony 209
loony bin 209
loop 34
loop-di-loop 251
loop-the-loop 117, 143
loopy 209, 280
loose 79

loot 5
lord bless us and save us 129
lord save us 129
lorry 43
lose the place 209, 247
lose the plot 209
lose your lunch 187
lose your marbles 209
louser 138, 240
love a duck! 261
loved up 295
love handles 184
love juice 195
lovely jubbly 261
love muscle 184
love truncheon 184
lowballing 34
low-budget 133
low rider 165
L-plate 51
lubricate 113
luck out 219
Lucky Country 177, 229
lucky seven 108
lug 265
lulu 275
lumber 51, 247
lunchbox 184
lunk 219
lunker 180
lunkhead 219
lurch 240
lurgy 204
lurk 66
lush 58, 113
luvvie 24
luzz 259

**M**
MacGuffin 24
mack 43
Mackem 253

macky 258
mad as a meat axe 233
Madchester 255
made guy 48
made man 48
made up 251, 255
madly 269
mag 19, 269
magalogue 34
maggoty 113
magic mushrooms 54, 290
magic sponge 77
Magpies 253
mainline 54, 282
make 195
make a move on 195
make like 219
make out 195
make out like a bandit 219
maker's name 82
make time with 219
make with 219
make your bones 48
makings 54
malarkey 280
mall rat 219, 295
mam 255
mamzer 219
man-boobs 184
Manc 177, 255
maneater 195
mang 247
mangarly 27
mangary 27
manky 99
man on! 77
manor 15, 43
mantrap 195
man upstairs 174
map 184
map of Tassie 229
marabunta 237

marching powder 54
mardy 256
mare 75, 138
mark 43, 269
marley 249
marmelize 125
marrow 253
martin 265
martini shot 24
Mary 229
mary 72
Mary Jane 54
mash 117
mask 105
massive 70, 237, 295
matlo 149
maulers 184
maund 265
mavin 219
max out 121
mazuma 121
McGuffin 24
McKenzie Friend 10
meal ticket 275
meat and two veg 184
meatball 138, 219
meathead 138, 219
meat rack 195
meatspace 66, 297
meat wagon 165
mebs 240
Med 177
medic 62
medico 149
meet a sticky end 206
megabucks 121
megillah 219
Melvyn Bragg 143
member's bounce 87
Mendoza line 95
men in white coats 209
mental 209

mentalist 58, 209
Merc 165
Mersey Funnel 251
mess up 125
Met 15
meth 54
Michelle 82
Mick 169
mick 174, 223
mickey 223, 240
Mickey Finn 280
Mickey-Mouse 285
Mickey Mouser 143, 177
Mick Jagger 113, 143
micro 66
microdot 54
middy 8, 113, 229
midfield dynamo 77
midfield general 77
midgie 180, 247
mighty 269
Migra 219
milf 299
milko 149, 229
milk run 5, 285
milk shake 89
milk train 5
mill 43, 84, 265, 267
millie 249
Milton Keynes 117, 143, 161
mince pies 143, 184
minces 261
mind-blowing 290
minder 280, 295
minge 184
minger 59, 247
minging 59
mini ramp 102
misery 270
misfortune 201
miskin 256
mission-critical 35

missis 201
miss the boat 275
missus 201
Mister Big 15, 43
mittens 43
mitts 85, 184
mix it 125
mizzle 270
MO 15
moaning minnie 5, 285
moat 99
Mob 15, 48
mobbed up 48
mobility 267
mobster 15, 48
moby 251
moccasin telegraph 223
mods 62
moffie 235
mog 180
moggie 180
moke 171, 180, 229
mollymawk 180, 233
mom 201
Monday-morning quarterback
   93
mondo 101, 219
money grab 219
money shot 29
mong 59, 138, 180, 229
monged 59
mongo foot 103
monkey 55, 121, 180, 233, 275
monkey suit 161
monkey's wedding 145, 235
mono 99, 204
monster 107
monstering 299
Montezuma's revenge 187, 204
monthlies 133, 188
moody 43, 261
mooi 235

mook 219
moola 121
moon 290
moon-eyed 113, 219
Moonie 174
moonrock 55
moonshine 113
moonshiner 113
moon shot 95
mopery 10
mopoke 138, 229
moppet 26
more bang for your buck 219
morkins 256
morning glory 89
mortal 113
mortaller 240
mosh 295
mossie 180
mot 240, 270
mother 138
motherfucker 138, 280
motherless 240
mother's ruin 113, 202
Motor City 177
motorway madness 165
Motown 177
motser 37, 121, 229
mountain dew 113
mountainy 240
Mountie 223
mouse 125, 267
mouse-milking 219
mouse potato 66
mousetrap 118, 285
mouth off 287
move your bowels 133, 188
moz 229
mozzie 180
Mr Big 15, 45
Mr Todd 105
muck 107

mucker 201, 285
mudder 89
mudhook 8
mudlark 89
muff 184, 267
muff diver 195
muffin-fight 118
muffin top 161, 299
mug 61, 125, 184, 244, 275
mugger 125
mug punter 37
mug shot 15
mule 15, 55
mullah 125, 261
mullahed 113, 261
muller 125, 261
mullered 113, 261
mulligan 87, 118
mulligrubs 267
mumbo-jumbo 174
mumper 267
munchie 240
munchies 55
munchkin 149
munge 66, 99
munt 235
munter 59, 297
muntu 138, 171, 235
muppet 59
murphies 118
muscle Mary 72
mush 184
mushmouth 219
muslin 8
muso 22, 290
mutha 138
mutt 180
mutt and jeff 143
mutton 265
my bad 219
my goodness 129
my word 129

# N

nab 43, 265, 267
nabes 24
nadgers 184
nads 184
naff 27
nag 180
NAI 10
nail 195, 270
nailed 101
nailed on 37
naked 31
Nam 290
nana 184
Nancy-boy 138
nang 59, 261
nantee 27
nap 37
napoo 278
napper 184, 270
narc 15, 43, 219
nark 15, 43
narky 275
nat 157
natter 255, 285
natty 237
naturals 29
naughty 195, 229
naughty bits 184
navvy 149
neck 275
ned 247
neddy 89, 229
needful 121
needle 113, 275
negatively privileged 133
nellie 180
nellie duff 143
nelly 180
nelson 82
nerd 138
net 37, 78

nethead 66
netiquette 66
netizen 66
Netspeak 66
nettie 253
never-never 121
never up, never in 87
neves 37
nevis 37
new chum 229
Newfie 177, 223
newky broon 253
newshound 19
News of the Screws 19
nice weather for ducks 145
nick 15, 43, 51
nickel 51
nicker 121
nifty 275
nigger 138, 171
niggle 265
nightcap 75, 89
nightmare 75
nightwatchman 82
nig-nog 5, 138, 172
nim 267
Nimby 154, 295
nineteenth hole 87
nine, ten, jack 82
Nip 169, 285
nip 44, 145, 265
nip and tuck 12
nipper 44
nippers 44
nit 285
nite 280
niterie 24
nixer 149, 240
nix my dolly 270
n/o 37
Noah's ark 229
nobble 44, 89

nobbut 255
no better than she should be 133
noble art 85
noble science 85
no-brainer 219
noddle 265
noddy 19, 211
noddy suit 5
noggerhead 259
noggin 184
nollie 103
no-mark 138
nonce 51
non-com 5
non-con 174
no-no 285
non-U 154, 155
noodle 22, 184
no offers 37
no oil painting 133
nooky 195, 280
nooner 219
nope 275
norks 184, 229
north and south 143, 184
North–South runner 93
nose 16, 44, 270
nosebag 118
nose candy 55, 280
nose grind 103
nosh 118, 261
noshery 118
nosh-up 118
nostrils 16
not a happy bunny 133
not all there 209
notchel 10
not half bad 275
not know a B from a bull's foot 265
not long for this world 206

not playing with a full deck 133, 209
not the full shilling 209
not the sharpest knife in the drawer 133
no way 290
no way José 290
nowt 255
nsg 26
nub 267
nubbin 99
nubbing-cheat 267
nubbing-cove 267
nudger 251
nuke 118, 287, 295
number 55, 161, 206, 290
number-cruncher 66
number nine 5
number one 8, 133, 188, 270
numbers game 48
numbers racket 48
Number Ten 157
number two 133, 188
numbnuts 139, 219
numpty 247
nurdle 83
nut 24, 125, 184, 209
nutcase 209
nuthatch 209
nuthouse 209
nutjob 209, 292
nutmeg 78
Nutmeg State 178
nuts 107, 184
nutter 209
nutty 209
nympho 195
nymph of darkness 133

## O

oak 62
oaken towel 270

oater 24, 26
obbo 16
ob-gyn 12
ocker 229
OD 55, 287
oddball 209
odds and sods 282
OE 233
ofay 172
off 91
officer down 16
off-message 157
offsider 229
off the hook 70
off your chump 209
off your face 59
off your head 209
off your nut 209
off your onion 209
off your rocker 209, 275
off your tits 59, 297
off your trolley 209
oggin 8
ogle-fakes 27
oh my God 129
oik 154
oiled 270
OK 275
old-age pension 108
Old Bill 44
old boy 201
old college try 62
Old Contemptibles 278
Old Dart 177, 229
old-fashioned way 97
Old Firm 247
old girl 201
Old Harry 174
old king cole 143, 152
old man 201
Old Nick 174
Old Scratch 174

old sweat 5
old woman 201
ollie 103
omadhaun 240
omi 27
on 108
on a line 256
oncer 121, 174
one and one 240
one-eight-seven 16
one-eyed trouser snake 184
one foot in the grave 206
one-horse town 177
one-night stand 22, 195
one of them 292
oner 121, 125
one sandwich short of a picnic 209
one-time 70
one-two 78, 85
on ice 51
onion 184
onion bag 78
onkus 229
onliner 67
on-message 157
on the bash 44
on the batter 113
on the beach 8, 152
on the broo 247
on the club 149
on the dole 152
on the fritz 220
on the game 44
on the in 51
on the knocker 121, 229
on the lam 220
on the lash 113
on the money 220
on the nod 121
on the nose 37, 229
on the numbers 93

on the outs 220
on the piss 113
on the pull 195
on the rag 133, 188
on the razz 59, 113
on the road 22
on the run 44
on the sick 149
on the slate 121
on the Social 292
on the street 152
on the streets 44
on the take 44
on the wagon 113
on tour with the National 51
on your beam ends 121
on your bike! 290
on your last legs 206
on your uppers 121
oof 121
ooftish 121
open 24
open a can of whoop-ass 125
open card 107
oppo 282
orthopod 12
Oscar 229
Ossi 169
Other Side 233
ou 235
our kid 251, 255
out 72, 297
outdoor 256
outfit 35, 48
out for the count 85
out of order 292
out of sight 275
out of the screws 87
out of your skull 113, 209
out of your tree 209
outsider 247
overindulge 133

overshot 267
over the top 278
over the water 251
owner 8
own the line 105
owt 255
Oxo cube 143, 261
Oz 177, 230

**P**
p.a. 26
pack 44
pack a sad 233
packet 121
pad 51, 282
paddles 91
Paddy 169, 270
Paddy's Wigwam 251
paddy wagon 16
paddy-whack 125
pads 105
paint 97
painters 133, 188
paint job 165
paint the black 95
pair 83
pakeha 233
Paki 139, 169, 172
Paki-bashing 292
pal 267
palatic 253
palimony 10, 292
paloney 27
palooka 85, 139, 220
pansy 139
pantile 174
pap 19
paper 31
paperhanger 44
paper-pusher 149
paper-stainer 149
paper the house 25

pappy 201, 270
paralytic 113
parcel 37
pardon my French 133
park 27, 31, 75
parky 145, 255, 275
parleyvoo 169
part brass rags 8
party 280
party hat 195
party ledge 99
pass away 134, 206
passman 51
pass on 134, 206
pastie bap 249
pasting 125
patrico 174
patsy 220
pave 240
pavee 240
pavement pizza 134
paw 267
pay a call 134, 188
pay a visit 134, 188
peach 44
Peach State 178
peachy 280
peanuts 121
pearlies 184
pearl necklace 29
pearly gates 184
pea-souper 145, 223
peck 118
pecker 185, 220
peckerwood 220
pecs 185
pee 188
pee down 145
peeler 25, 275
pee-pee 188
peepers 185, 270
peg 83, 185

peg it 206
peg leg 275
peg out 206
peke 180
Pelican State 178
pen 51, 220
pen and ink 143
pencil-pusher 149
penguin 5
penguin suit 161
penny-a-liner 19
penny ante 107
pennyboy 249
pen-pusher 149
pepper 223
Pepsi 223
perform 230
perishing 145
perk 35, 118, 275
perp 16
perv 230
pesky 270
pet 253
peter 44, 185
peterman 44
Pete Tong 143
petrolhead 165
PFO 13
PGT 13
pharming 67
phat 70
Philadelphia lawyer 10
Philistine 149
phishing 67
phiz 185, 267
phizog 185
phoney 275
phreaking 67
physical 78, 125
physio 75
pi 174
pic 275

picayune 220
pickle 265
pickled 113, 267
pickney 237
pick the eyes out of 230
pick up 195
pick-up joint 195
pictures of the Queen 261
picture taker 167
piddle 188, 270
piece 44
pie chucker 83
pie-eyed 113
pig 44, 275
pigboat 8
pigeon 44
pig out 118
pigskin 93
pike 267
pike out 230
pikey 139, 172
pile 270
pill 79, 149
pillock 139, 290
pill-pusher 12
pills 185
pimp 165
pinch 16, 44, 267
pineapple 5, 278
ping 79
pinhooker 89
pink 72, 105
pink ceiling 149
pinko 157, 282
pink oboe 134, 185
pink pound 35
pink slip 152
pins 185, 265
pint of plain 240
pious fraud 174
pip 5
pipe 103, 251

pipe-layer 157
pip emma 5
pipsqueak 165, 278
piss 188
piss artist 113
piss down 145
pissed 113, 220, 280
pissed off 285
pisser 185, 258
pisshead 113
piss-up 113, 287
pit babe 91
pix 282
pixilated 113
pizzazz 282
PJs 161, 290
place 37, 89
plank spanker 22
plant 25, 206, 267
plastered 113
plastic 121, 292
plastic money 292
plastic Paddy 240
plates of meat 143, 185
platter 282
playa 70
play away 134, 195
play away from home 134, 195
player 70
player hater 70
play footsie 195
play for the other team 134
play pocket billiards 195
play the field 134
play the pink oboe 195
play up 204
play with yourself 196
plebe 5
pling 67
plod 44, 292
plonk 278
plonker 139, 185

plonko 113, 230
plop 188
plough 63
plover 267
pluck 63
plug 35, 87, 125
plug-ugly 44
plumb 83
plump 125, 145
plunger 5
plunk 126
poacher 78
pocky 265
poddy 180, 230
poes 235
pogey 223
poindexter 139
point break 101
point Percy at the porcelain 134, 188
poison pill 31
poke 196, 276
poky 51
pol 157
Polack 169
politico 157
poll 63
Polly 180
polo mint 167
polone 27
pom 169, 230
pommy 139, 169, 230
pomp 235
Pompey 177, 259
pom-pom 5
ponce 44
pond 177, 270
pongo 5, 169, 230
pontoon 51
pony 121, 270
pony and trap 143, 188
poo 188

pooch 180
poof 139
pooftah 139
poontang 185, 196
poop 188
pooped 220
pop 48, 55, 118, 201
po-po 70
pop off 270
poppa 201
poppers 55, 290
poppies 241
poppy 121
pop shot 29
pop your clogs 134, 206
porangi 233
pork barrel 157
pork pie 143
pork sword 185
porky 143, 262
porn 29, 290
porno 29
pornshop 29
porridge 51
porridge wog 262
posse 70, 295
postal 126
postdoc 63
postgrad 63
postie 149
pot 37, 55, 75, 282
pot-belly 185
pothead 55
POTS 67
potty 280
poultice 121, 230
pound 37
pour 26
powder room 134
powder your nose 134, 188
power breakfast 35, 295
power dressing 35, 295

power lunch 35, 295
pox 204
poxy 280
prad 180, 270
praiser 26
prang 5, 165
prat 139, 185, 265
praties 241
prayer 93, 97
preach 174
preachify 174
preemie 12, 220
preggers 285
prelims 63
premed 63
pre-owned 134
prequel 25
pressie 282
press the flesh 158
previous 16, 44
prex 63
Prez 158
prick 185, 265
prig 44, 265
prim 12
prior 16
private eye 282
pro 44
Prod 174
Proddie 174, 247
professional foul 78
prog 63, 118
prole 154
prop 85
prophet 37
proposition 196
props 70
protection 48
prough 249
pruck 249
prune 5, 139
pseud 290

psycho 209, 285
pub 276
pubes 185
puck 241
puck bunny 223
puckeroo 233
pud 118
pudding 196
pug 85
puke 188, 267
pukka 244, 270
pull 16, 44, 89, 196, 276
pull-out quote 19
pull up 16, 44
pull your punches 85
pumpkin positive 12
pump ship 188
pum-pum 237
punani 237
punce 230
Punch-and-Judy hitter 95
punch-drunk 85
punch out 95, 126
punchy 85
punter 37
puppies 185
puppy-walker 16
pushing and shoving 91
pushing up daisies 134, 206
push the envelope 35
puss 105, 180, 185
pusser 8
pussy 139, 180, 185, 196, 285
put on the long finger 241
put out 196
put out to grass 85, 152
put the make on 196
put the pedal to the metal 91
put to sleep 134
put up 105
put up the shutters 35
put your bib in 230

putz 139, 185, 220
pyjama cricket 83

**Q**
quack 149
quads 107
qualities 19
quant 32
quare 241
quare hawk 241
quarterdecker 8
quarter-pipe 103
queen 251
queer 72
queer-bashing 126, 290
quickie 83, 113, 196
quid 121, 267
quim 185, 270
quit the scene 207
quod 51

**R**
rabbit 16, 83, 87
rabbit and pork 143
rabbit food 118
rabbito 230
rabbit punch 85
race face 91
rack 185
racket 149
rack off 230
radge 247
rag 19
rag day 63
rag-fair 5
raggery 161
raggy 258
raghead 139, 172
rag-out 19, 150
ragtop 165
rag trade 161
rag week 63

raid 32
raider 89
rainbow 204
rain cats and dogs 146
rain like a cow pissing on a flat
  rock 146
rainmaker 150
rake 241
raking it in 121
ramp 44
rampsman 37
R&R 220
randy 196
rap 44
rap sheet 16
rark 233
rasher 241
raspberry ripple 143, 185
rasps 118
rat 150
rat-arsed 113
ratbag 139
rat catcher 251
rat-catcher 105
ratpack 19
rat race 285
rat run 165
ratted 113
rattler 126, 180, 276
raunchy 290
raver 287
reader 44
readies 121, 282
recce 5
receiver 44
recon 5
red 158
red and white 253
red biddy 113
redcap 5
red cent 121
redcoat 223

Red Devils 5
red-eye 113, 224
red hat 5
Red Lane 185
red-light district 196
redneck 139, 154
red ned 113, 230
rednose 251
redpoint 99
redser 241
redskin 172
reds under the bed 158
red-top 20
reducer 78
reefer 8, 55
ref 75
reffo 139, 230
refreshment 134
reggo 166, 230
reject 97
relax your cacks 249
rellies 201, 230
reload 87
rent boy 196, 290
rents 201
represent 70
res 220
resting 25, 134
rest room 134
result 75
retread 158
retrosexual 299
reverend 174
reverse cowboy 29
rez 220
rhino 121, 267
rhinocerical 267
riah 27
rice queen 73
Richard the Third 143, 188
ride 166, 196
ride and a rasher 241

rig 166
rim 196
ring 44, 185, 276
ringer 44, 89
riot 105
rip-off 290
ripped 113
ripper 230
ripping 276
ripsnorter 146
roach 55, 180
roach clip 55
roadie 22
road rage 126
roasting 196, 299
Rock 224
rock 55, 97
rock chopper 174, 230
rocket scientist 32
rock house 55
rocks 185
rod 185
roger 180, 185, 196
rogue dialler 67
rogues' gallery 16
roids 75
roll 44, 196
rolled over 105
Roller 166, 287
roll-in 103
rolling in it 121
roll in the hay 134, 196
roll out 35
Roman candle 5
romcom 25
ronnie 241
roo 180
roof 37, 99
roofie 55
rooinek 172, 235
roomie 220
root 196, 230

rooty 5, 244
ropable 180
rope-a-dope 85
ropey 204, 285
rort 37, 230
rorter 230
rorty 230
Rory O'More 143
Roseland 177
Rosie Lee 118, 143
rosy 113
rotgut 265
rouf 37
roughie 230
rough trade 73, 196
rough up 126
round-ball game 79
rounder 107
roundhouse 85
round the bend 209
round the houses 144, 161, 262
round the twist 209
round-tripper 95
route one 78
Roy 161
royal flush 107
rozzer 45, 276
rubber 196
rubber cheque 121
rubber dollies 241
rubber johnny 196
rubbidy 113
rubby 224
rub out 48
ruby 85
Ruby Murray 118, 144
ruck 51, 126
ruddock 265
rude boy 237
rugger 80
rugger bugger 80
rum 270

rumble 126
rummy 114
rumpy-pumpy 196
runabout 166
run interference 93
runner 37
runners 230, 241
runs 188, 204
rush 55, 287
Russki 169, 278

## S

sab 105
sack 93
sackless 253
saddler 181
sad sack 220
safe 59, 196
Sally Army 174
Sally Gunnell 87
salt 8
salt-junk 118
Salvo 174, 230
sambo 139, 172, 230, 241
samey 280
Sammy 5, 118
S and M 29, 196
sandshoe crusher 83
Sandy 169, 270
san fairy ann 278
san ferry ann 278
sanger 230, 241
sannies 247
sap 276
saphead 270
sarge 5
sarmie 235
sarnie 118, 290
satin and silk 118, 144
Saturday night special 16, 126
sauce 114, 220
saucebox 265

sausage dog 181, 282
saved by the bell 85
savvy 270
sawbones 12, 276
sawbuck 121
Sawney 169, 270
sawney 267
scab 150, 270
scaffie 247
scag 55
scald 241
scaldy 241
scally 251, 255
scam 45
scandal sheet 20
scanger 241
scanties 161, 282
scarf down 118
scarfie 233
scarper 276
scattermouch 8
schemie 154, 247
schizo 209
schlemiel 139
schlep 139
schlimazel 220
schlock 220
schlong 220
schmeck 220
schmo 139, 220
schmuck 139, 185, 220
schmutter 161
schnook 139, 220
schnorrer 220
schnozzle 185
schoolie 61, 230
sci-fi 287
scissor sister 297
sclaff 87
scoff 118
scofflaw 10
scone 185, 249

scoop 241
scoosh 247
scope 235
scorch 166
scorcher 146, 276
score 55, 121, 196
Scotch mist 146
Scouse 177, 285
Scouser 177
scrag 185
scram 280
scrambled eggs 5
scran 118, 255
scrap 126
scrape 126
scrapper 75
scratch 88, 241
scream 45, 161
screamer 20
screech 224
screw 45, 51, 150, 196, 270
screw around 196
screwball 209
screwy 209, 276
scrimshank 5
script kiddie 67
scroggin 230
scrote 292
scrub 70, 89
scrubber 139, 276
scrum pox 80
scrumptious 118
scuffer 251
scumbag 197
scutler 258
scuttered 241
scutters 241
scuzzbag 220
scuzzball 220
scuzzy 220, 292
sea lawyer 8, 181
seat cover 167

seconds 118
secure accommodation 134
see 107
see a man about a dog 134, 188
seeing-to 126, 262
see you next Thursday 134
seller 90
serve 230
sesh 114, 295
settler 37
sewing machine 166
sewing-machine leg 99
sex bomb 290
sex goddess 282
sex kitten 197, 287
sex on a stick 197
sex on legs 197
sexpert 290
sexpot 197
sex up 299
sex worker 134
shack up 201
shades 161, 241
shaft 185, 197, 270
shag 197, 276, 282
shagger 197
shag-me shoes 197
shake down 45, 91
shake'n'bake 97
shamateur 75
shampoo 114
shamus 45
shank 51, 88
Shanks's pony 166
shaper 35
shareware 67
shark and taties 233
shark biscuit 101
shark repellents 32
Sharon 154
sharp 161
sharp end 99

sharpy 27
shaver 265
shedload 297
sheeny 172, 174
sheep-biter 265
sheep-dip 114
sheep-shagger 139, 155
sheet 146
sheila 230, 276
shekels 122
shelf 45, 230
shemale 197
shenanigans 276
shepherding 80
sherbet 114, 230
sherbet dab 144
sherman tank 144, 169
she's apples 230
shicker 114, 230
shickered 230
shift 118, 241, 265
shill 45
shimmy 161
shindig 287
shine 172
shiner 126
shirt-lifter 139
shit 55, 270
shit and a shave 51
shitfaced 114
shit-for-brains 139, 292
shithead 139
shithouse 270
shits 188, 204
shitter 185
shiv 40, 126
shiver my timbers 129
shock 204
shoeing 262
shonky 230
shoo 90
shoo-in 75, 90

shoot blanks 197
shoot-'em-up 67
shooter 16, 45, 83, 114, 126, 276
shoot hoops 97
shooting gallery 55, 287
shooting iron 126, 270
shoot the breeze 220
shoot the curl 101
shoot the pill 87
shoot the tube 101
shoot up 55
shop 45, 51
short 114
short and curlies 185
short stack 107
short stuff 88
shot 12, 114
shoulder 38
shoulder knot 10
shoulder surfing 45
shout 114, 230
shoutline 20
shout-out 70
shovelware 67
showbiz 25
showboat 75
shower 139
Show Me State 178
shrapnel 122
shred 101
shrink 210, 290
shrooms 55
shtick 25
shtup 197
shuffle off this mortal coil 134,
  207
shufti 285
shunt 91, 166, 292
shut the door 91
shyster 10
sian 244
sick as a parrot 292

sickie 150, 204, 287
sicko 210
side 211
sidekick 201
sidewalk surfing 101, 103
significant other 201
sign on 152
silk 10
silko 241
silver screen 25
silver surfer 67
silvertail 155, 230
silverware 75
simoleon 122, 220
simp 139
sin-bin 80
sing 16, 45
singing from the same hymn sheet
  158
singleton 201
sinker 118
sis 201, 235
sitcom 211
sithee? 255
sit on the splice 83
sitrep 5
sitter 78
siwash 139, 172
six feet under 207
six-pack 185
sixty-nine 197
sizzler 146
skag 55
skank 59, 220, 237
skanky 59
skatepark 103
skate rat 103
skaterboy 103
skatergirl 103
skeef 235
skeet 70, 197
skeeter 181

skell 16
skelly 247
skew-whiff 270
skid lid 91, 166
skier 83
skim 45
skin 241
skin flick 25, 290
skinful 114
skin game 45
skinny 161
skinny-rib 161
skin-pop 55
skins 22, 55
skinsman 22
skint 122, 276
skin up 55, 290
skipper 265
skite 230
skitters 188, 204
skittle out 83
skive 61
skivvies 161, 220
skivvy 150, 161, 230
skollie 235
skoosh 247
skrimshank 5
skunk 55
sky 78
sky parlour 270
sky pilot 5, 174, 276
slack 197
slag 139, 188, 230
slam dunk 97
slammer 51, 114
slanger 55, 220
slap 99
slap and tickle 197
slap-happy 85
slaphead 139
slapper 139
slap-up 118

slash 188
slasher 12
slasher film 25
slasher movie 25
slats 185
slaughtered 114, 295
sleaze 139
sleazebag 139
sleazeball 139
sleb 155
sledging 83
sleeper 25
sleeping policeman 166
sleep with 134, 197
sleeveen 241
slewed 114
slicks 91
slimy 267
sling ink 20, 150
slit 185
Sloane Ranger 155, 292
slog 83
slog your guts out 150
sloppy joe 118, 161
sloppy seconds 197
slosh 126
sloshed 114
slot 6
slued 114
slug 126
slugfest 85
slugger 85, 95
slurb 177
smack 55, 285
smacker 122, 197
smackhead 55
smack the pony 197
small screen 211
smart 67
smartarse 139
smartass 139
smartypants 276

smash 122
smashed 114
smasher 270
smear 99
smelt 267
smile 114
Smoke 177, 262
smoke 270
smokey 167
smokey bear 167
smokey in a plain brown
  wrapper 167
smoko 230
smoot 20
smouch 172, 174
smug 63
snaffling lay 270
snafu 6, 285
snag 231
snakebite 114
snakeboard 103
snakes alive 108, 129
snapper 20, 150, 241
snarf 118
snarler 233
snatch 45, 185, 276, 282
snazzy 161, 282
snifter 114
snip 12, 161
snit 220
snitch 45, 185
snitchers 45
snob 270
snog 197
snoot 185
snootful 114
snort 55, 114
snot 188
snotrag 162, 276
snotty 8
snout 16, 45, 51, 185
snow 55, 220

snowball 56
snowbird 56
snowdropper 45
snow-eater 146
snow-gatherer 45
snowjob 220
snow queen 73
snuff it 207
snuff out 126
soak 114, 126
soap 25, 197, 212
soapland 197
soash 251
s.o.b. 140, 221
sob sister 20
soccer 78
soccer mom 201
social 152
sock 126, 267
sockdolager 126
socked in 146
socko 26
sod 140
soda jerk 150
soft 241, 255
soft lad 251
soft spot 201
soixante-neuf 197
soldier 48, 118
solid 244
solo 29
some pup 249
something for the weekend 134,
  197
sonofabitch 140, 221, 267
Soo 224
Sooner State 178
sorry-assed 221
sort 126, 262
sorted 56
soul food 118
sound 251

soup 45, 101
souped-up 282
soup strainer 185
soup up 166
southpaw 85
soutie 235
soutpiel 235
souvenir 45, 231, 278
sov 122, 276
sow your wild oats 134
sozzled 114
SP 38
space cadet 56, 292
spaced out 56, 290
space opera 25
spacey 56
spade 140, 172
spadger 181
spag 140, 169, 231
spag bol 118
spam 67
spammer 67
spank 75
spanker 267
spank the monkey 197
spare tyre 185
spark 150
sparks 8, 150
spastic 140
spaz 140
spaz out 59
spazzy 59, 140
speak 105
spear carrier 25
spearing 93
spear tackle 80
special K 56
speed 56, 290
speedball 56
speed cop 166, 280
speedfreak 56, 166
speedo 166

speedy 241
spend a penny 134, 188
spew your ring 188
spic 140, 172
spide 249
spiflicate 270
spike 6, 93, 114
spin 51
spinach 88
spin doctor 158
spine-bashing 231
spinny 224
spit 201, 270
spitcher 8
spit curl 162
spitting 146
splash and dash 91
splash out 122
splash page 67
splatter film 25, 292
splatter movie 25, 292
splice the mainbrace 8
spliff 56, 282
split beaver 29
splitter 204
split the trees 146
splog 67
spoken for 201
spondulicks 122
sponge 114
sponger 267
spooge 197
sport of kings 90
spot the loony 210
spring 51
springer 38
sprog 6, 201, 270, 285
sprung 114
spud 118
spud-bashing 6
Spud Island 224
spunk 188, 197, 231

spy in the cab 166
spyware 67
squaddie 6
square 118, 155, 162, 285
square-bashing 6
square eyes 212, 290
squarehead 169
square up 122
squeak 20
squeal 45
squeeze 45, 201
squid 122
squiffer 22
squiffy 114, 276
squirrel ranch 210
squirrel tank 210
squirt 140
squish 61
squits 188, 204
squitters 188, 204, 267
stabber 241
stacked 285
stag 32
stag film 29
stair rods 146
stake out 16
stalkerazzi 20
stalking horse 158
stall 78
stall the ball 241
stand up 201
stand-up guy 221
star 51
start 150
starve the bardies 129, 231
stash 56, 270
stat 12
steady 201
steamer 38, 118, 231
steaming 45, 114
steever 241
stepney 244

steps 108
stew-can 8
stewed 114
stick 83, 88, 101
stick fighting 241
sticks 78, 90, 177
stick up 45
sticky 67
sticky dog 83
stiff 38, 45, 51, 88, 126, 207, 276
stiffener 114
stiffie 197
stiffs 78
stiffware 68
stiffy 197
sting 16, 45
stingo 267
stinker 9
stinking rich 122
stinko 114
stinks 61
stir 51
stitch up 45
stompie 235
stoned 56
stone dead 88
stone me 129
stoner 56
stone the crows 129
stonewall 83
stonk 6
stonker 126, 231
stonkered 114
stonkers 114
stony-broke 122
stoolie 45
stool pigeon 45
stooze 122, 299
stop a bullet 126
stotter 247
strafe 278
straight 45, 56, 197

straight arrow  221
straightener  46
straight flush  107
straight man  25
strain the spuds  134, 188
strap  140, 241
strapped for cash  122
Strat  22
streaker  292
street cred  292
streetwalker  134, 265
strep  12, 204
strep throat  12, 204
stretch  51, 166
stretcher  267
strewth  129
strides  162, 231
strike it rich  122
strill  27
Strine  231
strip  97
striper  9
stripes  181
stroke  97
stroke mag  29
stroll on!  262
stroppy  287
strummel  265
strung out  56
stubble jumper  224
stubby  231
stuck on  201
stud  198, 280
studly  198
stud muffin  198
stuff  198
stuffed shirt  155
stuffer  56
stumblebum  221
stunner  276
stunt  70
stunt cock  29

stupe  140
sub  20, 122, 150
subbie  150
sucker punch  85
suck face  198, 221
suck off  198
suck the monkey  114, 270
suds  114
sudser  212
sugar  56
suicide blonde  162
suicide jockey  167
suit  150
summat  255
Sunday punch  85, 126
sun dodger  9
sundown  162
sunnies  162, 231
sunny side up  118
Sunshine State  178
sunshower  146
superwaif  162
supp ben  152
sus laws  10
swab  9, 270
swabby  9
swaddler  175, 241
swag  46, 270
swagsman  46
swak  235
swap spit  198
sweat  6, 221, 270
sweats  162
swede  185
Sweeney  16
Sweeney Todd  144
sweetener  46
sweetie  201
sweet on  202
sweet science  85
sweet sixteen  108
sweety  201

swell 155, 162, 270
swept 233
swindle-sheet 35, 150
swing 46, 198
swing both ways 198
swinger 287
swinging 162, 287
swing the lead 6
swipe 46
swipes 115, 270
swish 140, 162, 282
swiss roll 144, 241
switch hitter 198
swiz 276, 282
swizzle 115, 270
swot 61
swy 51, 231
syebuck 270
syrup of fig 144

## T

T 97
ta 271
tab 56, 253
table-setter 95
tacho 166
tackies 162, 235
tackle 185
taddie 181, 247
tadger 185
Taffy 169, 267
Taig 140, 175, 249, 267
tail 83, 140, 185, 267, 271
tail-end Charlie 6, 285
tailgate 166
take a hike! 221
takeaway 93
take out 6, 78, 126
take the chequered flag 91
take the Fifth 10
talkies 282
talking head 212

talk on the porcelain telephone 188
talk to the hand 59
Tally 247
tammy 247
Tan 241
tangoed 299
tank 51, 221
tankbuster 6
tanked up 115
tanky 158
tanner 122
tape 115
tape-measure shot 95
tapes 6
tapping 78
tar 9
ta-ra 255
tar heel 178
Tar Heel State 178
tarpaulin 9, 267
tart 202
tash 285
Tassie 178, 231
taste 48
tater 96, 118
taters in the mould 144
TATT 13
Tatts 231
taxing 59
taxi squad 93
tbh 73
T Dot 224
tea 56
teacher's pet 61
tea fight 118
tea leaf 144
teapot lid 122, 140, 144, 172
tea room 73
teaser 212
techie 68, 295
technicolour yawn 134, 188, 290

technobabble 68
technofear 68
technojunkie 68
technospeak 68
Ted 162, 287
Teddy boy 162, 287
Teddy girl 162, 287
teeny-bopper 162, 290
telephone numbers 122
tell 107
telly 212
tenderloin 178
ten-four 16
ten-man rugby 80
tenner 122, 276
ten-percenter 25
term of endearment among
  sailors 134
Terries 6
Texas Leaguer 96
Texas Mickey 224
Texas wedge 88
that ain't hay 221
the boonies 176
the boot 200
the elbow 200
the lift doesn't go all the way to
  the top floor 134, 210
the lights are on but nobody's
  home 135, 210
the missis 201
the old heave-ho 200
the o.o. 26
the real McCoy 276
thesp 25
the whole nine yards 221
thick 38, 70
thickhead 140
thickie 140
thicko 140
thingumabob 271
third degree 11

third half 80
thirteen-man game 80
thrash 22
thrash metal 22
threads 162
thread the needle 93
threepenny bits 144, 185, 188
threequel 25
three score and ten 108
three sheets in the wind 9, 115
throat 204
throw 75, 85
throw shapes 242
throw up 271
Thunderer 20
thunderthighs 140
tick 122
ticked off 221, 287
ticker 32, 185
ticket 6
tickety-boo 280
tickle the ivories 22
tick-tack 38
tic-tac 38
tiddled 115
tiddley 9
tiddly 115
tidy 276
tie one on 115
tiger country 88
tiger line 88
tiggywinkle 181
tight 115
tightarse 140
tightass 140
tightener 118
tightwad 122, 140
tiki tour 233
tilbury 271
tile 162
timbers 83
timbit 224

time 46, 51
time-pass 244
tin 122
tin bath 144, 262
tin fish 9
tinkle 189
tinklebobs 259
tinny 115, 231
tinpot dictator 158
Tinseltown 25, 178
tip down 146
tip it down 146
tippy 162
tips 38
tipsheet 32
tired and emotional 20, 135
tissue 38
tit 185, 267
titfer 144, 162
tit for tat 144
tit-man 198
titty 185
tittybabby 256
titty-bar 198
tizzy 282
TK 244
toady 231
toast 207, 237
toastie 118
tober 27
todger 185, 276
Tod Sloan 144
toerag 140
toey 231
togs 162, 233
toke 56
tom 16, 46
Tom and Dick 144
tomato can 85
tomfoolery 144
tommy gun 126
tom tit 144, 189

ton 83, 122, 166
tonk 185, 231
tonsil hockey 198
ton-up boy 166
tony 267
Tony Blairs 144, 162
Tony's den 108
tool 185
tooled up 46
tools of ignorance 96
Toon Army 253
toonie 224
toot 56, 115, 231, 244, 271
tootle 166
toots 282
top 126, 271
top banana 25
top bollocks 186
top-drawer 155
top-kick 6
top of the head 38
top of the hour 20
top of the shop 108
topper 258
toppy 32
tops 282
topspin 20
torch 46
Torygraph 20
tosher 63
toss 198
tosser 140
total 221
totem pole 150
touch 46
touch base 35, 295
touch up 198
touchy-feely 292
towel 126, 271
towelhead 140, 172
townee 63
toyboy 295

toy dolls 144
toys 249
Tracey 155
track 83
tracks 56
trade 73
traffic 91, 93, 265
trail 212
trailer trash 155, 297
trainspotter 295
tramlines 56
trannie 295
tranny 290
trap 46, 186, 231
traps 22
trashed 115
tree-hugger 297
trenches 93
trendy 290
Trev 59
Trevor Nunn 63
trey 97
tribulation 267
trick 46, 70
trick cyclist 210
trilbies 186
trip 56
tripehound 231
triple witching hour 32
trippy 290
Trojan 68
Trojan horse 68
troll 68, 73
trollies 162
troppo 231
Trot 158, 290
trots 189, 204
trouble and strife 144, 202
trout pout 299
truck 103
truck and trailer 80
tsotsi 236

TTFN 285
TTFO 13
Tube 166, 262
tube 101, 115, 212, 231, 247
tubes 12
tub-thumper 175
tubular 101
tuck 119
tuckahoe 178
tucker 119, 231
tuck shop 61
tufter 105
tummy 276
tummy tuck 12
tune 236
tunes 59
turd 189
turd-burglar 140
turf 90
turf accountant 38
turkey 25
turkey-shoot 6
turn 56
turn in 267
turn off 267
turn over 46
turn up your toes 207
turn your arm over 83
turtle dove 144, 162
tush 186, 221
tushie 186, 221
tussock 256
tutty pegs 256
tux 162
twankay 115
twat 186
tweak 20
tweedle 46
tweedler 46
twenty 167
twenty-four-seven 297
twicer 175

Twickers 80
twink 73
twinkie 73
twin killing 96
twirler 83
twist 115
twister 146
twitchel 256
two and eight 144
two-bulb 242
twoccing 16
two-eyed steak 119
two fat ladies 108
two little ducks 108
two point four children 202
two-pot screamer 115, 231
Tyke 255
tyke 175, 231
typo 20
tyre biter 242

## U

U 155
uey 166
uglies 80
ulu 244
ump 75
unc 202
uncle 244
Uncle Arthur 242
Uncle Charlie 96
Uncle Dick 144
Uncle Sam 178, 276
underachieve 135
underboss 49
undergrad 63
undergraduette 63
understandings 271
under the table 115
under the weather 115, 135, 204
undies 162
unhip 162

uni 63
unlucky for some 108
up-and-down 88
up-and-under 80
upchuck 189
upper 56
upper crust 155
upper storey 271
upright-man 265
upskirt 29
up the duff 285
up the jumper 80
up the pole 6, 115, 280
up the river 51
up west 262
up yourself 285
usual 115

## V

vac 63
vada 27
valium picnic 32
vapourware 68
varda 27
varsity 63
vee-jay 22, 212
veep 158
veg 119
vegetable garden 99
veggie 119
veggies 119, 287
velvet 38
verbal 16
vert ramp 103
very dab 247
vic 16
vig 46
vigorish 38, 46
village bike 140
villain 16
-ville 276
vino 115

vino collapso 115
virus 204
visibly moved 20, 135
voddy 115
voetsek 236
Volunteer State 178
vowels 122
VPL 295
vroom 166
vrot 236

## W

wack 221, 251
wacker 251
wacky 210
wad 119, 122
waddle 32
wage plug 231
wag it 61, 256
wag off 61, 255
wagon 242
wake up and smell the coffee 297
walk 11, 16
walker 202
walk home 75
walk it 75, 282
walkover 75
wall 78
wallaby 152
wallah 244
wallop 115
walloper 46, 231
wall pass 78
Wall-Streeter 32
wally 140
walt 249
walthead 249
wang 186
wank 198, 276
wanker 140
wanksta 70

wanky 292
warby 231
ward heeler 158
warm 126
warrantable 105
wash 35, 46
wash-up 231
WASP 172
wasted 56
water-cooler moment 212
water dog 9
watering hole 115
water sports 29, 198
watery grave 88
wawa 224
way to go 221
wazoo 186, 221
wazz 255
weapon 186
Weary Willie 152
webhead 68
wedding tackle 186
wedgie 61
wedgies 162
wee buns 249
wee champion 249
weed 56
Wee Free 175
weegie 178, 247
weenie 119, 186
weeny 186, 271
weeny-bopper 292
wee onions 249
weepie 25, 280
weigh off 46
well away 115
well hard 262
well-hung 198
well I never 129
welly 166
we need to talk 135
Wessi 169

West Brit 242
wet 115, 146, 158, 231
wetback 172, 221
wets 91
wetware 68
wet your beak 49
wet your whistle 115
whack 49, 271
whack off 198
whaler 231
whale tail 162, 299
wham bam thank you ma'am 198
whammo 26
whanau 233
whang 186
wharfie 150, 231
what about ye? 249
what it is 70
what's-its-name 267
what's up 70
what's your poison? 115
what's yours? 115
wheeler-dealer 290
wheelhouse 96
wheels 166
when pigs fly 267
when the balloon goes up 278
whiff 88, 96
whiffled 115
whip 59, 70
whipper 249
whipper-in 90, 105
whirlybird 166
whistle 163
whistle and flute 144
whistled 115
white knight 32
white lady 115, 231
white lightning 115
whites 83
white settler 169, 247
white squire 32

white stuff 56
whittle 265
whizz 56, 221
whizzbang 278
whizzer 46
whoopee 198
whop 126
whopper with cheese 12
whup 126
widdle 287
wide boy 283
widow 115
wifebeater 163
wifie 247
wig 11
wigger 59
wig out 221
wigs on the green 242
willy 186
win 265
wind 85, 237
Windies 83
Windy City 178
wine 237
wing 265
wingding 221
winger 6
wingman 11
winker 166
winkle-pickers 163
Winnie the Pooh 108
wino 115
wipe 271
wipe-out 101
wire 16, 46, 119
wired 56, 68
wiseass 221
wise guy 49
with it 163
wix 59
wobbly duck 93
wog 140, 172, 204, 231

wojus 242
wolf 119
wolly 17, 119, 262
wonga 122
wonk 63
woodbine 170, 231
wooden overcoat 135, 207
woodentop 17
woodie 101
woodshedding 22
woodwork 78
woofter 140, 295
wool 251
woolly 163, 181
woollyback 181, 251
Woop Woop 231
wop 140, 172
wop-wops 233
word 70
word up 70
worker 88
working girl 46, 135
work over 126
works 56
worm food 207
worrywart 221
would you believe it 130
wowser 231
wrecked 115
wrinkly 140
wrist 38
wristlets 46
write-off 283
write yourself off 6
wrong side of the tracks 178
wrong 'un 83
wuss 140, 292

## X

xis 38
X's and O's 93
XTC 56

## Y

yada, yada, yada 221
yahoo 83, 271
yakka 231
yakker 96
yamp 256
yampy 256
Yank 170, 178
Yankee 170, 178
yard 59, 122
Yardie 237, 295
yegg 46
ye gods 130
ye gods and little fishes 130
yellow 276
yellow jack 204
yestergay 73
Yid 140, 172, 175
yike 126, 231
ying-yang 221
yips 88
yob 283
yobbo 283
yock 25
yockers 242
yodel in the canyon 198
yok 25
yoke 242
yomp 6
yonks 290
yoof 59, 295
Yorkie 181, 287
you can say that again 283
your balls are beef 249
your man 242
your mother 59
your mum 59
your only man 242
your woman 242
you wouldn't read about it 130
yo-yo 140, 242
Y2K 297

yummy mummy 202, 299
yuppie 155

## Z
za 290
zap 212, 244
zapper 295
zebra 93
zhoosh 27

zhooshy 27
ziff 231
zilch 285
zing 221
zinger 20, 221
zip 221
zit 204
Z-list 153
zonked 56, 115